About Reinvention

➤ Reinvention represents some type of change, a departure from what came before or an embellishment of something that was in place.

➤ Reinventing yourself is exciting. With lengthening life spans and an increasingly multicultural society, you are exposed to more viewpoints, ways of seeing the world, pastimes, and modes of thought than your counterparts of generations ago.

➤ Reinvention includes getting your mind in gear for change and reinventing your physical self, your career, your relationships, and other aspects of your life.

➤ You don't have to be the same person you have been, living the same life you've been living, doing the same things you've been doing. The opportunity to repeatedly reinvent yourself is within your grasp.

➤ Reinvention is a chance to renew yourself, a chance to take on a new hobby, a new sport, a new pastime, or a new cause.

➤ Reinvention is about making your own path. The common denominator to all those who are on any kind of quest for reinvention is that they recognize that life affords continual opportunities for renewal.

➤ The longer you live, the more opportunities you have for reinventing your life!

Possible Reasons for Reinvention

People want different things in life. Some want ...

➤ A better life.
➤ To make more money.
➤ A stronger body.
➤ Life to be more interesting.

➤ To be more respected.
➤ To know God.
➤ To be happier.
➤ A stronger relationship.

Values

Reinvention is largely a question of values.

➤ What do you value in life?
➤ What merits your time and energy?
➤ What is worth looking foolish over?

➤ To what are you willing to commit?
➤ What is worth trying over if ...
➤ What off...

alpha
books

Self-Talk That Stifles Reinvention

➤ "I shouldn't have done that."
➤ "It looks like this is going to be one of those days."
➤ "I never get this right."

➤ "I really botched that."
➤ "Why did I do that?"
➤ "This probably isn't going to work."

Small Steps

Sometimes initiating the smallest task on a project will get you on the high road to major change. Here are some examples:

➤ Making a phone call
➤ Joining an organization
➤ Rearranging your closet
➤ Dropping a service
➤ Seeking assistance
➤ Rearranging your calendar

➤ Subscribing to a publication
➤ Creating a file folder
➤ Writing a letter
➤ Clearing your desk
➤ Prioritizing tasks
➤ Setting up a reward system

➤ Visiting the library
➤ Clearing out a drawer
➤ Making a presentation
➤ Buying a resource tool
➤ Going on the Internet
➤ Visualizing yourself as successful

Web Sites That Support Reinventing Your Health

➤ American Cancer Society: www.cancer.org
➤ American Council on Science and Health: www.acsh.org
➤ American Diabetes Association: www.diabetes.org
➤ American Heart Association: www.amhrt.org
➤ Center for Science in the Public Interest: www.cspinet.org
➤ Food Allergy Network: www.foodallergy.org
➤ International Food Information Council: www.ificinfo.health.org
➤ Tufts University Nutrition Navigator: www.navigator.tufts.edu
➤ U.S. Food and Drug Administration: www.fda.gov
➤ USDA Nutrient Database: www.nal.usda.gov/fnic/cgi-bin/nut_search.pl

To Develop More Internal Focus

➤ Shift your focus from the external things in your life to your internal self.
➤ Get away from the hustle and bustle of life and create a private space all your own.
➤ Take the time to stop on occasion, just to catch your breath.
➤ Treat yourself to a trip to a spa.

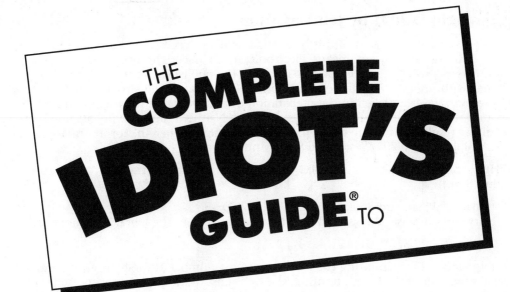

THE COMPLETE IDIOT'S GUIDE® TO

Reinventing Yourself

by Jeff Davidson

alpha books

201 West 103rd Street
Indianapolis, IN 46290

A Pearson Education Company

Publisher
Marie Butler-Knight

Product Manager
Phil Kitchel

Managing Editor
Jennifer Chisholm

Senior Acquisitions Editor
Renee Wilmeth

Development Editor
Michael Thomas

Senior Production Editor
Christy Wagner

Copy Editor
Jan Zunkel

Illustrator
Jody P. Schaeffer

Cover Designers
Mike Freeland
Kevin Spear

Book Designers
Scott Cook and Amy Adams of DesignLab

Indexer
Angie Bess

Layout/Proofreading
Svetlana Dominguez
Mary Hunt
Heather Hiatt Miller
Ayanna Lacey
Stacey Richwine-DeRome
Gloria Schurick

Contents at a Glance

Contents

18 The Makings of a Leader   **187**

19 Speakers Are Leaders   **197**

Foreword

Congratulations on deciding that the time is right for personal reinvention, or simply to explore the possibility of personal reinvention.

What is reinvention? Reinvention is any type of change, from the material to the spiritual, in which you become a whole person or a different person, hopefully a better person, but certainly a changed person. Is it a simple matter of changing one's hair color or learning a new language? For some, this may be all the change they believe is needed for them to feel whole. For many, though, reinvention goes deeper than physical appearances or academics. Reinvention is immensely personal and no one can tell you what it is for you. Luckily, someone can tell you how to get there.

In the desire to reinvent one's self, many questions arise: How do I go about reinventing myself? Why do I want to change? What should I change? Would I be happier if I reinvented myself? These questions are all to be expected. Change is awkward, especially if the needed guidance is not available.

Well, you've got that guidance here in *The Complete Idiot's Guide to Reinventing Yourself*. You began reinventing yourself when you purchased this book. So, take a deep breath—you're already on the way to a new you!

Jeff Davidson tackles a difficult but common concern in present-day adult life. If you are familiar with his other books, especially those in *The Complete Idiot's Guide* series, then you know that you will be aptly led on this road to change. Jeff converts voluminous masses of information on reinvention and turns it into an enjoyable, easy-to-read guide.

A Guide, Not a Manifesto

Thankfully, Jeff does not suppose that this is the only resource you'll want on the path to reinventing yourself. He has included numerous resources, from books to Web sites, from which you can glean more information on the areas of your life that you would like to reinvent.

Jeff is going to guide you through different types of reinvention that are within your grasp. You choose for yourself what you would like to change. In the six parts of this book, Jeff does everything from helping you develop a plan, to identifying obstacles in your personal and professional life, to enumerating the important aspects of philanthropy. In short, Jeff makes it easy for you.

You always hear the phrase "Change is good." Why, then, do more people not reinvent themselves? In this day and time, we are afforded a unique opportunity, historically, in which it's possible to be the type of person we would like to become, despite age, race, or gender. I believe that the reason more people do not reinvent themselves is that they believe change is too hard to attempt. With this book by your side, you don't have to be one of those people.

Prepare Thyself

I suggest that, during your reading, you do some things to help you get the most out of this book. Be prepared to answer some tough questions about yourself and be honest when you answer. That's the only way that true reinvention will be possible.

Also, use a pencil, pen, or highlighter to mark any passages that catch your eye. This makes the experience a more personal one for you, and it also makes it easier to go back and see what you thought was important.

Take your time and enjoy this book. You are embarking upon a remarkable journey to reinvention. Notice I used the word "journey" and not "excursion." The path you took to become who you are today was not traversed overnight, so don't expect true reinvention to be attained quickly. I wish you all the best in this exciting endeavor!

Marcia Wieder, author of *Making Your Dreams Come True* and founder of Dream University

Introduction

Reinventing Your Life Is Your Choice

You have a book in your hands that could change your life. Somewhere along the path from where you started to where you're heading, you've recognized that you are the captain of your soul and the master of your fate. You have the opportunity and the ability to change as it fits your circumstances or your desires. What better time than now, in the early years of the third millennium, to engage in the wondrous process of reinvention?

In this book, we will examine what it means to reinvent yourself, leverage your life circumstances, and metamorphically emerge as a new version of you! Henry David Thoreau once said that most men live lives of quiet desperation. Unlike the serfs of the Middle Ages, puritanical restrictions of the 1700s, and the conformity of America in the 1950s, each of us has wider latitude, perhaps wider than ever before, to embark upon new personal journeys, whether they be changes in lifestyle, appearance, vocation, avocation, or mindset.

If you are familiar with *The Complete Idiot's Guide* series, then you know that this book will be a fun and easy read, while covering important ground to help you achieve your objectives. Twenty-seven chapters, each in bite-sized portions, offering wit and wisdom in extremely reader-friendly language, will help get you where you want to be.

Part 1, "Getting Started on the New You," gives you a framework for "getting your act together and taking it on the road." You'll learn how to make the best of where you are, and move on from there. You'll discover how to identify what obstacles may be holding you back, blast through procrastination, and take your place on the high road to reinvention.

Part 2, "Getting Your Mind in Gear," will help you to focus your mental energy on your reinvention goal. You are a powerful entity, and once you effectively put your mind to work for you, you're already halfway toward achieving your outcome. All that's left is execution!

Part 3, "Reinventing Your Body," examines the physical you. Are you getting enough rest, the right amount of exercise, and an adequate mix of nutrients? We also focus on going even further in the physical realm by redesigning your constitution through sports, practitioners trained in bodily manipulation, and medical procedures.

Part 4, "Reinventing Your Career," provides you with the insights and the edge you need to move on, either in your current line of work or in the work that you would rather do. This section asks penetrating questions while offering nitty-gritty advice to help you reinvent your career from what it is to what you know it can be.

Part 5 is called **"Reinventing Your Relationships."** Your quest for reinvention may well involve others, so reinventing your relationships with the people around you, in many respects, is the most important aspect of reinvention. Changing yourself is within your grasp; changing others is often illusionary, but changing your relationship with others is entirely possible and is within your grasp.

Part 6, "Reinventing Other Aspects of Your Life," contains an eclectic yet important lineup of topics that consolidates and unifies issues referred to throughout the book, and offers you the proper send-off with which to get started on the high road to reinvention.

Your future is ripe with opportunity, presuming that you are a student of what you read and actually commit to act upon the advice offered throughout. If you intend to get the most out of this book, then after you've gone through it a few times, no one else will want it—you will have marked up pages, highlighted passages, and used stick-'em pads or paper clips to note important sections. Perhaps you will have photocopied some pages, and torn some pages out because you're ready to act quickly on what you've read! After you've used the book, gotten great value from it, and turned it into a shambles, you'll probably want to go buy a second copy to keep in pristine condition and 10 to 15 more copies for your closest friends!

Extras

Stay alert to helpful observations, tips, warnings, and definitions generously allocated throughout the pages of this book to help you along your path to reinvention. Here's what they look like:

Reinvento Observes

Observations and advice from a mythical sage.

Tip

A quick recommendation worth heeding.

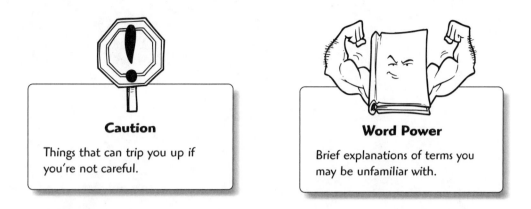

Caution

Things that can trip you up if you're not careful.

Word Power

Brief explanations of terms you may be unfamiliar with.

Acknowledgments

This book could not have been published without the support and enthusiasm of the fine folks at Pearson Education. Of all the authors in the world, they chose me to write this book so that it would be available for you. Thanks to Marie Butler-Knight, my publisher, and Renee Wilmeth, my acquisitions editor, for having the vision and wherewithal to initiate this project. Thanks to Jennifer Chisholm, the managing editor, Michael Thomas, development editor, Christy Wagner, production editor, and Jan Zunkel, copy editor.

Thanks also to Lynn Hickerson in International Sales, Debbie Parisi in Special Sales, Vickie Skelton in Public Relations, Eve Tabin in Electronic Rights Sales, Gardi Wilks in Promotion, Rachele Schifter in Subsidiary Rights, Jeannie McKay in Communications, Dawn Van De Keere in Marketing, and Kerry Cordero and Dianne Fortier in Business Development.

Thanks to Brent Winter, Brian Lawler, Tashia Zeigler, Sharon Askew, and Christie Koch for their original writing and editorial assistance as well as research, reviews, and copyediting.

Thanks to Susan Davidson for word processing assistance and, most importantly, to Valerie Davidson, age 10½, for showing Daddy just how easy reinvention can be.

Trademarks

Part 1

Getting Started on the New You

Whether you live another 40, 60, 80, or 100 years (don't laugh—it may soon become the norm), nowhere is it written that you have to be the same person, living the same life, doing the same things, the whole way through. Today, unlike a generation ago, the opportunity to reinvent yourself is alive and well and within your grasp.

In Part 1, we'll look at what reinvention is and what it isn't, and how to leverage the circumstances in your life. But you have to be willing to assess the truth about where you are and where you want to be. Are you ready to chase away the demons that could be holding you back? Are you ready to overcome the impetus of staying put, which keeps most people, for most of their lives, right where they are? If so, turn the page and get started on Chapter 1, "What Is Reinvention?"

What Is Reinvention?

In This Chapter

➤ A chance for renewal, the opportunity to change

➤ What reinvention is not

➤ Who needs quiet desperation?

➤ Developing an attitude

Since she first wrote these stirring words, many people have been inspired by author Marianne Williamson and her 1992 book, *A Return to Love:*

> "Our deepest fear is not that we are inadequate. Our deepest fear is that we are powerful beyond measure. It is our light, not our darkness, that most frightens us. We ask ourselves, who am I to be brilliant, gorgeous, talented, and fabulous! Actually, who are you not to be?

> "You are a child of God. Your playing small doesn't serve the world. There's nothing enlightened about shrinking so that other people won't feel insecure around you. We were born to make manifest the glory of God that is within us. It's not just in some of us. It's in everyone, and, as we let our light shine, we unconsciously give other people permission to do the same. As we are liberated from our own fear, our presence automatically liberates others."

In many ways this brilliant piece of prose is what this book is about. Okay, perhaps your quest to be something new, something more than simply an extension of what you were before, isn't so grandiose. Maybe you don't buy the part about being born to make manifest the glory of God within you. Perhaps the rallying cry to let your light shine, unconsciously give other people permission to do the same, liberate your fear, and automatically liberate others doesn't resonate for you.

Regardless, each of us, at various points throughout our lives, is bound to feel held back, not fully able to express our creative selves. This is what reinvention is all about: a chance to renew yourself. A chance to take on a new hobby, a new sport, a new pastime, or a new cause. Maybe your quest is to start your own business. Maybe it's to become a marathoner. Maybe it's to do volunteer work. Maybe it's to amass great wealth. Maybe it's to travel the world.

Movement That Matters

As used in this book, *reinvention* means significant, noteworthy movement from point A to point B, for whatever point A and point B represent for you. Self-reinvention could happen in as little as a day, indeed even a moment, depending on what leads up to it. More often, however, it takes weeks, if not months, of "moving into that new territory" and waking up one fine morning to find that you are a new person.

The Path Less Trodden

In his poem "The Road Not Taken," Nobel laureate Robert Frost wrote, "Two roads diverged in a wood, and I—/ I took the one less traveled by,/ and that has made all the difference." Reinvention is about making your own path. Maybe your path is along a well-traveled road, or a less-traveled road, but in any case, the route is up to you. For many people today, life is speeding by at an uncomfortable pace. They wake up in the morning, and their first thought is that they are already behind. From there, the pace just seems to accelerate.

If you are a student, a young career professional, a veteran career professional, a mom or a dad, a homemaker, a retiree, or anyone who holds any kind of position of responsibility, chances are that on too many days, and too many times throughout the day, you feel a bit more time-pressed, a bit more pressured, and maybe a bit more anxious than you would have cared to be at this point in your life.

So, for you, perhaps the quest for self-reinvention is along some prior path with a slower pace. If you're just breaking into the career world, embarking on some new enterprise, or joining a new community, maybe you find the pace to be exhilarating and very much to your liking.

Word Power

Reinvention is noteworthy movement from point A in your life to point B, for whatever point A and point B represent for you.

Your Chance for Renewal

The common denominator to all those who are on any kind of quest for reinvention is that they recognize that life affords continual opportunities for renewal. Indeed, with life spans around the globe increasing in every region, mathematically, the sheer opportunities for renewal have never been greater for a multitude of individuals than right now.

The Opportunity to Change

Reinvention represents some type of change, a departure from what came before or an embellishment of something that was in place. The nature of humans being what it is, even the most positive types of change often represent upset, upheaval, or dislodging.

Are You Seeing Things?

Achievement theory has long held, and science is now proving, that by first holding a vision in your mind of what you want to achieve, measurably if not infinitesimally, you move closer toward the achievement. In his book, *You'll See It When You Believe It,* author Dr. Wayne Dyer *elucidates* on the power of belief in the pursuit of any quest, professionally or personally, as well as individually or collectively.

While this book is not about social reinvention, reinvention of a whole society is entirely possible. Once the United States had slavery; now it would be unthinkable. Once women could not vote, as hard as that is to fathom, and had to march in the streets to become enfranchised. Once cigarette smoking was socially acceptable, even chic; now smoking is widely regarded as a cancer-inducing habit that causes great pain and suffering throughout society.

Speedy Changes

As entire societies can change, so, too, can individuals. At the individual level, your options are nearly unlimited. The speed with which you can effect change is far

Reinvento Observes

"Different strokes for different folks." This axiom is never more true than when it comes to a person's quest for reinvention.

Reinvento Observes

Speaking of mathematics, the ancient mathematician and philosopher Archimedes once said, "Give me a lever long enough and a place to stand, and I will move the earth." In your own life, obtaining the right lever at the right time may be the spur that leads to great and wondrous personal reinvention.

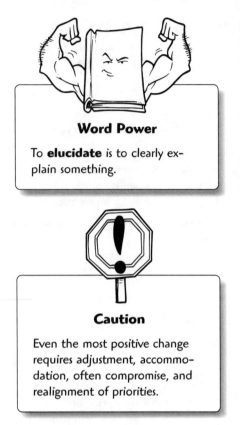

Word Power

To **elucidate** is to clearly explain something.

Caution

Even the most positive change requires adjustment, accommodation, often compromise, and realignment of priorities.

greater than that of a community or larger society, and the minor adjustments and modifications are up to you.

Consider this: In late 1989, I sent a proposal to Rick Horgan at Warner Books for a book titled *A Layman's Guide for Saving the Planet.* This was to be a book that would walk readers through their homes, room by room, and show them how to be environmentally responsible. Rick sent me back a rejection letter saying that he thought the proposal had merit, but that the editors at Warner felt that no one in America realistically would change their "cozy, comfortable lifestyles."

Four months later, another book was published, *50 Simple Things You Can Do to Save the Earth,* and it became a worldwide bestseller, endorsed at the highest levels of business and government, including the White House. Several other environmental books quickly followed, with many of them selling very well. People *were* willing to recycle, use less energy, and conserve when practical. (At that point, I sent a photocopy of Rick's letter back to him, with a note at the bottom that said: "Dear Rick, People *can* change.")

It's My Choice

Talk to a hundred different people about why they want to change and you're likely to get a hundred different reasons. Some want …

➤ A better life.

➤ Life to be more interesting.

➤ To be happier.

➤ To make more money.

➤ To be more respected.

➤ A stronger relationship.

➤ A stronger body.

➤ To know God.

Ask yourself: What are your reasons for wanting to change? By pinpointing your reasons, you may find more fuel for your reinvention!

Ready, Set, Self-Actualize

Philosophers and psychologists, from the ancient Greeks to Abraham Maslow, contend (and rightly so) that each of us contains some element within that prompts us to seek happiness and fulfillment. The process has been termed "self-actualization," although some people, for whatever reason, are not able to engage it.

Maslow once wrote that *self-actualization* and *self-transcendence* were the epitome of self-expression, being all that one was capable of being. After years of study, he concluded that very few people achieve self-actualization.

One way to achieve self-actualization is by eliminating the value-judging of others, which may seem to be an impossible goal to achieve. Yet, just by attempting it, you can activate higher levels of self-esteem. The attempt itself is a fruitful exercise and any level of the attempt yields a payoff.

Hierarchy of Needs

Dr. David McClelland undertook pioneering research in illuminating a hierarchy of human needs, including the need to relate to others, the need for personal power, and the need for achievement. In recent years, he has also been among the most prominent researchers in exploring the potential connection between mental functioning and career or personal success.

Word Power

Self-actualization is the legitimate personal quest for happiness and fulfillment; the epitome of self-expression; to become all that one is capable of becoming.

Word Power

Self-transcendence is the notion of living your life for purposes other than self-gratification. The self-transcendent person finds a purpose higher than the self.

Currently a professor at Boston University, McClelland earned much of his fame while at Harvard University. For several decades, he studied the potential links between what one thinks about and what one achieves. Ultimately, McClelland became convinced that even men and women of humble origin could break ranks and redesign their lives. So, there's hope for each of us!

How Do People Begin Their Reinvention?

Some people write a mission statement that spells out what they want to achieve in life. Some hire a life coach or a personal coach and meet with this professional on a regular basis in pursuit of incremental progress. Some people write their own eulogy or obituary—in essence, starting from the end of their lives and working toward the present, listing their achievements (many of which have not occurred yet). Then, they use that document as a blueprint for proceeding in life. How and where you start is not nearly as important as the fact that you *do* start.

Jeff Davidson, Best-Selling Author and Motivational Speaker, Dies at 116

Tahiti, Sunday May 15, 2067—Jeff Davidson died yesterday at age 116 of heart failure following a brief but completely painless illness. Active all his life as a speaker and author, Davidson's book *The Complete Idiot's Guide to Reinventing Yourself* became a worldwide best-seller early in the century, resulting in requests for him to speak at the highest levels of government and at many of the largest conventions and gatherings on all seven continents.

Davidson's mission was to inspire, educate, and challenge career professionals, as well as people everywhere, to achieve a healthy balance by living and working at a comfortable pace in our sped-up society. He achieved this by teaching that people gain a finer understanding of the principles that lead to breathing space by teaching alternatives to high-pressured days, without requiring radical changes in how people live or what they do. He also provided the tools and support people need to meet the ongoing challenges they face.

Davidson was honored throughout the world for his accomplishments in speaking and writing. He was knighted in Great Britain early in this century, appeared four times on the cover of *Time* magazine, and was consistently cited as one of the 10 most admired men in the world. In all, Davidson wrote 124 other books including dozens of books for Macmillan such as *The Complete Idiot's Guide to Managing Stress, The Complete Idiot's Guide to Managing Your Time,* and *The Complete Idiot's Guide to Reaching Your Goals*.

Beside his 18-room villa in Tahiti, Davidson had homes in Chapel Hill, North Carolina; Storrs, Connecticut, where he was an avid UConn basketball fan and the team's most generous benefactor; McLean, Virginia; Sausalito, California; Grand Cayman Island; Ko Samui, Thailand; and Montreaux, Switzerland. Rumored to have an estate in excess of $850,000,000, Davidson is survived by his wife, ex-model Julie, 28, and his three children, six grandchildren, and nine great-grandchildren in six countries.

Upon learning of his passing, U.S. President Laura Alsop, a close friend of Davidson's, commented, "A great mind has passed from this earth. There will never be another human being like Jeff Davidson."

A Journal Entry a Day

Some people start a journal, writing their thoughts and observations in it every day. They use this as a living document that chronicles their lives' journeys. In itself, this begins to serve as an incentive tool on a daily basis.

In the quest to reinvent one's self, some turn to spirituality and conversations with God. Confession or simply discussion, conversation with a spiritual advisor, has long proven to be a highly effective method of enhancing one's soul.

A World of Ideas

The following list, loosely grouped by topic areas, represents a multitude of other ways that people have found to be useful in the quest to reinvent themselves:

Tip

Journal writing can be powerful because, after all, you know that you need to add something to your journal for that day, and furthermore, it becomes a cathartic and emotional connection to self-progress. Having to make a new journal entry will get you up and moving and recognizing your journey.

➤ *Nature:* Camp for two fabulous weeks in a national park. Learn the names and characteristics of surrounding trees and flowers. Drive on all the back roads in your county or state. Visit your local parks and walkways. Become a naturalist.

➤ *Lifetime:* Set lifetime goals. Build in travel time before you retire. Identify the five events in your life that you have always wanted to attend.

➤ *Business/career:* Begin a forced savings plan at work to meet your retirement goals. Invent something. Develop a philosophy. Conduct your own original research. Become an authority on something. Run for office. Speak at a meeting or local conference. Convert a passionate hobby into a business.

➤ *Travel:* Take a cruise. Be in the front row to hear Pavarotti sing. Take a five-mile walk along the Great Wall of China. Visit our neighbors to the north—Canada. Attend the Christmas Mass at the Vatican or the Wailing Wall. Ride the old Patagonia railroad the length of South America. Spend a week with a friend whom you need to see. Go to Hawaii and learn to surf. Go on safari to shoot (photograph) big game. Take a road trip through the United States.

➤ *Physical feats:* Learn to inline skate. Run a marathon or compete in a triathlon. Learn T'ai Chi. Learn a martial art. Learn ballroom dancing. Walk to work and everywhere else you can. Try fasting. Invest in and follow workout videos. Become certified in scuba diving.

➤ *Mental exercises:* Go back to college. Learn how to interpret dreams. Trace your ancestry. Spend a year reading only classical literature. Study your own religion and others. Increase your vocabulary. Write a memoir.

➤ *Hobbies:* Learn to play an instrument. Learn to sculpt or paint. Start an aquarium. Take up photography. Learn to fly a plane. Speak Japanese, Russian, or Farsi fluently. Sew a quilt. Plant an inside herb garden. Hire a coach.

➤ *Affiliations:* Act in a play. Join in a Renaissance festival as a costumed character. Join the historical preservation society. Get involved in politics. Live in a group house. Join a local band. Begin monthly dinner parties inviting people you've wanted to know better.

➤ *Give:* Maintain an urban street garden for the enjoyment of others. Create or change your will to include some philanthropic bequests. Help someone learn how to read or do math. Become a mentor. Become a Big Brother or Big Sister. Adopt a charitable organization as your favorite and help them over the next decade. Coach a team. Adopt an animal from a local shelter.

What Reinvention Is Not

Is being elected to public office a form of reinvention? How about getting a facelift? How about re-enrolling in school? The answer in all three cases is: It depends.

In the case of running for office, if it represents a logical extension of what you've been heading for in your career, if you don't particularly feel new, renewed, or otherwise inspired, it would not represent a reinvention.

In the case of a facelift, certainly if it is your third or fourth, that would not represent reinvention. If there was no new "you" behind the face—i.e., your mindset had not changed—that would not be a reinvention. However, if you felt younger, more vibrant, more attractive, or if you simply achieved some type of new start on the current phase of your life, then who is to say that you haven't reinvented yourself?

In the case of re-enrolling in school, imagine a scenario in which your boss said that you had to take a course. Or you couldn't get the kind of job you were seeking with the education that you currently had. So you march down to the local community college or major four-year university and re-enroll. Does that represent a reinvention? Most people would probably say "no."

Present and Accounted For?

In all three cases, running for office, having a facelift, or re-enrolling in school, some of the common denominators that would likely be present, and, more conclusively, would cement the fact that you are on the road to reinvention, would include the following:

➤ It is a conscious choice, a self-initiated goal, something that you want to do, something you have actively chosen to do, and something that you are looking forward to doing.

➤ However external the change may be—a change in your title, your face, or your level of education—a deeper, more satisfying, more fundamental change has taken place internally.

➤ In all likelihood, the activity is something for which you have planned a long time. You didn't do it on the spur of the moment; you weren't told to do it and you didn't fall into it. It was part of your contemplation and careful consideration.

➤ The resulting change or activity—i.e., winning public office, having a successful facelift, passing the course that you took—is not an end in and of itself.

A Larger Issue

In each case, there is something larger behind it:

➤ In seeking public office, presumably it is to serve others, to do good for your community, county, state, nation, or world.

➤ In the case of having a facelift, perhaps it is to match the inner you that was already feeling younger and more energetic. Perhaps it is to find a new mate, to maintain your competitive edge in a public position, or to celebrate long-term success.

➤ In the case of re-enrolling in school, it could be to improve your mind, to strengthen your resumé, to bolster your position at work, to achieve a better job, to obtain a higher-paying job, to prove that you could do it, to match the educational level of those in your family, to complete something that you had forsaken years ago, or one of dozens of other reasons.

Who Needs Quiet Desperation?

As I conveyed in the introduction, noted philosopher and author Henry David Thoreau made the bold and decisive statement, "Most men lead lives of quiet desperation." I surmise that that was an accurate and revealing statement, which helped to describe the 1840s and still rings true to most people even in the twenty-first century. The difference is that it doesn't need to be that way. The amount of reinvention-related resources available today to the typical individual in Western and industrialized nations is nothing short of awesome. You don't have to sit and hope for guidance or inspiration.

And in Just Minutes ...

A trip to the local library, or a PC connected to the Internet, is the door to a world of new ideas. In hours or minutes, not days, weeks, or months, you can easily amass a wealth of high-quality references on virtually any topic of interest to support your reinvention quest.

You simply have no excuse today not to get started on the road to whatever it is you think represents a valid change in your life. If you don't have a PC at home, or you are not connected to the Internet, most libraries today afford you the opportunity. If you have never connected to the Internet, the reference librarian can get you started in a matter of minutes.

If you are not familiar with the top search engines, you can become proficient with them in less than five minutes. Then, too, a stroll through any magazine store, with the hundreds upon hundreds of specialized magazines available, will further bolster your quest, as will a stroll through any bookstore, where between 40,000 to 140,000 titles might be in stock.

From Keeper of Our Borders to Keeper of Our Children to Statesman: General Colin Powell

"I come before you ... a fellow citizen who has lived the American Dream to the fullest. As someone who believes in that dream and wants that dream to become reality for every American."

—Colin Powell at his military retirement speech, 1993

Colin Luther Powell was born in the United States to Jamaican immigrants on April 5, 1937. He attended the City College of New York and served there as a cadet in the Reserve Officers Training Corps. It is from this experience that Powell gained his entry into the ranks of the United States Army. Later, he received a Master of Business Administration degree from George Washington University.

Powell was a battalion commander in Korea, heading the 2nd Brigade 101st Airborne Division and V Corps. He also served two tours of duty in Vietnam, from 1962 to 1963 and 1968 to 1969, prior to serving as the Chairman of the Joint Chiefs of Staff.

Medals of Honor

Widely recognized for his leadership during the Persian Gulf War in 1990, Powell retired from the U.S. Army in September of 1993, but not before receiving numerous military decorations, including the Defense Distinguished Service medal, Bronze Star medal, and the Purple Heart. He also received honors in the civilian arena, including the Presidential Medal of Freedom, the Congressional Gold Medal, and an honorary knighthood from the Queen of England.

In 1995, he published his autobiography, *My American Journey,* and went on a national book tour. Although rumors abounded that he would run for president during the 1996 election, Powell announced that he would not pursue any political office. He had different plans in mind.

A Different Kind of Leader

Once chairman of the most powerful armed forces in the world, Powell chose to become a leader of a different kind of entity. For several years he served as chairman of "America's Promise," an organization that asks Americans to take responsibility for the education of their children, and to realize that everyone has a personal stake in the life of a child.

Powell also found time to be a member of the Board of Trustees of Howard University and of the Board of Directors of the United Negro College Fund. He served on the Board of Governors of the Boys and Girls Clubs of America and was a member of the Advisory Board of the Children's Health Fund. In 1997, President Clinton gave him the position of the General Chairman of the Presidents' Summit for America's Future.

Talk about reinventing your life! Colin Powell rose through the ranks of the U.S. Armed Forces as protector of our rights, during times of peace and war, continued to give back to our country by supporting its youth, and now is the U.S. Secretary of State in President George W. Bush's cabinet, the first African-American to hold the position.

The Least You Need to Know

➤ Reinvention is significant, noteworthy movement from point A to point B, for whatever point A and point B represents for you.

➤ Reinvention represents a departure from what came before or an embellishment of something that was in place; often even the most positive change represents upheaval.

➤ Even men and women of humble origins can break ranks and redesign their lives. So, there's hope for each of us!

➤ You have no excuse today for not getting started if you want to change your life.

Chapter 2

Leveraging Your Circumstances

In This Chapter

➤ Your lifecycle and your life

➤ Before and after major change

➤ Predictable milestones

➤ Letting the seasons tell you

➤ Letting your age tell you

Each day you live, the opportunity exists for reinventing your life! Regardless of your longevity, a number of predictable lifecycle events that you will experience may prompt you (or force you!) to reinvent yourself.

Into Each Life Some Rain Must Fall

More than 30 years ago, researchers Thomas R. Holmes and Richard Rahe published a social-readjustment rating scale in the *Journal of Psychosomatic Research,* which, among other things, revealed that into one's life a lot of rain will fall. The social-readjustment scale represents a snapshot indicator of the relative impact of predictable events in life and, for our purposes, times at which self-reinvention may be desirable or necessary.

Though the scale has been modified over the years, the original, reprinted on the following page, remains a classic, and is a reminder not only that into each life, including yours, some rain must fall, but also that some rainbows will appear.

Social Readjustment Scale

Number	Life Event	Mean Value
1.	Death of spouse	100
2.	Divorce	73
3.	Marital separation from mate	65
4.	Detention in jail or other institution	63
5.	Death of a close family member	63
6.	Major personal injury or illness	53
7.	Marriage	50
8.	Being fired at work	47
9.	Marital reconciliation with mate	45
10.	Retirement from work	45
11.	Major change in health of a family member	44
12.	Pregnancy	40
13.	Sexual difficulties	39
14.	Gaining a new family member (e.g., through birth, adoption, moving in)	39
15.	Major business readjustment (e.g., merger, reorganization, bankruptcy)	39
16.	Major change in financial state (a lot worse or a lot better than usual)	38
17.	Death of a close friend	37
18.	Changing to a different line of work	36
19.	Major change in number of arguments with spouse (regarding child-rearing, personal habits)	35
20.	Taking out a mortgage or loan for a major purchase (e.g., for a home, business)	31
21.	Foreclosure on a mortgage or loan	30
22.	Major change in responsibilities at work (promotion, demotion, lateral transfer)	29
23.	Son or daughter leaving home (e.g., marriage, attending college)	29
24.	Trouble with in-laws	29
25.	Outstanding personal achievement	28
26.	Spouse beginning or decreasing work outside the home	26
27.	Beginning or ceasing normal schooling	26

Social Readjustment Scale (continued)

Number	Life Event	Mean Value
28.	Major change in living conditions (e.g., building a new home, remodeling, deterioration of home or neighborhood)	25
29.	Revision of personal habits (e.g., dress, manners, associations)	24
30.	Trouble with boss	23
31.	Major change in working hours or conditions	20
32.	Change in residence	20
33.	Changing to a new school	20
34.	Major change in usual type or amount of recreation	19
35.	Major change in church activities (e.g., a lot more or a lot less than usual)	19
36.	Major change in social activities (e.g., clubs, dancing, movies, visiting)	18
37.	Taking out a mortgage or loan for a lesser purchase (e.g., for a car, TV, freezer)	17
38.	Major change in sleeping habits (much more or less sleep, or change in part of day when asleep)	16
39.	Major change in number of family get-togethers (more or less than usual)	15
40.	Major change in eating habits	15
41.	Vacation	13
42.	Christmas	12
43.	Minor violation of law (e.g., traffic tickets, jaywalking, disturbing the peace)	11

Source: Holmes and Rahe's Social Readjustment Rating Scale, Journal of Psychosomatic Research, *November, 1967.*

Given that you don't get hit by a truck tomorrow on Main Street, chances are that your life and lifecycle follow some predictable patterns. At each point along your journey, whether it be because of mental or emotional pain or deprivation, a greater level or awareness, or consciously directed free will, you have the opportunity to reinvent yourself.

So let's examine how to leverage circumstances throughout your life, for the rich potential that various life passages may hold in terms of change.

Word Power

A **lifecycle** is the typical course of events in a person's life.

Tip

Visualize your new life in your new location and take only that which supports it.

Word Power

The **status quo** refers to things as they are. In other words, if things stay the same and nothing changes, one is said to be maintaining the status quo.

Following the Lifecycle

Following college, marriage, getting a good-paying job, and so on, eventually most people move from their current residence. You'd think, with all of humankind's technological breakthroughs, someone would do something about the onerous task of relocating. After all these years, there doesn't seem to be any way around loading and unloading every single thing you own, one item at a time, into a car or truck. You can hire people to do it, but the process of moving is no less disruptive. You have address cards to fill out, phone numbers to change, utility bills to reconcile, utility companies to call, and a ton of other activities to manage.

Seizing the Move

Determine ahead of time the specific changes that you want to be in effect after your move. Decide up front whether something will make the move, be sold, or be given away. This forces you to make decisions you wouldn't otherwise make when you're in the middle of a long-term lease and aren't considering relocating.

More than the physical move itself, there's something about the moving process that is akin to changing. It's a departure from the *status quo*. A move, like the start of a new year, is a place marker. It's an interval between one era and the next, namely, the time between when you lived in the former residence and when you moved to the new one.

In the new location, perhaps you not only want a new couch, but matching chairs and light fixtures to go with it. Perhaps your whole attitude changes. Maybe you decide it's time to upgrade your lifestyle and do more entertaining or to associate with more movers and shakers.

You may be moving because you got a raise. In either case, the raise or the move, you have a new vantage point from which to view your life. From that vantage point spring opportunities for reinvention unlike anything you've experienced.

New Perspectives for New Times

If you're married or are living with a significant other, a move can be a wonderful time in which to mutually reinvent yourselves. Perhaps you agree to let your partner have more space in the new location, or you agree to set up a home gym and buy some of those exercise machines advertised ad-nauseam on television.

Before and After a Job Change

Looking for a job when you don't have one is hard. Looking for a job when you do have one is still not an easy task. Starting a new job represents a wide variety of challenges. In all these cases, though, is a great opportunity for reinventing yourself.

Unemployed and Looking

As emotionally nerve-wracking and financially trying as looking for a job can be, it's one of the clearest opportunities you'll have in life to contemplate the type of changes you want to make. After all, when else do you get clear, uninterrupted stretches for determining exactly what's important in your life and career?

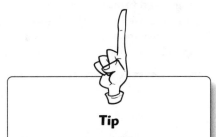

Tip

Whether it's a move or any other transition in your existence, exploit—in the positive sense of the word—the opportunity to reinvent yourself consistent with where you want to be in life.

Still, it's easy enough to get caught up in the notion of "I've got to find a job, and find one now!" as your job search wears on. The feeling of desperation can haunt you if you're not careful. Early in my career, I had a couple bouts of unemployment and, by the fourth and fifth month, started to feel as if I would never be employed again. I was young and didn't know better, and I let it affect my sense of self-worth. After all, wherever I went and whatever I did, I was among the unemployed. Couldn't people tell? It was as if I was somehow glaringly deficient.

With Crystal Clarity

Recognize that the crystal clarity you can bring to establishing goals related to your next job may help you get a job that's more consistent and more aligned with what you want to do in life and where you want to be at this age.

Here are some potential *goal statements* that may serve as starting points from which you could begin to reinvent yourself:

➤ To land the right full-time job by June 30 of this year with a salary of 10 percent more than my last position.

➤ To be employed in my industry as a manager at $38,500 or more within 120 days from now.

Word Power

A **goal statement** is an objective or desired result that is written down, measurable, and has a specific time frame.

➤ To land a sales position with a top EDP manufacturer with a 10 percent commission rate, to begin at the end of this quarter.

➤ To gain a summer internship with one of the Silicon Valley Internet service providers, at an average of $15 per hour or more, two months prior to the start of the season.

➤ To gain a year-long appointment to the special task force at my same salary, starting with the next fiscal year.

Reinvento Observes

If you're currently unemployed, realize this is simply a transition period in your long-term career. Perhaps you got fired or left your previous job under less-than-pleasant circumstances. Maybe you're new in the work place and have never had a career position. You may be re-entering the career world after many years. In any case, you're where you are for a reason, and you have before you the marvelous opportunity to set your sights on what is most appropriate, challenging, and enjoyable for you.

Milestones for the Taking

Here's a brief list of other potential career milestones around which you may find yourself naturally inclined to entertain the notion of reinventing yourself:

➤ You receive the largest pay increase in your career history.

➤ You are appointed by your organization's top officer to be on a special task force.

➤ You are elected to be an officer in your professional association or group.

➤ You are interviewed by a national publication.

➤ Your biographical information is published in a Who's Who directory.

➤ You are awarded an honorary degree.

Here are other possible noncareer-related milestones:

➤ You are asked to be on a special committee supporting your town council.

➤ Your local newspaper requests your views on a community issue for their opinion page.

➤ A literary magazine decides to publish your poem.

Accenting the Positive

Whenever any of the above types of events occur, given the new situation, you may find it fitting and appropriate to re-examine your life. For example, a four-year scholarship may mean that, instead of your son or daughter working the summer before entering college, the whole family can go on an extended vacation.

What's happened in your life lately that represents a milestone? What's on the immediate horizon that represents a potential milestone? And—here's one to put down in the book and ponder—what milestones have passed without your giving them much fanfare that you could now use to reinvent yourself?

Before and After a Mate Change

If you're in a relationship, particularly a long-term relationship, and it ends, whether your heart is slightly broken or seemingly crushed beyond repair, life moves on. Having your significant other leave you is heavy-duty. Divorce is heavy-duty. Even if you were the initiator of the breakup, the loss of a significant other can have a profound impact on you. However, from such developments can come new opportunities.

Reinvento Observes

At any given time the United States alone has some 15 million widowed persons, according to Jarrett Bennett, a certified financial planner in Fairfax, Virginia, and author of *Making the Money Last*.

Before

If you know your relationship is not going to make it, you have opportunities to make serious changes in your life.

Many psychologists believe that we have lessons we need to learn, and so we attract partners who will help us learn such lessons. Some people believe that we are attracted to those who seemingly have what we lack, so in our quest to be complete, we want a relationship with this person to complete us.

In either case, until we learn the importance of being relatively whole and complete individuals in and of ourselves, we're bound to repeat the same type of relationship mistakes with subsequent partners; thus, if you're breaking up with or divorcing your significant other and haven't learned more about yourself and your needs as a result of your relationship, you run a significant risk of replicating your prior relationship.

After

Whether you've just found someone new or you're in a long-term relationship, you potentially have the opportunity to view your mate in a new light. Perhaps it's time to talk about your relationship for the coming week, month, year, or five years. If you're in that in-between time, looking for somebody and not sure when and where he or she will appear, then get clear about what you're looking for in your next relationship. Ask yourself some questions:

➤ What kind of person do you want to meet?

➤ What level of commitment are you willing to offer?

➤ What level of sacrifice are you prepared to make?

➤ In what kind of activities do you want to engage?

➤ How much energy will you devote to the relationship?

➤ Will you be a better listener this time?

You can convert all these types of issues into goal statements, which will help ensure that you will achieve these reinvented relationship standards. Take the last one, for example. How might "Will you listen better this time?" appear as an established goal?

➤ To listen to my partner for at least 10 uninterrupted minutes at least three times a week during every week of the relationship.

If you mean business, once you're in a relationship with someone, and you intend to make it last and to be a better listener, you could share this goal with your partner! Not willing to share? Perhaps you're not as serious about being as good a listener as you had originally thought.

Don't Wait Until You're Desperate

People often wait for significant pain before they make major changes in their relationships. When one partner or the other threatens to leave, then, and sometimes only then, will the other partner agree to make changes.

Letting the Seasons Tell You

Here is a simple list of months and events throughout the year. Each of them represents an opportunity for you to clarify and focus more on what you want.

Month	Opportunity
January	New Year's: beginning of new you
February	Presidential birthdays: role model meditation
March	Spring approaching: time of rebirth
April	Daylight savings time: get outdoors!
May	Spring cleaning: relieve yourself of clutter
June	Graduations: celebration of movement into the world
July	Independence Day: renew your sense of patriotism
August	Dog days of summer, vacations: rest, reflect, renew
September	Labor Day, back to school: get back into a learning mode
October	Halloween: get playful, fantasize
November	Harvest, Thanksgiving Day: truly give thanks
December	Holidays, vacations: visualize world harmony

The climate in which you dwell, the temperature on a daily basis, and the weather at the moment can all be contributing factors to the changes you make. Spring is nature's rebirth. The very term "spring cleaning" arises from the fact that after raising windows closed all winter to keep the cold out, spirits begin to rise with the temperature, and it's much easier to engage in a thorough cleaning of your home. You can keep windows open and fans on as you transport debris. You can more easily change vacuum cleaner bags when it's warm outside. You can beat rugs outside. You can more easily clean windows. It's less treacherous to get up on your roof than it was when ice and wet conditions prevailed.

So, too, at various times during the year, you may find incentive to tackle projects that, at other times, you wouldn't touch with the proverbial 10-foot pole.

Caution

Changes under duress have a nasty habit of lasting only as long and the duress is present. What's more, while someone else can impose change on you, the changes have to be internalized, i.e., made your own, if they are to be effective.

Letting Your Age Tell You

Age can be a useful factor in reinvention. The mere fact that you turned 30 or 40 might be enough of an incentive for you to buckle down and try something new. A birthday ending in zero is a huge event. When you turn 30, 40, 50, or 60, you've passed a stage in life you'll never pass again. What a wonderful time to move into your next phase. You can use it the same way people use New Year's or the start of a new decade to spur themselves on.

On the Wings of Your Upcoming Age

If it's been a long-term notion of yours to clear the cellar of all its clutter and convert it into an office, and you're going to be 40 in two weeks … guess what? If you aim to convert the cellar into an office in the next two weeks, you're likely to proceed with more energy and focus than you would at some other time. After all, you've chosen to finish before you turn 40.

So, you plot your strategy. It will take a couple of days to clear everything out. Use one day for total cleaning. Take two days to have contractors paint, rewire, close off one area and expand another. Take a half-day at the office supply store to round up a desk, office equipment, paper, files, a bulletin board, a clock, and an answering machine. Another half-day can be used to call the phone company to get an additional phone line and call other utilities as the need arises. Another day to two days can be used to catch up on all the other things for which you may have budgeted the time too tightly.

Easy Marks

Certain traditional age markers are independent of any personal ones you might choose to act upon. The age of 16 is, of course, when many people get their automobile license. Others include age 13, becoming a teenager; age 17 or 18, graduating from high school; age 21, attaining the legality to consume alcohol; age 21 or 22, graduating from college; age 24 or 25, continuing education in graduate school, medical school, or law school. Finally, at age 30 you are (as 1960s radicals famously proclaimed) no longer to be trusted!

Age 40 has traditionally been a milestone, as in the expression "Life begins at 40." So many youthful people are in their 40s these days that age 50 is pretty much what 40 used to be. Age 65 is a traditional retirement age. Age 74 is a milestone in that it's considered to represent the average life span for American men, and age 79 is the average life span for American women, but these averages are rising fast.

Reinvento Observes

How about acknowledging the anniversary of your reinvention once it's finally in place?

Age 80, becoming an octogenarian, has been, in recent decades, held as a rite of passage. Age 90 is even more exclusive. Age 100 will garner you a postcard from the President.

Happy Anniversary

Your first anniversary is a milestone. Each anniversary represents the opportunity for reinventing yourself and your relationship. A twenty-fifth anniversary is certainly notable, and every five-year interval after that, admirable. Fiftieth anniversaries are rare, but you may be among the lucky few who celebrate it.

A sixtieth, seventieth, or seventy-fifth anniversary (they do happen) will land you mention in a national publication and on your local news, if not on NBC's nightly weekend report. The point is to use all of these milestones and more as incentive to keep establishing what you want in life.

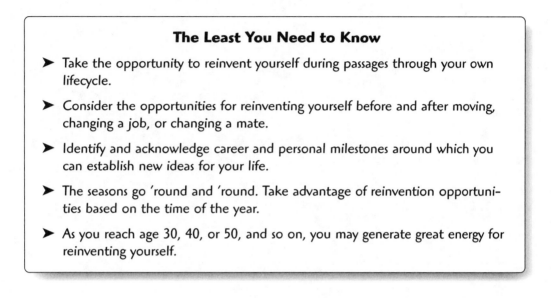

The Least You Need to Know

➤ Take the opportunity to reinvent yourself during passages through your own lifecycle.

➤ Consider the opportunities for reinventing yourself before and after moving, changing a job, or changing a mate.

➤ Identify and acknowledge career and personal milestones around which you can establish new ideas for your life.

➤ The seasons go 'round and 'round. Take advantage of reinvention opportunities based on the time of the year.

➤ As you reach age 30, 40, or 50, and so on, you may generate great energy for reinventing yourself.

Chapter 3

Assessing Where You Are

In This Chapter

➤ Where you are

➤ Where you can be

➤ Where you want to be

➤ Measuring the gap

So often in life, we look for answers everywhere but within. Many people write to Eppie Lederer, an 83-year-old woman from Sioux City, Iowa, seeking her counsel, although she has no particular credentials for dispensing advice. She receives more than 1,000 letters a day. Lederer (more widely known as Ann Landers) has a full-time staff of seven employees to handle the mail. Her biggest competitor is her sister, pen name Abigail van Buren, better known by her column, "Dear Abby."

A faster and more effective way to solve many problems, though, is to engage in self-assessment, which can lead to reinventing yourself. In this chapter, we'll discuss issues that will enable you to do the following:

➤ Get to the root of challenging issues you face.

➤ Take more responsibility for where you are in life.

➤ Decide on a course of action for reinventing yourself more quickly and easily.

Are these issues of at least passing interest for you?

Who Am I Kidding?

Despite where you are in the cycle of life, you may be relatively clueless as to where you are in the context of a specific situation. For example, a close friend—let's call her Sue—has been working in a large organization for many years. During this time, Sue has watched countless others in the organization forge ahead, obtaining promotions and salary increases while she seems to be in a career-long rut. It's not that Sue lacks intelligence or talent. Indeed, she has oodles of both. What, then, is her problem?

The Truth About Where You Are

Sue has never stopped to assess the truth about where she is in the organization. That is, she hasn't stopped to consider her strengths and weaknesses, what courses or skills she needs to acquire in order to continue along an upward career path. She has little idea as to how she is perceived or regarded by others, especially by those who have the power to help advance her or hold her back in her career.

Reinvento Observes

Without doing the internal "headwork," which is actually the groundwork it takes to get to the truth of where she is, it's unlikely that Sue is going to move up in the organization.

As the years go by, Sue moans and groans about missed opportunities, about others getting the "breaks," and about how the entire organization is riddled with favoritism. She has spent more time railing against the system than working within it. Yet she has no intention of leaving her post. She feels secure, almost comfortable, in her relatively low-level position.

Regardless of her vague reinvention plans, do you think that Sue is going to move even one iota?

In his book *On Becoming a Leader,* Warren Bennis, Ph.D., says, "I cannot stress too much the need for self-invention. To be authentic is to literally be your own author, to discover your own native energies and desires, and then define your own way of acting on them." Until Sue discovers her own native energies and desires, her chances for promotion are nonexistent.

The Truth About Where You Are 2

Someone else I know—let's call him Bob—is far less skilled than Sue; however, he is rising continually, if slowly, in his organization. He continually assesses his strengths and weaknesses. Bob …

➤ Is not defensive when he becomes aware of one of his shortcomings.

➤ Routinely assesses what he needs to do next in order to correct or compensate for the situation.

➤ Routinely reads books in areas where he could stand to be more knowledgeable.

➤ Volunteers for assignments at work that broaden his skills and capabilities.

➤ Takes courses at local colleges or through other adult education programs, often paying for them himself.

It is not easy to hold a full-time job, raise a family, and take nightly courses. Yet, Bob is honest with himself. He knows the consequences of *not* furthering his education, *not* addressing his professional weaknesses, and *not* progressing along his desired path. These consequences are far more expensive in the long run than taking action now to shore them up.

Change Requires Action

Jack Canfield, co-author of the *Chicken Soup for the Soul* series along with Mark Victor Hansen, says, "Everything that you want is out there waiting for you to ask. Everything that you want also wants you. But you have to take action to get it." The most appropriate action plan follows rigorous self-examination as to the truth about your current situation and clarity about what you want.

People who aren't willing to engage in self-assessment also have a hard time admitting that they made a mistake, saying "I'm sorry," or owning up to a wide variety of other behaviors. Conversely, think about the candidate running for office who, during a debate, or at some point along the campaign trail, makes a mistake and admits it. Survey data shows that the populace often receives such candidates more warmly after having made a mistake and then admitting it afterward.

Caution

Don't you often find that the most lamentable people you know are the ones who aren't honest with themselves? They seem to dwell too often in a netherworld where they internally gloss over some glaring personal deficiency, falsely believing that other people are not aware of it.

Others Love Self-Disclosure

People graciously allow for the faults and foibles of others when one is sincere, gracious, or forthright about them. From the standpoint of successfully reinventing your life, you need to assess where you are and where you want to be. Such an assessment is facilitated by first acknowledging to yourself the truth about where you are.

Word Power

An **axiom** is a truism of life, a premise that people accept as valid.

As the *axiom* goes, "If you can't be truthful with yourself, with whom can you be truthful?" If it's been a while since you engaged in this kind of exercise and this kind of thinking, then the first step is to take responsibility for where you are in life. Sure, you had some bad breaks; things that didn't go your way; people who have treated you badly. Everyone can say the same.

"How Did I Arrive at This Point?"

When total up all that you have done, all that you have experienced, and where you are right now, you have to concede that the vast majority of decisions were yours. You certainly were the only one who accompanied yourself every step of the way, and by all reason, must assume responsibility for where you are.

Caution

If you aren't responsible, then you're irresponsible. There is no middle ground here.

When I've followed a path that has led to considerable pain and gnashing of teeth, my favorite question is, "How did I get into this?" The answer to this question is more involved than initially meets the ear.

When writing this book, for example, I encountered some tough situations involving heavy travel and hosting of guests, concurrent with chapters being due. While you were watching the in-flight movie on that trip to the coast, I was mulling over notes, organizing pages, creating new passages, and proofreading old ones.

Fully answering the question, "How did I get into this?" involves understanding my *etymology.*

The Etymology of Me

Rather than taking you back to the start of humankind, I'll start with my parents who were born to parents of Byelorussian ancestry and grew up in New England. Because my grandparents were blue-collar workers, desirous of having their children

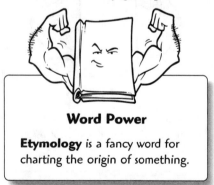

Word Power

Etymology is a fancy word for charting the origin of something.

go on to higher education, both of my parents graduated from college and were highly literate. Because of their value system, I surmise that I had good verbal skills at a young age.

At Ocean Beach Park in New London, Connecticut, my parents met, eventually married, and had children. Then they moved to Bloomfield, Connecticut, which was blessed with good schools. I was placed in the accelerated class. I went on to college and graduate school, majored in marketing, and thereafter got an MBA.

I didn't learn to write formally until I started my first job as a management consultant. Following each consulting engagement, I had to prepare a final consulting report, which was anywhere from 12 to 30 pages. I actually learned how to write correctly during this time.

After my father's death in 1977, I moved to Washington, D.C. Eighteen months later, my older sister died from a thrombosis—an arterial blood clot. This threw me into mental and emotional turmoil for more than a year. I went on a self-help journey, taking every course on health, nutrition, and stress reduction that I could find.

Trail Guides

On my path, I met an author by the name of Jefferson Bates, who inspired me to join the Washington Independent Writers. I became interested in this group and even became an officer of the association. Because of my written articles, I was asked to speak, which I enjoyed also.

I then joined the National Speakers Association, where I was exposed to some of the leading thinkers, literally, in the world. I began to develop higher expectations about myself, which led me to a series of mentors and empowering people, and ultimately to Robert Fritz's book, *The Path of Least Resistance,* wherein I learned about the power of making profound choices.

As I delved further into my now-dual profession of writing and speaking, I noticed that the pace of civilization seemed to be speeding up, and more people were in a frenzy more often throughout the day. I wrote a book called *Breathing Space: Living and Working at a Comfortable Pace in a Sped-Up Society.* From that, I eventually caught the eye of the publishers at Alpha Books, who asked me to write a book called *The Complete Idiot's Guide to Managing Your Time.*

While writing that book, I continued to fulfill speaking dates at conventions and conferences. Clearly, the rigors of the dual profession I chose would often lead to some rather tight deadlines and require some highly innovative solutions to avoid scheduling conflicts. So it was for this book as well.

In a brief history, I've described to you precisely how I got into the situation wherein I had to mix a heavy travel schedule with writing a book. My etymology leads to one inescapable conclusion: I choose to be doing this.

Consider the alternative. If you don't take responsibility for your present circumstances, you'll have a difficult time reinventing yourself. After all, if you're not in control, you're out of control!

The Etymology of Jeff Davidson

In a nutshell, here's my path. What would yours look like?

Grandparents emigrated → America

Hartford, parents → Traditions

Cultural factors → Verbal skills

Good schools → Accelerated classes

Friendships → Aptitude, era

Management consulting → Learned to write

Father's death → Moved to Washington, D.C.

Sister's death → Self-help journey

Joined Washington Independent Writers

Wrote books → Met Jeff Bates

Joined National Speaker Association

Exposure to leading thinkers

Higher expectation for myself

Wrote books → Noticed by Alpha Books

Heavy speaking schedule → Manuscript due

Reinvento Observes

If you're willing to accept most of the responsibility for the circumstances in which you currently find yourself, your quest for reinvention will be greatly accelerated.

Where You Can Be

Now, here is a concept so simple that it becomes profound: If you chose where you are, you can choose where you're going! But this may not mean what you think it means. A spate of books in the last half of the twentieth century (and I presume that the trend will continue at least in the first decade of the twenty-first century) offer a lot of blather about being anything you want to be, going anywhere you want to go, and so on. This is ridiculous when taken literally.

Only a handful of people in a generation can be president of the United States, no matter how many hundreds of thousands want to be president. A vertically challenged individual (someone who can't jump) will never win an Olympic medal in the high jump. I could go on, but you get the point.

Choosing Challenging Goals ...

I wrote an entire book about setting and reaching goals, called *The Complete Idiot's Guide to Reaching Your Goals.* In it, I discuss at length how to set challenging, yet appropriate, goals. Suffice it to say here, merely wishing on a star or desiring something spectacularly out of reach for most people usually represents an inordinate challenge that will only frustrate and confound them.

Nevertheless, the reinvention goals that you choose can still be quite magnificent. Ben Stein, host of the television show *Ben Stein's Money,* says, "The indispensable first step to getting the things that you want out of life is this: decide what you want." I add: after you decide, put your goals in a drawer for a few days before taking them out and looking at them again. Hone your goals; refine them; solidify them; put them away again. Repeat the process.

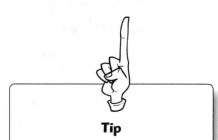

Tip

When you find yourself or your opportunities restricted in some way, ask yourself, "How did I get into this?" Give yourself time for an extended, thoughtful answer; maybe outline your etymology! Most of the time, you'll find that you got into this because of choices you made.

... And Committing to Them

When I was 26 years old, I could dunk a basketball. It was my golden year for leaping. At age 41, I had trouble even touching the rim. So I set myself the goal of being able to dunk again in my 40s. I started doing exercises at the gym, including leg-lifts with various weights. I improved my jumping somewhat, but couldn't get close to dunking the ball.

As time passed, I realized that I wasn't going to be able to dunk again with my present level of commitment. I further realized that I wasn't willing to raise my level of commitment. Theoretically, it's possible for a 40-something male to dunk a basketball. In revisiting this quest, I realized that what I was really after was the ability to stay in top condition, and that dunking a basketball was simply a manifestation of the underlying quest.

Finding the Underlying Issue

Today, at age 50, I am no closer to dunking than I was a few years ago, but my aerobic fitness level is comparable to that of a 25-year-old.

The underlying issue for me was to maintain a peak level of fitness and not necessarily to dunk a basketball. (Don't get me wrong—if I could stuff again, it would be a wonderful world.)

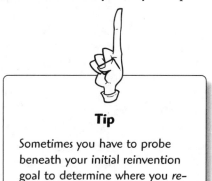

Tip

Sometimes you have to probe beneath your initial reinvention goal to determine where you *really* want to be.

Assess and Win

A variety of assessment tools exist today to help you determine your skills and aptitudes, which essentially pinpoint where you currently are. For example, some vendors, such as Carlson Learning based in Minneapolis, administer a wide variety of assessment tools. The Meyers-Briggs personality indicator test is popular among many, as is the Campbell Interest and Skills survey. Many career and vocational assessment centers within universities, secondary schools, and vocational and adult learning centers also administer such tests.

Some people find great utility in getting data about themselves that confirms or perhaps contradicts their long-held self-assessments. In any case, it makes sense to get to "know thyself."

Charles Garfield, Ph.D., in his book *Peak Performers,* writes:

> "Self-mastery calls for thorough familiarity with one's mental and emotional strength. And it calls for sustaining a commitment to personal growth—the understanding of what makes you tick as an individual as well as professional development."

Tip

If you have never taken such a test, it might be an enjoyable and worthwhile experience for you. At the least, you learn a few new things about yourself. At the most, you may decide to make a 180-degree turn in your career, hobbies, or other pursuits.

Where You Want to Be

Once you've done the spade work for getting to the truth about where you are in life and have taken responsibility for where you are, and if you have a pretty good handle on your skills and capabilities, you're in a prime position to map out where you want to be—what aspect of yourself you wish to reinvent.

To tap the level of brainwave activity in which you do some of your most profound thinking, some people find it appropriate to meditate (see Chapter 6, "Resting Your Mind and Your Body"), to take a walk in the woods, or to get away from noise and distractions however they can. Some choose to go on vacation, simply take a drive in the country, or even more simply, sit on the back porch.

Contemplate Your Values

Having found such a quiet space, literally or figuratively, and determining where you want to be, is largely a question of values. What do you value in life? To what are you willing to commit? What merits your time and energy?

Going a step further, what is worth trying, even if you fail and fail spectacularly? What is worth looking foolish over? What, in retrospect, would have been worth the effort, although at the time you didn't think it was worth the time or the money?

I find that looking out of the window from 30,000 feet up in an airplane is a marvelous time to reflect on where I have been, and where I want to head. Many people have tremendous moments of awareness while mountain climbing; others get it hiking in nature. Still others are able to sit in a favorite chair and have new insights spring forth.

Some people experience the "eureka moment," in which an explosion of energy and insight comes at an unpredictable time. Some do their best thinking in the shower. Some actually are able to use commuting time to great effect.

Caution

Don't censor yourself. You can always cross things out later. But if you don't record some of your wonderful ideas, like the proverbial slippery fish, they may be gone for good.

Contemplate and Capture

If some thoughts come when you are not near a pen and paper, a PC or Palm top, or a pocket dictator, then soon as you're in proximity of such recording devices, capture as many of your thoughts as you can. Flood your page or your screen with ideas.

Measuring the Gap

If where you are and where you want to be are miles apart, depending on your time, energy, resources, and level of commitment, you likely have considerable work ahead. As with all well-chosen and challenging goals, you'll need to map it out. Instead of biting off more than you can chew, formulate a plan. Create bite-size action steps that lead to accomplishment.

In the case of a large gap, you may decide that you only wish to go half as far, and having achieved that much, determine if you want to go the rest of the way. At all times, keep the quest within the bounds of possibility.

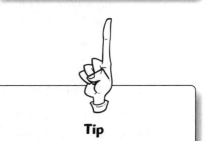

Tip

If the gap between where you are and where you want to be is sufficiently wide, then perhaps you need help. Look for a mentor or others with the same goals. Look for a trailblazer, somebody who has already gone down the same path, who can give you insights that could shave weeks, months, or years off your path.

Now for Some Real Work

The larger the gap, the more likely it is that you will need help to be successful. Fortunately, you have a number of strategies, including coaches, partners, team members, and other affiliations.

Working with others is rarely a substitute for engaging in real work on your own. In fact, coaches and others are likely to add to your overall task, because they will point out things that you didn't see and, in many cases, convince you of the need to accelerate your efforts.

The Least You Need to Know

➤ In the words of Warren Bennis, Ph.D., "To be authentic is to literally be your own author ... to discover your own native energies and desires and then define your own way of acting on them."

➤ When you total up all that you've done and experienced, and where you are right now, you have to concede that most of the decisions in your life were yours.

➤ Given that you choose where you are, you can choose where you're going!

➤ Sometimes you have to probe beneath your initial reinvention goal to determine where you *really* want to be.

➤ Determining where you want to be is largely a question of values.

Feed Your Head

Once you have made the decision to reinvent some aspect of your life, have considered where you are in the lifecycle process, are ready and able to leverage your circumstances, and have figuratively or literally measured the gap between where you are and where you want to be, the next major supporting element along your path is to "feed your head," as Grace Slick belted out in the Jefferson Airplane song, "White Rabbit." With what do you want to feed your head? Positive thoughts, good vibes, and a vision of succeeding!

Look Past the Facade

All around you, illusion prevails. Even stories carried by the press that represent the positive aspects of humanity are somehow tinged so that you feel like an outsider looking in. The photos of celebrities and models that adorn magazine covers are routinely airbrushed to perfection. Profile pieces in the popular women's magazines typically convey an ideal lifestyle complete with a tastefully adorned large home, wonderful *cherubic* children, and an adoring spouse for those who happen to be featured in this month's issue.

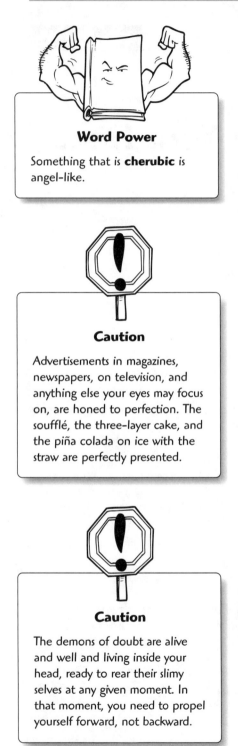

Word Power

Something that is **cherubic** is angel-like.

Caution

Advertisements in magazines, newspapers, on television, and anything else your eyes may focus on, are honed to perfection. The soufflé, the three-layer cake, and the piña colada on ice with the straw are perfectly presented.

Caution

The demons of doubt are alive and well and living inside your head, ready to rear their slimy selves at any given moment. In that moment, you need to propel yourself forward, not backward.

Why shouldn't they be? Artists first laid out how the ad should look; then designers, arrangers, and prop professionals ensured that the vision would be flawless; and the magazine, newspaper, television commercial, or other advertising medium accommodated the advertiser by ensuring that the image conveyed would represent nothing less than perfection.

An Imperfect, but Real, Life

Flash forward to your own life, replete with obstacles, where things don't always go as planned, where frustrations and irritations abound. Your spouse is less than ideal, and so are you, for that matter! Your children are not cherubic, you don't live in a mansion, and you don't bake perfect soufflés. How, then, would you ever imagine that you could accomplish some major reinvention of your life? Aren't such lofty aims reserved for and achieved by the people you read about? Do you really think you can pull this off? I mean, after all, who are you?

Against All Odds

Consider, as well, what could possibly be holding you back in your quest. Immediately, a plethora of answers appear. At any given moment, for whatever you want to accomplish, you will always have more convincing, more compelling, and more numerous reasons for *not* proceeding than for proceeding. Proceed anyway.

If you continually conjure up visions of lethargy, illness, dysfunctional relationships, isolation, or depression, why would you ever expect to get from point A to point B?

Cranial Readjustments

In overcoming potential psychological impediments to your quest, realize that reinvention is *awareness*. Awareness is that ability to notice your surroundings, to ascertain situations, and to recognize that you're hardly the first or the worst to go down the trail you're on.

When I come up against roadblocks in my quest to achieve a breakthrough (not always on the order of reinventing one's life!), I ask myself a key question: Am I the only one who has ever attempted this? Realistically, the answer has to be no. So, if I am not a pioneer in what I'm trying to achieve, this means that somebody else, someplace else, has done what I am trying to do. That prompts a few other questions:

Word Power

Awareness enables you to recognize that others have faced the same challenges that you face, and that they have been successful, and may have had far fewer skills, capabilities, or energy than you. Still, they overcame obstacles, and, ultimately, triumphed.

➤ Can I find such a person?

➤ Can I find an article or Web site that has information on what this person did?

➤ Can I learn from the experience of others?

I Can't Be the Only One

When I face a frustration or irritation and attempt to design a solution, I reflect on this statement: "I can't be the only one who wants to solve this problem. I can't be the only one who has been tripped up by this problem." If it's a computer-related issue, I look at the FAQs—frequently asked questions—that accompany Web sites, instruction booklets, and so on.

For larger issues, this simple process of becoming aware works just as well. You want to transform your relationship with your spouse? You want to take a six-month sabbatical? You want to switch professions completely? You want to go from bagged out to bust? In every case, someone has done it before you. You either know about such a person, or can read about such a person, somehow, some way, if you simply do a little digging.

Fight for Objectivity

Closely related to the goal of developing greater awareness is that of striving for objectivity. I gave a speech in Paris last year, at a symposium of pharmaceutical researchers. After the presentation, at a reception that evening, one of the attendees asked me about my seemingly high level of productivity, energy, and enthusiasm. She asked if I ever feel down, to which I replied, "Of course."

She then asked, "Well, what do you do to get yourself back up?" I thought about the question for a moment, recognizing that, as simple as it sounds, I had never been asked that before. Then, the answer emerged. "I fight for objectivity." I explained to her that I try to relate my situation to something else, perhaps the minor obstacle that I face compared to the situation of someone who truly faces a life-diminishing or life-threatening condition.

The Quest for Balance

The year 1996 was incredibly tough for me. In many ways, it was the most stressful year for me since my father and sister died 18 years before. It certainly was my most stressful year in business. I had computer malfunctions that lingered for more than seven months—first the hard drives, then the software, then a virus, then more hard-line problems; it seemed endless. I lost tens of thousands of dollars in missed opportunities, down time, and out-of pocket repair costs.

All the while, I kept thinking about two other individuals whose situations helped me to keep mine in balance. The first was Sergei Grinkov. He was a skater from Russia who had won two gold medals in the pairs figure skating with his long-time sweetheart and wife, Ekaterina Gordeeva.

The Grinkovs had moved to Simsbury, Connecticut, where they lived an almost idyllic life. They had a wonderful home, a three-year-old daughter, many friends, wealth, and fame. Their mutually enjoyed profession sustained them.

Reinvento Observes

General Colin Powell, in his book, *My American Journey*, said that most of the obstacles that we face today won't look quite so big or bad after a night's sleep.

Word Power

Cranial relates to the head, and more specifically, to your skull.

One day, while working out on the ice with his wife, Sergei dropped dead. No warning, no nothing. He was 28 years old.

Christopher Reeve, as everybody knows, was a talented actor, a family man, and a sportsman. He played soccer, swam, and rode horses. His public appearances, his messages, and his spirit for life in general, since he was thrown from a horse and forced into quadriplegia, have inspired everyone.

Model Yourself

An easy "*cranial* readjustment" to help chase away the demons, or anything else that could be holding you back in your quest to reinvent yourself, is to model yourself after someone else. Pick someone you know, or know of, whose actions, behaviors, or achievements appear to be within your capability.

In the simplest terms, if you know Joe down the hall is able to accomplish XYZ, and you know that if Joe can do it you can do it, then, in this sense, Joe has served as a simple model for you.

If you admire a celebrity, a sports star, an author, or some other highly accomplished individual, perhaps you can emulate some aspects of that person's behaviors and achieve high accomplishment.

As a variation, choose selected traits and characteristics from a number of people, the aggregation of which adds up to the type of behaviors, the level of achievement, or the kind of person that you would like to be. Consider, for example, the aggregation of individuals in groups such as the U.S. Women's World Cup Soccer team, an *Apollo* space mission crew, or the Human Genome Project Team.

Read and Succeed

Reading promotes awareness and objectivity. For whatever you want to accomplish, you're likely to find a bevy of good books on the topic these days. Buy or borrow from the library 6 to 12 good books on the topic of your choice, and read one a month for the next 6 to 12 months, and you can't help but feed your head with the right kind of insights and breakthroughs that will propel you along.

Take the books along with you when you travel and on vacations. Dwell on the magnificence of what noted authors have been able to capture on page. Blend your own thoughts with theirs, and come up with your own vision of what you want to achieve, following your unique path.

Collect and Win

If the spirit moves you, start a clipping file of articles you encounter that inform or inspire you. These might come from magazines, Web sites, newspapers, or anything in between. Let your packet grow! You can always weed out the duplicates and less important materials later. The mere fact that you started a file folder is an excellent initiative in support of your desired outcome.

It has been said that whatever you think about expands. So, too, whatever you read about. To paraphrase the ancient philosophers, "As a man thinketh, so shall he be." Reading facilitates thinking. You can literally read your way into a new mindset. You can change the way that you think as a result of your reading. With particularly effective reading material, you can be a different person by the time you turn the page.

Caution

When modeling after others you want to be careful not to pick someone whose achievements you regard as so grand that, for modeling purposes, there will be little or no effect on your behavior. For example, Mark McGwire has 554 career home runs. If you are a 37-year-old male who is mediocre at baseball, don't put yourself down for not keeping up with McGwire. Be realistic.

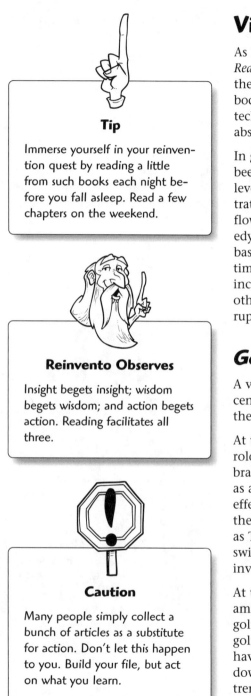

Visualize and Realize

As I discussed in my book *The Complete Idiot's Guide to Reaching Your Goals,* visualization is a powerful tool on the path to achieving any desired goal. A growing body of evidence indicates that using visualization techniques can aid in one's performance—even in the absence of practice sessions!

In general, basketball free-throw percentages have been dropping for several years at the pro and college level. It appears that this shot requires greater concentration than a standard jump shot taken during the flow of the game. Visualization could be used to remedy this lack of concentration. For example, a study of basketball players revealed that visualization during time away from practice enabled half of one team to increase their foul shot percentages above those of the other half of the team, who participated in uninterrupted practice with no visualization!

Get in the Zone

A variation on the theme of visualization is deep concentration, or what many people refer to as being "in the zone."

At the University of Chicago, researchers, led by neurologist Dr. John Milton, are actually studying the brains of professional golfers. Because golf is regarded as a sport that requires largely mental skills to ensure effective physical execution of all strokes, it has been the subject of intense scrutiny. A golf champion, such as Tiger Woods, is able to focus so intently on his swing before he actually takes it, that the results are invariably outstanding.

At the University of Chicago, the research team is examining on a neurological level what happens to golfers when they enter the "zone." Nine top female golfers with the Ladies Professional Golf Association have volunteered for this study. A long, green carpet down the laboratory hallway, as well as other accoutrements of the golf course, help volunteer LPGA participants to achieve their focused state, while wired to sophisticated diagnostic equipment that charts brain patterns.

The theory is that brain activity during visualization mirrors that of actual physical movement. Milton hopes that, one day, stroke victims will be able to visualize themselves walking as a prelude to having them actually walk.

Do-It-Yourself Psych Jobs

In his book, *What You Say When You Talk to Yourself,* Dr. Shad Helmstetter says that the quality of our lives, let alone our capacity for reinvention, is dependent upon our self-talk. All day long, that little voice within us is saying things like, "I shouldn't have done that," "I really botched that," "It looks like this is going to be one of those days," "Why did I do that?" "I never get this right," "This probably isn't going to work," "I'm always messing up," and "I don't have a chance at this." In saying such things we are actually predicting our fate with reasonable accuracy.

Dr. Helmstetter says that if you were told at an early age that you're just no good at a particular skill, the chances, unfortunately, are that you may have convinced yourself that you are no good at it. Hence, you go about your life collecting evidence to confirm this erroneous notion until it becomes your own. "Well, of course I'm no good at XYZ; I've never been good at it." Yet, such pronouncements, carefully maintained and nurtured by your subconscious, are not your destiny.

If even half of Helmstetter's findings are correct, this means that it is vitally important to set up your immediate environment so that it will support you around the clock. In addition to taping affirmations on cassette and posting positive messages throughout your home and office, here are additional tips for establishing a highly positive environment:

➤ Subscribe to positive magazines such as the *Optimist, Real Simple,* or *Guideposts.*

Reinvento Observes

Being "in the zone" is an altered state of consciousness that enables people to concentrate so intently on their desired objectives that their resulting actions are often excellent and automatic, helping them to accelerate their progress toward the goal.

Caution

Negative phrases, which can take hundreds of forms, literally direct our lives in ways we wouldn't allow if we were conscious of what was going on. Each of these statements is a powerful limiter of what we experience and accomplish in a day, week, in our careers, and in life. The subconscious part of our mind takes in everything we're exposed to and carefully files it away.

➤ Bookmark the Web sites of organizations that publish the above magazines as well as other positive Web sites such as "Destination Hope," at www.desthope.com; "Holistic Online" at www.HolisticOnline.com; "Planet Link" at www.planetlink.com; "Positive Press" at www.positivepress.com; and the "Prosperity Meditation Center" at www.Positive-place.com.

➤ Read positive books such as John Templeton's *Is Progress Speeding Up?, The Laws of Life,* and *Golden Nuggets,* which can be ordered at www.templetonpress.org.

➤ Watch positive and uplifting movies and videos such as *Chariots of Fire, Apollo 13,* and *Jerry Maguire,* and old-time movies such as *Singing in the Rain, Yankee Doodle Dandy, Going My Way,* or *My Fair Lady.*

➤ Hang around with positive and uplifting people—you know who they are.

➤ Listen to positive, upbeat television and radio talk shows, forsaking the shock talkers, and the *Jerry Springer*–type shows that highlight people who seem to take delight in airing the details of their menial lives. What shows can you tune into instead? Try the History Channel, The Learning Channel, and Arts & Entertainment. On the radio, tune into NPR's *People's Pharmacy, All Things Considered,* and *Market Place,* to name a few.

➤ Read positive and uplifting books, particularly biographies of those who overcame great odds such as Helen Keller, Roger Banister, Victor Frankl, John McCain, James Stockdale, and Nelson Mandela.

➤ Read poetry, which has been described as "prose packed under pressure."

➤ Read the words of great philosophers and learned men and women throughout the ages.

If Not You, Who?

What if your reinvention represents something that no one has ever done before, at least to your knowledge? Does that mean that you shouldn't proceed? Geraldine Ferraro was the first woman to run for vice president of the United States. Joseph Lieberman was the first Jew to run for vice president of the United States. Someday soon, an African-American and a Hispanic American will be running for vice president or president of the United States. No one has done it before, but that needn't stop you! For every noble pursuit, someone has got to be the first to attempt it.

Someone was the first to step on the Moon, just as someone was the first to sit in the front of a segregated bus. Someone was the first to swim the English Channel. Think about your life and all that you have accomplished up to this point and what you want to do in terms of reinventing it. So what if ...

➤ Your quest represents a first for humankind, your gender, or your ethnic background?

➤ It represents a first for a person of your age, income, demographic background, or heritage?

➤ No one in your state, county, town, or neighborhood has done it before?

➤ There is no particular role model since you are treading on entirely new ground?

If the little voice within you says to proceed, then follow it gladly. You become the role model. You become the one from whom others gain inspiration. Carve your own path; mark your own trail ... you belong there.

Chuck Colson: From Watergate to the Gates of Heaven

At one time, Chuck Colson was one of the most powerful men in America. He was the Special Counsel to President Richard Nixon, and heavily involved in the Watergate Scandal. Heavily involved, perhaps, in watering down the truth.

At his trial, Colson admitted to knowing all about the workings of the Watergate break-in as well as the illicit and illegal money involved in the caper. His justification at the time was that there were no limits to his dedication in getting Richard Nixon re-elected in 1972. After the fallout of the Watergate Scandal, Colson was sentenced to a prison term. It is during this time that his reinvention began.

Giving Hope to the Hopeless

Having the time to reflect, Colson came upon the writings of C. S. Lewis. These deeply affected him and prompted him to search for God. Ultimately, Colson founded an organization called "Prisoner Fellowship," a ministry to inmates, which gives them the opportunity to seek God by changing their hearts.

Because of his prominence in the Nixon White House and the seemingly dramatic turnaround he achieved, Colson was widely covered by the media. At first, many people were skeptical, but in time Colson's reinvention proved on many levels to be authentic. Today he has a daily radio broadcast, titled *Breakpoint,* which gives news and views from the Christian perspective. Although many still are wary of him, he continues to be a major player in the conservative, Christian world.

Colson has been busy on the speaking circuit. For example, he has spoken at the annual convention of the National Association of Evangelicals, at various seminaries, as a commencement speaker, and on the Reverend Jerry Falwell's broadcasts.

He has been awarded the title of Honorary Doctor of Law, which may seem ironic considering his time in jail prior to his re-invention.

A Lesson to Be Learned

Colson, although kept at a distance by some people because of his extreme leftist views, is a man from whom we can take a lesson. He was a part of one of the most prominent scandals of the twentieth century. Yet he considers this involvement and eventual punishment to be the lifesaver that he needed to become right with God. Colson's life teaches us that even the most awful and humiliating times can be used to reinvent our lives.

Colson did not crawl into a hole; instead, he became a new man, one who went from hiding the truth from people to one who is trying to show his truth to people. You may not agree with his views, but you can certainly learn from his reinvention.

The Least You Need to Know

➤ For any given reinvention there are a variety of obstacles and roadblocks that can hold you back, few of which are insurmountable.

➤ Develop a positive internal dialog so that you stay more focused, more of the time.

➤ Surround yourself with positive and uplifting messages including what you read, what you watch, and with whom you associate.

➤ Read at least a book a month, on your area of focus, for the next 6 to 12 months.

➤ Visualize, visualize, visualize yourself succeeding, and you increase the probability that you will succeed.

Chapter 5

Overcoming the Impetus of Staying Put

Does this sound like you?

➤ You never file your taxes on time.

➤ You send out greeting cards too close to the occasion for them to arrive on time.

➤ You shop for presents at the last minute.

➤ You see a doctor only months after suspecting that something is wrong.

➤ You have desk drawers that are jammed with stuff—but you'll "get to it one of these days."

➤ You initiate some task *after* the deadline.

Much of what you may need to do to achieve a desired outcome may not please you while you're doing it. Jogging for many miles to reduce your waistline or saving more and spending less won't necessarily make you feel better on any given day. Eventually, when your waistline is at the trim target you've chosen, or your savings account has grown to a healthy balance, you understand that less-than-pleasing now means highly pleasing later.

If Not Now, When?

In his various speeches and exhortations about the need for civil rights in the United States, the Reverend Jesse Jackson was wont to say, "If not now, when?" So it is with the quest to reinvent your life. The impetus of staying put, staying where you are, is a real and pervasive problem for people everywhere seeking to change.

When we draw upon some of the simplest notions of physics, it's easy to understand why the impetus of staying put is so strong. Sir Isaac Newton's First Law of Motion, more commonly known as the theory of gravity, holds that a body at rest tends to stay at rest, and a body in motion tends to stay in motion.

Reinvento Observes

Any time you have discretion over the order in which you tackle steps, handle the seemingly unpleasant elements first. If you do what you like to do first, and save the unpleasant things for last, the probability of procrastinating increases. In any case, get started now!

You and Sir Isaac

Newton's laws, as applied to your life, work this way: Suppose that you're 32 years old. That means everything that you have ever done up until this point, every word that you have ever read, every word that you have ever said, every time that you have even put your head upon the pillow, has contributed to the development of who and what you are in this world right now.

So, if you're 32 years old, you're 32 years in the making (plus, of course, nine months). The viewpoints that you've formed, the habits that you've developed, and the entity that you've become, are just perfect—a perfect you. You have the ability to change. You have the ability to reinvent yourself. However, you have to overcome the hurdle that 32 years of being you presents.

If you're 42, then, understandably, all other things being equal, overcoming the impetus of staying put is even greater. Even more so at 52 and 62.

Less to Change

Conversely, at 12 and at 22 you've lived a lot less; you're relatively more open, more impressionable, and more easily adaptable to change. Studies have shown that young children can pick up a second and third language far more easily than adults can. So, too, children can learn a musical instrument or become proficient at a particular sport by starting early.

If you are 42 or over, this isn't to say that your path to reinvention will be measurably harder than that of a 32-year-old or 22-year-old, because you have other "gifts" to work with. For one, your wisdom and experience are likely to be more pronounced than those of your younger counterparts.

Motivation Is Enough

If you have experienced emotional pain, some kind of deprivation, or simply a strong desire to seek another direction in life, it really doesn't matter what age you are.

When asked why he was reading the voluminous *Lives* of Plutarch at the then-advanced age of 85, former justice Oliver Wendell Holmes replied, "To improve my mind." Late Grandma Moses, renowned for her paintings, didn't take up the discipline until her 80s, and then painted well past age 100.

Reinvento Observes

If it was easy for you to make changes to your life in the past, then it may be easy for you to make changes now. What's most important, though, is your motivation.

What's Holding You Back?

If age isn't necessarily a barrier to reinventing your life, then what keeps so many people from taking the first step? As it turns out, habitual behaviors—or habits, for short—have far more impact on daily activities than we might imagine. Research has shown that the more often you engage in a behavior, the stronger the neuronal pathways in your brain develop to increase the probability that you keep doing what you're doing.

Reinvento Observes

If you drive home from work the same way every day, month after month, year after year, it may be difficult for you to even consider taking another route, unless traffic is so bad that you'll try anything! If you are involved in the same exercise regimen or lack thereof, chances are that you are going to continue on that same path. Alarmingly, research also shows that if you continue living by these habits long enough, your potential for creativity literally shuts down.

Deep in your 40s, decades of habitual behavior, habitual thought patterns, and a habitual life, all but ensure that your level of creativity in approaching life will be but a fraction of what it might have been 10, 20, and 30 years ago. All of which, I repeat, is not to say that you can't change. Chances are, however, that you will have to have extraordinary motivation.

Yes, Now, and How

It is an axiom of life that if you are seeking a change, the best possible time to begin is now. If not now, when? Like the dieter who was always going to start next week, without making a commitment to change now, you find that next week doesn't seem to come. The false promise of beginning something next week, next month, or whenever, is really a disguised form of procrastination.

Victor Kyam, one time CEO of the Remington Company, said, "Procrastination is opportunity's natural assassin."

Procrastination Is Your Enemy

The energy and anxiety that you invest in putting off an activity often consumes more energy than it would take to actually do the activity. If you have a notion to reinvent some aspect of your life, but have been continually putting it off, you actually may be draining your batteries! You may be sapping yourself of the vital energies that you could have harnessed to get started and succeed in your quest.

Take Action, Gain Satisfaction

If procrastination is your enemy, then action is your friend. Respecting Mr. Newton— if a body in motion tends to stay in motion, even the smallest action can get you out of your inactivity and started on the path to some change in the quest to reinvent your life. It's better than no action at all. A small action could consist of …

Caution

Contemplation of a change does have value. Germination has value. When a desired change has marinated in your mind to the point where it is starting to get soggy, you need to get started! So often the changes we put off making, once we actually get started, require less effort, less energy, and less time than we thought!

➤ Making a phone call.

➤ Visiting the library.

➤ Going on the Internet.

➤ Subscribing to a new publication.

➤ Joining an organization.

➤ Creating a file folder.

➤ Clearing out a drawer.

➤ Rearranging your closet.

➤ Writing a letter.

➤ Making a presentation.

➤ Dropping a service.

➤ Buying a resource tool.

➤ Seeking assistance.

➤ Clearing your desk.

➤ Visualizing yourself as successful.

➤ Setting up a reward system.

➤ Rearranging your calendar.

➤ Prioritizing tasks.

Blasting Through Procrastination

Some people can't get started on making a change in their life because they're waiting for the perfect moment or, worse, waiting until they know conclusively that the change will succeed. This type of mindset represents a trap that will keep you from ever moving to point A from point B.

Julia Cameron, author of *The Artist's Way*, says, "*Perfectionism* is not a quest for the best. It is the pursuit of the worst in ourselves, the part that tells us that nothing we do will ever be good enough …"

If you're waiting for the time when you think the change will perfectly succeed, think again. You're wasting precious time, and your quest is losing. At all times, you're but a work in progress. My friend, Jim Folks, a management trainer, says, "You can only be where you are." And, I might add, you can only become what you will become next.

If this is all too philosophical for you, then here it is in shorthand: Let go of perfectionism. There won't be a perfect time to change, and your change won't be perfect. Proceed anyway.

Word Power

Perfectionism is the practice of attempting to make things perfect, and it is often a disguise for not proceeding or for being discontent.

➤ The winning lotto ticket?

➤ A big raise or promotion?

➤ Your children to grow up?

➤ Your name in lights?

➤ A sunny day?

➤ A female president?

➤ A rainy day?

➤ Someday?

Break On Through to the Other Side

Here are a variety of ideas for helping you to break through any self-imposed limits to getting started on something:

➤ Share your deadlines with others for the support they may offer.

➤ Clear your desk of everything, except the materials related to the task at hand.

➤ Visualize yourself having completed the task you're toiling with.

➤ Give yourself constant small rewards as you complete certain small parts of the undesirable task.

➤ Allow yourself to have some break time.

Off-Your-Duff Strategies

Let's look at the many ways you can blast through the obstacles that thwart your ability to get started.

Get Some Rest!

If you're having trouble starting a task, perhaps you're tired. When you're well rested and well nourished, you have the best chance of doing your best work. Conversely, when you don't have enough sleep and haven't eaten well, even the simplest tasks can loom larger than they really are.

After you feel rested, get organized. When you "divide and conquer," you have a good chance of overcoming procrastination. Regard each task before you as a distinct entity. When you tackle a five-minute job, and gain the satisfaction of having it all done, you have more energy, focus, and direction to take on another five-minute job.

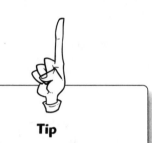

Tip

If your ignorance on a subject is holding you back from completing the task, find knowledgeable people and ask them for help. They may be able to give you a running start, which can be as good an incentive as anything. Once your questions are answered and you feel more confident about the task, you can begin.

Suppose you do five of those five-minute jobs, and with each job you feel a sense of victory, however minor. This spurs you to do the next job and then the next. In this manner, five of the 5-minute jobs can actually be easier than one 25-minute job.

And in Just Five Minutes ...

If you're having a hard time getting started, promise yourself that you'll engage in the task for *only* five minutes. After five minutes, you have the option of stopping or continuing. Fortunately, many times, once you get in motion, you're more than willing to continue.

If you face many projects at once, don't be afraid to trade one off for another.

➤ Seek a partner, even for a few minutes, who can help you get started. It helps especially if you can find someone who has already had to tackle what you currently face.

➤ If you find you simply can't tackle the harder task first, play one task off against another. If task A is terrible, but task B is worse, then perhaps in this context task A doesn't look so bad, and you can get started on it.

Identify the Lingering Issue

Sometimes it's difficult to get started because you haven't identified some lingering issues that are affecting your feelings toward the task.

➤ Perhaps you're ambivalent about the task.

➤ Perhaps you think it's unnecessary or unworthy of you.

➤ Perhaps you resent doing it—i.e., you weren't able to say no in the first place, and now you have to make good on your earlier promise.

Identify the reason for your procrastination and blast through it. The reason is only an excuse to not get the job done.

Get a Jump-Start

Often a jump-start is all you need so that you can stop procrastination. The mere act of turning on your PC, popping a video into the VCR, or flipping on your pocket dictator may be enough to get started on a task that you've been putting off. For example, suppose your car conks out on the side of the road, and your battery gets a jump-start. All of a sudden, the engine is *revving;* this is certainly not a time to turn off the car. You want to keep it running for a good 20 minutes.

Word Power

Revving is the same as humming or operating at optimum capability.

Likewise, once that PC boots up and your hard drive is humming, you may experience a jump-start in your ability to delve into the project.

Look for an Easy Win

For whatever you're trying to tackle, if you can find some element of it that you can complete quickly and easily and get an easy "win," that's a far-easier method of getting started than tackling some difficult portion of it first.

By getting organized, an easy win, you have a better handle on the project. The supporting items are

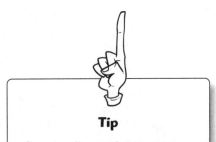

Tip

Occasionally, simply organizing materials, putting them into smaller file folders, stapling items, or rearranging the order of things represents a good, early win.

in the importance of how you arranged them and the probability of your continuing on is reasonably assured.

The Reframe Game

Another way to tackle procrastination is to reframe the task. In other words, approach the job from a different perspective. When Tom Wolfe, the novelist, was working for *Esquire* magazine and was already past the deadline for an article, his editor gave him a wonderful suggestion. Wolfe was to start writing a letter to the editor, describing how he would approach the article and what he would put in it.

So, Wolfe submitted a draft that started off like a letter. Sure enough, by eliminating the first paragraph or two, and retaining the body of what Wolfe had written, the editor had the requisite material. Like Wolfe, you may not have trouble with the task, but simply with getting started.

Recruit and Win

No matter what you try or how hard you try, sometimes you still can't get started on the task you've been putting off and the associated stress begins to increase. This is a great time for your friends to prove how strong a friendship you truly have.

Don't be afraid to join forces with someone who has the same goals as you. This suggestion requires an extremely trustworthy friend, because your money will be involved. You give a friend $500 and you tell him, "If I don't finish this task by next Thursday, you get to keep the $500." This is not for the meek or the broke. And, if $500 means nothing to you, raise the ransom. When you find the right sum, I guarantee you'll finish the task on time.

Hey, Check Me Over

Did you ever stop to think that the reason you finish a task at work with such rapid precision is because you have a boss awaiting the results of your task? Perhaps you could ask a friend to check the task after it's completed and give him a deadline for when you should report to him.

While you don't necessarily want to treat personal tasks like assigned tasks, having to report your progress to someone will increase your odds of starting and finishing a job in a timely manner.

Don't Hesitate to Delegate

Here's something fun: Find a portion of the task that you can delegate, especially if there is a part that you are not good at doing or do not want to do. Let's face it, there are some tasks that, no matter how hard you try, how many lessons you take, and how long you practice, you're not going to be good at.

Plan Your Escape

Sometimes you have to escape from the every-day dealings so that you can begin your task. For example, you may have to clear your desk, have your receptionist hold your calls, or turn the ringer off on your phone in order to get started. That's okay. These distractions could be a reason for your procrastination, so eliminate them and give yourself an uninterrupted span of time.

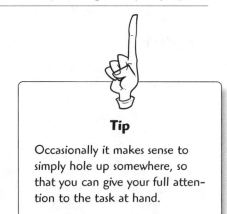

Tip

Occasionally it makes sense to simply hole up somewhere, so that you can give your full attention to the task at hand.

How to Avoid Slipping Back

Once you have set upon a course of action, you tend to stay on that path. However, obstacles to your progress are likely to appear. You may be fatigued. You may lose focus. You may become disheartened. It's crucial to devise some strategies at the outset that will keep you going along the path.

You repeat behavior that is positively reinforced. So, if you set up a series of rewards for yourself for accomplishing small steps on the path to reinventing some aspect of yourself, you have a greater probability of being successful. Rewards can take various forms. For accomplishing a particular activity or task, you may decide that calling or e-mailing a friend is sufficient reward for your accomplishment. For other people, it could be a stroll around the block, a favorite snack, a 20-minute nap, or a bubble bath.

Some people reward themselves by reading a favorite magazine or book, preparing and eating a favorite dish, watching a show on television, going to a movie, or engaging in some hobby. Still others reward themselves by buying something, getting a massage, sitting in the steam room at the gym, or sleeping longer the next morning.

A Small Reward for Each Step

If your plan consisted of 20 steps, and you plotted in advance how you would reward yourself for accomplishing those 20 steps, you would greatly increase the probability of your success. You could have some rewards repeated or have a different reward following each task. It's up to you.

For some people, simply allowing themselves to daydream is a reward. For others, it's taking no work home from the office, going a whole weekend without reading, playing a musical instrument, participating in a sport, taking off early without feeling guilty, or even doing a crossword puzzle.

Many people tie their rewards to the Internet, such as visiting a favorite Web site, playing a favorite game, checking up on sports scores or stock-market values, attending a forum, or visiting a chat room. For others, it's reading a *Dilbert* comic strip or the Lifestyle section of the newspaper.

Maintaining Momentum

Along your path to reinventing some aspect of your life, even if you're a master at overcoming the impetus of staying put, blasting through procrastination, and establishing a reward system to keep you on track, there will still be some down time. Sometimes you will be too tired; sometimes you won't have the right resources; or sometimes you will just feel out of sorts.

When these things happen, recognize that a brief delay along the path is just that: a temporary delay, not a catastrophe. My friend, Willie Jolley, wrote a book with a very clever title, which also serves as great insight as you proceed in your quest: *A Setback Is a Setup for a Comeback.* Keep these words in mind whenever you feel that your progress is waning.

The more challenging your reinvention, the more likely you are going to incur challenges. Staying put doesn't require much effort. Moving forward does. The best time to move forward is now.

The Least You Need to Know

➤ Right now is the most important time in your life.

➤ Procrastination is your enemy. The anxiety associated with a stalled activity can burn up more energy than would be required to complete the activity.

➤ In blasting through procrastination, action, even a small action, is your friend.

➤ Set up a reward system so that when you complete each step along your plan, you are positively reinforced to continue on your path to reinvention.

Part 2

Getting Your Mind in Gear

A mind is a terrible thing to waste—especially yours. If the creative component within you has been a little dormant in recent years, fear not! You can wake it up and put it back to work to reinvent yourself in wondrous ways.

In Part 2, we'll start off with the important notion of resting your mind and your body. Then we'll look at the many ways to stretch your mind. Some are effortless and some require what you might consider to be work. In any case, the chapters that follow enable you to get more of the neurons in your cranium firing more of the time. The younger you are, the easier it is to do. (Hey, isn't that the case too much of the time?) Still, even if you're a member of the 40-something, 50-something, 60-something-or-older group, it will all still work for you. Read on!

Chapter 6

Resting Your Mind and Your Body

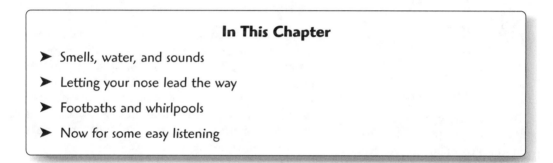

In This Chapter

➤ Smells, water, and sounds

➤ Letting your nose lead the way

➤ Footbaths and whirlpools

➤ Now for some easy listening

People reinvent themselves all the time without necessarily gearing up for the process, let alone engaging in any mind-relaxing, body-soothing rituals. Nevertheless, the following will sure help, if you have the time, inclination, and the curiosity. All the techniques discussed here are tried and true. They have been handed down through the ages, honed and refined, and are proven to be effective.

Aromatherapy: Smelling Good and Feeling Good

In perhaps an over-accented moment in history, Cleopatra, Queen of Egypt, seduced Mark Anthony, a Roman General, by surrounding him with heaps of rose petals—or, at least, that's how the story goes. Cleopatra herself was often found decked out in sequins, fabulous gowns, and colorful clothing that would make any peacock envious. And, Cleopatra bathed herself in the most alluring essences of the day.

Flash forward to today, where researchers at the Smell and Taste Treatment and Research Foundation based in Chicago, Illinois, conduct hundreds of tests annually to determine what smells have what effects. Dr. Alan Hirsch, neurologist and founder, says that an invisible universe exists at the tips of our noses.

Sex Machine

Hirsch conducted one study wherein he exposed 31 men to 46 different scents to discover which, if any, would excite them sexually. As it turned out, the combination of lavender and pumpkin pie actually increased penile blood flow by 40 percent! If you're wondering what scents sexually excited women, it turned out to be a combination of the smells of sweet licorice and cucumber. How is that for the power of *aromatherapy!?*

In another experiment, Hirsch determined that sniffing lavender oil when retiring for the evening was as effective as any sleep medication for some insomniacs!

Why Does the Nose Know?

How is it that the nose comes to be the center of such a mysterious and powerful universe? Right above the nasal cavity is the *olfactory epithelium.* This area, no bigger than your thumbprint, is home to millions of receptor cells in the cilia, which swim about in a layer of mucus. Though the actual process by which we perceive and identify odors remains a mystery, one day soon it is likely to be unraveled.

Until then, it's enough to know that the smells you perceive fire direct messages to the limbic system within the brain. The *limbic system* is that sacred chamber within your brain that has the greatest influence on your capacity for anger, memory, love, indulgence, and a lot of other primitive emotions and behaviors.

Your olfactory sensors, located in your nose and up, are directly connected to the brain. Unlike light images, which have to be translated before you can recognize them visually, aromas do not have to be translated. "Passing Go," and "collecting $200," they proceed directly to the brain. Hence, aromas are powerful memory triggers and evoke emotion via *neurotransmitters* in the brain.

Memories Are Made of This

Although they often are surrounded by its effects, most people entirely underestimate the power of scent. A single drop, for example, of what are called essential oils (plant extracts), found in any health food store, can make its way directly to your brain and trigger the chemical reaction that leads to the release of serotonin, increasing your feeling of health and well-being.

A single whiff of some scent that is pleasurable to you can literally help to generate a tidal wave of memories and feelings. Surprisingly, this mechanism has probably been in place since before you were born! Monell Chemical Scent Center, based in Philadelphia, is touting the notion that we all may have been impacted through scents absorbed by our mothers while in utero. And you'll be more likely to regard those scents as favorable later in life. If you happen to like thyme or lemon, chances are you got a whiff of it in the womb!

Word Power

Neurotransmitters—chemical messengers that trigger the brain to dispatch information—control brain-wave activity and patterns, your blood pressure, breathing, heart rate, glandular activity, and hormonal production.

Aromas in Everyday Life

Many natural substances help you feel calm and serene. For some people, the smell of pine works wonders; for others, it's lemon. Do you remember your last trip to a shopping mall where you got a strong whiff of the chocolate chip cookies baking around the corner? Or how about a whiff of pizza as the dough was rising?

Shopping mall designers have long known the power of scents. It's no coincidence that when you walk through the halls of a shopping mall, you're likely to catch a whiff of fresh-baked cookies, pizza baking in the oven, or sweet-and-sour pork. Designers develop the malls so that the food court smells will make their way to a good percentage of the people strolling by.

Reinvento Observes

In your quest for reinvention, when you surround yourself with smells favorable to you (for whatever reason they are favorable to you), you increase the probability of accomplishing what you set out to do.

Mmm, Mmmmm, Chocolate Chip

Dr. Alan Hirsch says that, "You do not have to be consciously aware of an aroma for it to have an effect," and in that sense, aromas can serve as invisible manipulators.

Real-estate agents have long known that homes sell more readily when potential buyers get a whiff of chocolate chip cookies or something else that was just baking in the oven before they arrived.

Used-car dealerships know that the "new car" smell in used vehicles attracts shoppers in ways that cars without the new-car smells have not. There is even a spray called "New Car Smell."

In Japan, companies have been experimenting for years with producing scents through ventilation systems to enhance worker productivity, reduce anxiety, and diminish stress. Japanese businesses have found that:

➤ Peppermint increases alertness.

➤ Lavender makes workers feel relaxed but not to the point of drowsiness.

➤ Citrus helps to energize the work force.

Judith Sachs, author of *Nature's Prozac,* suggests suffusing your home or work environment with the scent of soothing smells such as lavender, rose, pine, jasmine, or lemon.

Let's Do Another Root Canal!

Dentists, of all people, have found that when they scent their offices, patient resistance and fear seem to diminish. Even patients (get this!) having root canals, when immersed in a room primed with relaxing scents, exhibited less anxiety and higher levels of relaxation than those in unscented rooms. They even reported pain sensations less frequently.

If root-canal patients can experience this, you can certainly smell your way to less stress. Yet, you've long known that smells have powerful effects on how you feel and what you want to do. Think about the last time you were in close proximity to the fragrance of your significant other. My goodness, scientists tell us that you'd remember the scent your favorite aunt wore when you were three years old if you were to encounter it 30 years later.

One True Thing

Although there are a variety of delivery vehicles for aromatherapy products, the only true path that the oils can take in terms of affecting your mood and temperament is through your olfactory system. In short, you inhale the odors.

Inhalation crosses what is known as the blood-brain barrier and, ultimately, affects your central nervous system.

Take a Whirl in a Whirlpool Bath

If you played on any teams for your high school or college, chances are that you already know about the pleasures of a whirlpool bath. You and a few well-chosen friends get in, flip the switch, and soothe aching muscles through the gentle whirling motion of water.

Whirlpool baths come in a variety of designs geared to suit your individual needs. Most systems can direct water at various speeds and various pressures throughout the tub, giving rise to agitated water that makes its residents feel anything but agitated.

Footbaths for Foot Soldiers

Footbaths can play an important role in helping to relax your mind and body. Often used in backyards, footbaths can be far more relaxing than merely reading about them may suggest.

On a hot day, or when you have been using your feet extensively, a simple dunk in a soothing footbath can make all the difference. Add various salts and minerals to achieve maximum therapeutic effect.

Bathe Your Cares Away

One of the most effective ways to relax your mind and body is to draw a hot bath with bath beads, essential oils, or bubble bath, and simply sit and soak. A hot bath can be highly soothing. If you add oil of malacia, lavender, or other bath oils, your fatigued body and weary soul will receive an incomparable treat.

Caution

The long-running debate among aromatherapists that oils massaged into the skin also have an aromatic effect is proving to be untrue. Any delivery method that enables you to get a whiff of a given smell, be it through a facial steam device, nebulizer, massage, facial mask, or washing, essentially directs smells to your olfactory system. Hence, aromatherapy is a nose-based system.

Reinvento Observes

You can combine the effects of aromatherapy with massage. For example, drop essential oils into your footbath before giving yourself a foot massage. With the soothing aromatherapy-type soak prior to massage, once you step out of the footbath, you have a major head start on boosting your circulation, and on relieving tired and aching feet, warming them, and making them feel totally relaxed.

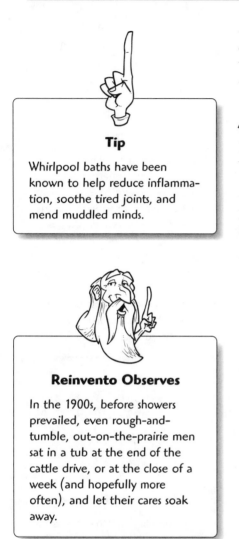

Consider the following. *Drug Store News* reported that one out of six households in America regularly turns to bath beads, bubble bath, or liquid bath additives as a haven in this hectic world.

Add Beads and Recede

Bath beads and bath additives in general come in a wide variety of options. Walk into Bed, Bath and Beyond, the Body Shop, or the bath section of any drugstore. You can have fruit-scented baths, such as peach, raspberry, and melon, which are widely regarded to be calming. Jasmine, citrus, and lavender are regarded as energy boosters. Most of the bath additives help to make your skin feel softer and, in some cases, smoother.

Fortunately, almost any bath bead or bath additive helps to soothe you. You can get fragrances with such names as Gentle Breeze, Peaceful Orchard, Soft Petal, and Botanical Garden. Keep a huge, warm bath towel handy; dry yourself off completely, and you're as new as you can get.

Dr. Avery Gilbert, based in Sacramento, says, "Because the bath engages almost all of the senses, it is a powerful way to influence our moods." The key, however, to getting the most from your bath, according to Gilbert, is to "tune into your desired emotional state or mood. Once the desired bathing mood has been identified, it can be enhanced through sensory inputs."

He suggests the glow of a flickering candle or the relaxing sound of soft music.

Soak Your Cares Away

If you put a few drops of the essential oil in your bath, you need only to lie back and soak for about 15 minutes. The steam and warmth of the bath help evaporate the oils and intensify the aroma. You come out of the bath with softer skin and a calmer mind.

If you keep your eyes closed, the aroma seems stronger and fuller. "You can almost name all of the blooms individually," says Rich. "The effect is caused by heat making the individual oils come in waves, so you can smell them singly and combined, with the result that they smell so different and divine you'll hardly recognize them."

Reinvento Observes

Cleopatra bathed in all kinds of oils. Mary, Queen of Scots, filled her tub with hot wine, and then soaked until, well ..., intoxicated. Ottoman Turks believed that physical cleanliness and personal hygiene (at least what was known about it back then) were essential on the path to spiritual holiness. The Romans built lavish public baths throughout their wide empire. The French soothed their weary bones in the natural springs that dot their countryside. The Japanese currently maintain ancient, intricate bath rituals.

Easy Listening

Easy-listening music, like your grandfather used to play, can have a dramatic effect on your being. Easy-listening music actually is easy to listen to, and that may be among the many reasons that teenagers bent on rock 'n' roll or rap find it to be kind of, well, you know ... boring.

Some people enjoy listening to soft rock or classical music while they work. They appreciate the easy listening and slow pace, or they like the absence of distracting words. Maybe they simply like a benign background noise. Regardless, these individuals find that listening to music is a simple measure that puts them in a better state to handle the challenges that come their way.

Music can help in the treatment of pain, depression, and anxiety, and can even help those in the grieving process or those facing terminal illness. Music can even produce physiological benefits, not just psychological ones. In his book, *The Art of Preserving Health, Book 4,* author John Armstrong in the 1760s told his reader, "Music exalts each joy, allays each grief, expels diseases, softens every pain, subdues the rage of poisons and the plague." Around 1700, William Congreve, a dramatist, uttered the famous phrase, "Music hath charms to soothe the savage beast."

Music in Surgery

Today, as a result of extensive research on the dramatic impact of music on the human psyche, we know that music can calm patients headed into surgery, reduce post-surgery healing time and the need for medications, and potentially lead to shorter stays in the hospital.

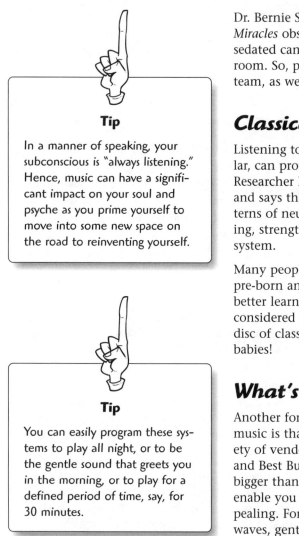

Dr. Bernie Siegel in his book *Love, Medicine and Miracles* observed that even patients who are heavily sedated can "hear" what's going on in the operating room. So, positive, uplifting statements by the medical team, as well as relaxing music, do have an impact.

Classical Music Can't Hurt

Listening to classical music, and to Mozart in particular, can promote learning, healing, and personal calm. Researcher Don Campbell calls this the Mozart Effect, and says that it can help to organize the firing patterns of neurons, which can stimulate creative thinking, strengthen your focus, and calm your nervous system.

Many people believe that playing classical music for pre-born and newborn infants can help to make them better learners. In fact, the State of Georgia recently considered providing all new parents with a compact disc of classical music they could play for their new babies!

What's That You Say?

Another form of easy listening that doesn't involve music is that of the soothing sounds of nature. A variety of vendors, including Sharper Image, Radio Shack, and Best Buy, offer soothing sound systems, usually no bigger than a radio or cassette player. These systems enable you to select the sound that you find most appealing. For example, you have your choice of ocean waves, gentle rain, wind whistling though the trees, or birds in the forest.

Most sound systems come with headphones for private listening as well as powerful speakers that could sound-condition an entire room or more. Personally, I've used a white noise machine and found it to be extremely effective when I want to mask sounds coming from another room or an external source.

White noise machines emit different frequencies and amplitudes of a droning, non-disruptive blanket of sound. The Sound Screen, developed by the Marpac Corporation, is a portable white noise device you can use to minimize the effects of startling or disruptive sounds outside your home or office. Here's the ordering information:

Sound Screen
Marpac Corporation
PO Box 3098
Wilmington, NC 28406-0098
Fax: 919-763-4219

Get Relaxed with Relaxation Tapes

Your typical bookstore, health food stores, and some gift and specialty shops offer relaxation tapes—cassettes designed specifically to assist you with resting your mind and body. Some tapes help you to focus on your breathing, which in itself can be a powerful and deep form of relaxation.

Some tapes offer affirmations. These are statements which, when repeated over and over, can sink into the depths of your psyche, and actually help you to move in your chosen direction.

Subliminal tapes are another form of cassette available to help you relax or achieve some other particular goal.

The Pros and the Cons

Our minds simultaneously operate at the conscious and subconscious level. The subliminal aficionados allege that our subconscious mind can interpret and process information at far-greater speeds than our conscious mind can. The subconscious mind, proponents claim, does not need to weigh the data or attempt to put things in order. When it hears a message repeated often enough, it acts on that message. The introduction of subliminal tapes has significant efficacy.

Caution

There has been much discussion and debate over the years as to whether subliminal tapes are truly effective. If they are, you need them in order to make progress toward your goals.

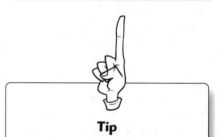

Tip

If you're curious about exploring the world of subliminal tapes, whether for relaxation, goal achievement, weight control, accumulating wealth, or any other reinvention focus area, simply get on the Internet and type in the words "subliminal tapes" on any popular search engine, and you will get dozens of hits.

Those opposed to the subliminal tape process argue that this is precisely the reason why it is best not to use subliminal tapes. Who wants a message directed to your subconscious over and over again, even if it is a positive message that you want to direct to your subconscious? Why not allow both your conscious and subconscious mind to work for you in unison to help you make progress?

67

2, 4, 6, 8, Let's All Meditate

Meditation is a technique for improving concentration and attention by focusing your mind on a single thought. While sitting comfortably, but in an upright position so as to remain alert, you focus your mind on a particular word or phrase or a particular vision, such as the flame on a candle, and you remain focused on it. This helps to slow down the mind, which in human beings, as you likely already know, tends to be frenzied—dashing about from here to there.

Covered at length in my book *The Complete Idiot's Guide to Managing Stress,* meditation enables you to concentrate better, because in quieting the mind, you end up with more clarity and ultimately more energy following mediation sessions.

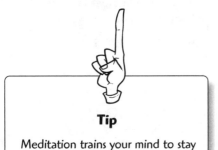

Tip

Meditation trains your mind to stay focused, and teaches you to control it when it wanders. The more you meditate, the longer your mind will be able to stay focused.

Combating Problems

A common problem during meditation is the experience of pain or discomfort. Things like itches, aches, and pains are common because your body's sensations are more noticeable while you meditate.

With your body and mind calm, however, you're able to notice more details. Sometimes you can turn these sources of discomfort into the object of your meditation. Observe them until they go away. Other times, it is just a matter of bad posture. If this is the case, adjust your posture so that your back is straight.

Some people fall asleep. When you relax, especially if your eyes are closed, your body might feel like it's time to sleep. If you fall asleep during meditation, you might simply be physically tired. Your time might better be spent taking a nap or sleeping in.

Enhanced focus through meditation can have a positive effect on the rest of your life. Not only can you focus more at work, but you can also control daily worrying and obsessing. With practice, you can lead your mind away from unhealthy fixations and trivial pursuits.

A Little a Day

Whatever technique you engage in to help relax your mind and body in your quest for reinvention, get in the habit of devoting at least a little time to it on a daily basis, or, if that is not possible, at least every other day.

Remember, at this moment, you represent the sum total of all the behaviors and habits you have accumulated in life. Giving yourself permission to get into a state of rest and relaxation for both your mind and body can represent a welcome departure from the daily grind. In that regard, it can be an important step on your journey to reinvention. However, the choice is up to you.

The Least You Need to Know

➤ Aromatherapy is a powerful method for evoking strong memories.

➤ Whirlpool baths, footbaths, and bathing in general are simple but effective methods for resting the mind and body.

➤ Easy-listening music is appropriately named. It is easy to listen to and relaxing.

➤ A wide variety of relaxation tapes are available today to help relax you and get you into whatever mood you desire.

➤ Meditation is an age-old technique that quiets the mind, yielding clarity and energy.

Chapter 7

Advanced Measures for Your Mind

In This Chapter

➤ From external back to internal

➤ Lamaze for the nonpregnant

➤ Flotation

➤ Dream interpretation

➤ Psychotherapy at home

Chapter 6, "Resting Your Mind and Your Body," told you how to put your mind and body at ease. Chapters 1 through 5 helped you to understand the changes necessary to turn your life into the satisfying, fulfilling experience you want it to be. In this chapter, we'll consider some advanced techniques for getting your mind in gear.

From External Back to Internal Focus

There is now more to see, do, and own than at any time in history, and tomorrow there will be even more than today. People are scrambling at a rapidly increasing pace to keep up with society. In addition to working more, making more, and spending more, we also are pressured to …

➤ Read the right books and magazines.

➤ Listen to trendy music.

➤ Buy fashionable clothes.

➤ Meet the right people.

➤ Go to the important places.

➤ See popular movies (before they leave the theater).

➤ Visit the hip Web sites.

➤ Take the best vacations.

We have to do, do, do all the time, and there's always more to be done. This unrelenting focus on external activity is the source of much of the unhappiness and despair of our age. This problem originally is social and cultural, not individual or personal, but if you're not careful, it ends up being individual and personal. It all boils down to what personal choices you make.

Reinvento Observes

We live in a society that values entertainment over enlightenment. We are constantly encouraged to look outside ourselves for satisfaction and fulfillment, and we're culturally discouraged from looking within ourselves or developing self-awareness.

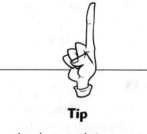

Tip

People who spend time not trying to accomplish anything often wind up sitting and thinking. Some doze off because when they give themselves a moment to rest, they realize how exhausted they are. It's okay to doze off at first! In time you probably won't feel the need.

Your Winning Key

You need to have time in your life when you're not trying to accomplish anything specific—even "relaxing" or "having fun." You need to have time when you can simply be, with no agendas and nothing to accomplish.

A constant, external focus is a good recipe for unhappiness, if only because self-awareness and self-understanding are the pillars upon which a satisfying and fulfilling life is built. The key to combating our society's pervasive sense of emptiness is to forge a relationship with yourself. Fortunately, it's relatively easy to begin forging this relationship! The first step is to carve out some space and time in which you truly, profoundly slow down.

Beyond Mere Relaxation

This slowing down goes beyond mere relaxation. When most of us are relaxing, we're still usually engaged in some sort of diverting activity, like reading, listening to music, having a drink, watching TV or a movie, or chatting with friends. As pleasant and enjoyable as these activities may be, they still pull you outside of yourself. These and other typical leisure-time activities fragment your attention and scatter your energies.

Pretty outdoor settings, such as parks, rivers, lakes, the beach, and hiking trails that provide ideal places for this time of nonaccomplishment are fine as long as they're not too noisy or crowded. If you desire a more ambulatory experience, then a pleasant walk can enable the same sort of return to the self.

You'll often find that spending quiet time with yourself will result in new thoughts and realizations that wouldn't have come to you otherwise. These thoughts and realizations are the seeds of your new self-awareness.

A Deeper Sense of Self

As you spend more time giving yourself space to simply be, you begin to notice a deeper sense of peace and stability in your life. The more time you can spend with yourself this way, the faster you'll notice a change in your frame of mind. Five minutes a day, three times a week, is better than nothing, while 15 minutes a day, everyday, is a lot better than that.

Carving Out the Space

For some people it makes sense to create a physical space in your home that you can use as your own personal retreat area. This should be a space that feels welcoming to you and in which you enjoy spending time—a spare bedroom, a study, the rec room, a converted basement, or perhaps a seat in a sunroom or a garden.

Wherever it is, it should be a place you can close off and make your own, a place where you feel safe and secure. If you need to, tell other family members that this area is now your personal space.

Do whatever it takes to create and maintain the *sanctity* of this area. That includes telling yourself that this is a space where you won't talk on the phone, pay bills, worry about problems, or do anything else that might compromise the nurturing and relaxation you receive from this place. When the world gets to be too much to handle, go to your retreat for rest and healing. You'll be glad you did.

Caution

Make sure you're not walking for exercise, however, or to reach a certain place or meet a certain person. You can do those things some other time.

Reinvento Observes

Establishing inner serenity requires the absence of an immediate goal. Getting your mind in gear for great things often requires a period of doing nothing. Your purpose should be no more than to exist in a peaceful state wherein you're not focused on achieving anything at all.

A Hop, a Skip, and a Jump

Top athletes have long known of the power of putting themselves into a mild trance before their turn to perform. Many Olympic athletes visualize themselves going through their routines, whether speed skating, gymnastics, or throwing the javelin, and they actually improve performance once they step into the competitive arena.

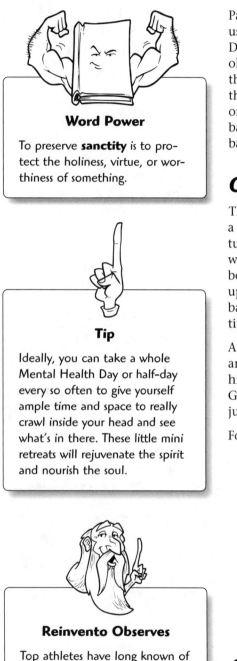

Word Power

To preserve **sanctity** is to protect the holiness, virtue, or worthiness of something.

Tip

Ideally, you can take a whole Mental Health Day or half-day every so often to give yourself ample time and space to really crawl inside your head and see what's in there. These little mini retreats will rejuvenate the spirit and nourish the soul.

Reinvento Observes

Top athletes have long known of the power of putting themselves into a mild trance before their turn to perform.

Particularly in Olympic track and field, athletes have used visualization to great effect. In the early 1970s, Dick Fosbury, an unassuming student from UCLA, revolutionized the world of high-jumping, leaping over the bar backward. Until Fosbury, everyone preformed the "western roll"—running to the bar, leaping off of one foot, and then attempting to clear it with their back to the sky and their front torso not touching the bar below.

One Big Flop

Then, Fosbury came along and figured out that with a slight change in approach, he could run to the bar, turn at the last moment, and leave his feet to lift off with the bar behind him. Then he would throw up both his hands to get the weight of his head and upper torso up and out over the bar, and arch his back to create a low resistance for his body to continue.

As his feet cleared the bar, he would flatten his back and hit the mat, hands still high over his head, with his face looking up toward the sky, as if to thank God for clearing yet another seven-foot-plus high-jump.

Fosbury explained his technique:

> "I began to develop my new style during a high school competition when my body seemed to react to the challenge of the bar. I became charged by the desire and will to achieve success. Then, I developed a thorough process in order to repeat a successful jump: I would psych myself up, create a picture, and feel a successful jump—the perfect jump, and develop a positive attitude to make the jump. My success came from the visualization and imaging process."

Counting the Steps

Years later, fellow high-jumper and Olympic gold medallist Dwight Stones also used visualization and imaging to achieve similar success. You could see Stones mentally counting out his paces, lifting off with his back to the bar, clearing it, and landing squarely in the middle of the mat.

Stones went through the same ritual before every jump, as did home-run champion Mark McGwire before his turn at bat. In essence, they saw it and then they did it. Stones didn't clear the bar every time, nor did McGwire hit a home run every time. These would be superhuman feats and no one, anywhere, using visualization and guided imagery, achieves absolute perfection each and every time.

But when the tally was done, McGwire with his 70 home runs and Dwight Stones with his gold medal, the results were clear. Visualization helped these superstars to achieve enough success enough of the time to supersede the performance of others.

Jackie Joyner-Kersee, perhaps the greatest female athlete of all time, put in long, hard hours on the track on her way to becoming a sprinting and jumping phenomenon. Yet, much of her training regimen involved sitting in a reclining chair with her eyes closed, mentally conditioning herself to have superior physical workouts. Marion Jones also frequently gets into a *meditative* state before hurtling down the track. The same techniques are available to you for athletic and nonathletic pursuits of all varieties!

Word Power

To be **meditative** is to be in a contemplative or reflective state.

Lamaze for the Nonpregnant

A simple technique for increasing peace of mind and self-awareness is just as close to you as the next breath you take. Breathing is something we all do, yet most of us never stop to consider whether there's a better way to do it. We all know that it's common for pregnant women to take childbirth classes that focus on the importance of proper breathing during labor.

Lung functioning and our manner of breathing have a strong, direct effect on both the quality and the length of our lives. This connection was demonstrated in a scientific analysis called the Framingham Study, which focused on the predictive power of *forced exhalation volume* (FEV) as a primary indicator for the length of an individual life span. The study found that the less a person's FEV was, the shorter his or her life was likely to be.

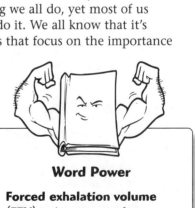

Word Power

Forced exhalation volume (FEV) is the amount of air a person is capable of forcibly expelling from his or her lungs.

Take a Breath on Me

Think about your own breathing for a moment and consider if any of the following are true:

➤ Do you often find yourself breathing shallowly or hardly breathing at all?

➤ Do you have trouble sleeping or have an irregular heartbeat?

➤ Do you breathe through your mouth a lot?

➤ Do you ever feel light-headed or like your breath doesn't go down in your lungs far enough?

These are signs that you're not breathing optimally. But you can use simple techniques to improve the quality of your breathing and increase your lung capacity. In fact, as few as 15 minutes of deep breathing a day would generate all the energy needed for the day.

One, Two, Three, Breathe

Here's a great breathing exercise you can do any time or anywhere. Standing or comfortably sitting, take a deep breath through your nose into your abdomen, so that it expands like a balloon. Continue the inhale so that the rib cage also expands. Then continue the inhalation so that the upper chest expands as well. This generates a deep breath.

Next, reverse the procedure by exhaling, first from the upper chest, then from the rib cage, and last from the abdomen. Tug inward on the abdominal muscles at the end of the exhalation to expel all the air. Repeat this cycle of inhalation and exhalation for up to 15 minutes.

Dare to Be Aware

Develop more awareness of your normal breathing throughout the day. Deep breaths, those that are more abdominal and use the diaphragm (the dome-shaped muscle in your abdomen) are more beneficial than shallow breaths that cause your shoulders to rise.

Did you know that there is a whole branch of alternative therapies called Breathwork? These therapies include Rebirthing and Holotropic Breathwork. Also, Pranayama yoga focuses almost exclusively on the breath, regarding breath as vital life energy. Pranayama yoga teaches that you can deepen and strengthen your bond with your own life energy by practicing techniques to control and manipulate the breath.

Indulging at the Spa

If rebirthing or Pranayama yoga sounds too "far out" for you, there are always vacation or retreat spas. Spas are the ultimate getaway from daily hassle. These are centers dedicated to renewing your entire being. The day revolves around an abundance of treatments, and to make life even better, they are often located in beautiful, exciting places and provide resort-like accommodations for their patrons.

As a guest at a spa center, your days include exercise, relaxation, pampering, and catered meals. Most retreat spas now operate with a focus on your whole being. Your time there is seen as a retreat from your daily life and a time to rejuvenate—physically, mentally, and even spiritually.

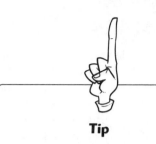

Tip

You have many opportunities today to easily gather information and education about systems of healing therapies and exercises that focus on the breath.

The Life of a Royal

A typical day of treatment at a resort spa might go something like this:

You wake up in a peaceful room (with a view) and fuel your body with delicious and wholesome food, planned and prepared for you by highly skilled culinary magicians. Then, there might be some time to exercise. Will you enjoy an aerobics class today? Or perhaps try some yoga to limber up instead? Maybe you have a massage scheduled, or a wonderfully relaxing hydrotherapy session.

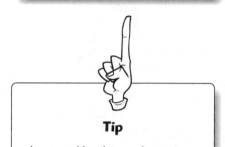

Tip

A retreat like this can be an invigorating chance for you to cater to your need for personal time. Or it might be a chance to bond with a group of people. Many spas and retreats now offer group packages, and some even tailor to corporate groups.

Sometime amidst this euphoria you enjoy another meal. Afterward, there might be time for meditation, or perhaps some reflective writing. The rest of the afternoon might pass while you enjoy a body-polishing treatment and an intensive facial. Dinner is wonderful and followed by plenty of time to rest up for tomorrow's intense schedule of pampering.

If you've got the bucks, you can have entire days filled with personal attention. One spa advertises a package including up to four treatment sessions a day. But by far the best part about it is that, unlike most vacations, other people plan the details of your day. This gives you the freedom to reap all the benefits of a holiday while others do your scheduling and prioritizing.

Float Me

Maybe you're having difficulty finding space and time to meditate or relax. If your environment is too chaotic or you're too easily distracted by your surroundings, you may want to consider entering an environment where almost all sensory input is cut off and you're left completely to your own mental devices. We're talking about sensory deprivation through flotation therapy, also called restricted environmental stimulation technique (REST—pun intended!).

You may have seen this practice dramatized in the 1980 movie *Altered States* with William Hurt and Blair Brown. While the film exaggerated the potential of this therapy (as films often do!), the title accurately describes the phenomena that most users experience.

Reinvento Observes

Most sensory input is cut off, enabling the user to enter a state of deep relaxation. The effect is like that of deep meditation or what one feels before falling asleep at night.

Your Own Water Bed

REST flotation requires the user to float on his or her back in a tub containing a 10-inch-deep solution of water and Epsom salt. The water is kept at a temperature of 94 degrees, and the salt is used to make the water so dense that the user floats effortlessly on the surface.

The rooms used for REST therapy are typically four feet by eight feet by eight feet. The walls, ceiling, and floor are covered with thick insulating material both to keep in the heat and to screen out any outside noise. REST rooms usually have light switches on the inside and are ventilated to provide fresh air. The user enters the room, shuts the door, turns off the light, and lies down in the water.

If you have the opportunity, give flotation a try. Surprisingly, many universities have REST tanks, although their policies vary regarding use by the public. Some employer-sponsored wellness centers are starting to include REST tanks, as are some larger health clubs.

Dream a Little Dream with Me

You may not have access to a REST tank, but you do have access to your dreams, a part of your life rich in opportunities for personal growth. Dreams are more than neurons randomly firing. They're the way your unconscious mind does its housekeeping. Dreams are places where we grapple with the issues that concern us—whether or not we realize we're concerned with those issues.

Sigmund Freud, the father of modern psychotherapy, was the first to elevate the significance of the human subconscious. Freud believed that dreams, when properly interpreted, could reveal the workings of the mind. Freud's one-time disciple, Carl Jung, took this idea further when he made dream interpretation one of the primary techniques of Jungian analysis.

You Can't Interpret What You Don't Remember

Before you can interpret your dreams, you have to remember them! If you think you're one of those people who never dreams, chances are you're wrong. Sleep physiologists tell us that virtually everyone dreams every single night, but we tend to only remember dreams when we wake up during them.

Here's how to grab hold of those elusive dreams:

➤ Put a pen and a piece of paper next to your bed before you retire for the evening.

➤ Go to sleep as you normally would.

➤ If you happen to wake up at any point during the night, there's a chance you may have woken up during a dream, in which case you should have some memory of it.

➤ Immediately write down everything you can remember about your dream.

➤ When you wake up, try to remember any dreams you may have had during the night.

➤ Write down every scrap of dream you can dredge up.

Reinvento Observes

You don't have to undertake analysis to interpret your dreams. The dream-related teachings of Freud and Jung, as well as the wisdom of many other teachers and sages, have been distilled into books, programs, courses, and even Web sites that will help you interpret your own dreams.

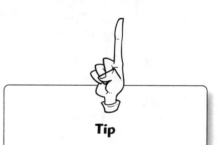

Tip

If you're not satisfied with your progress using these methods, you can set your alarm to wake you up during the middle of the night. You're almost sure to catch yourself in the middle of a dream.

If you practice the above on a daily basis, it will become easier for you to remember your dreams.

Tip

Your search for enlightenment need not be limited to books. Thousands of video and audio tapes provide similar information. You can also take courses and join discussion groups.

Caution

Accumulating information on self-improvement is easy. The problem is how to distinguish the useful from the useless. One way to choose well is to ask accomplished people what they might choose (or have chosen!).

Dreamscape Shorthand

Dream interpretation books are usually shelved in the self-help section of a bookstore. They may also be found in the psychology or New Age sections. These genres of publishing offer a cornucopia of advice, education, and wisdom for the discerning reader who wants to learn ways to grow and develop as a human being.

Once you have a dream down on paper, you can use dream-interpretation reference material to understand its relevance to your life. Different systems or philosophies may offer differing interpretations, so it's wise to use more than one reference and compare them to each other. Dream interpretation can provide a valuable—and endless—source of enlightenment and wisdom about your life.

Does It Work for Me?

Paradoxically, there's no one formula or set of criteria you can use to determine which book, system, or course is right for you. A method that works wonders for one person may wreak havoc for another. The book that changed your sister's life may only elicit yawns from you.

The best system for you to use is the one that works. Engage in some trial and error. The path that leads to riches will make it all worthwhile.

The Least You Need to Know

➤ For reinvention, shift your focus from the things *in* your life to your *internal* self.

➤ Get away from the hustle and bustle of life and create a private space all your own.

➤ Stop and catch your breath occasionally.

➤ Treat yourself to a trip to a spa.

➤ There is no one formula for determining which instructional materials are best for you, but when you find something that works, stick with it.

Chapter 8

Exercising Your Mind

In This Chapter

➤ Reshaping your mind

➤ Learning new things

➤ Finding your niche

➤ Going back to school

Your muscles get flabby and weak when they're not regularly exercised. So does your mind—and an out-of-shape mind is a huge obstacle to reinventing yourself.

Thought *Usually* Precedes Action

The world is populated by many people who buy self-improvement books, read them cover to cover, and put them on a shelf next to a bunch of other self-improvement books. Meanwhile, their lives continue, no different from before. You may know people like this. You may even be one. When people do this, it's often because they're not really thinking about what they're reading. The words flow past their eyes and into their brains, but no substantive thought takes place as a result.

Using the Right Equipment

Many of the books published today don't provide much mental exercise (especially fiction). As a die-hard fan of sword-and-sorcery novels once admitted to me, "All of these books are pretty much the same. I know how they're going to end. I just want

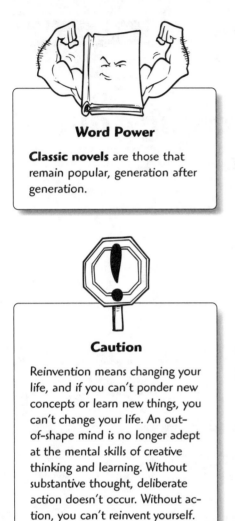

Word Power

Classic novels are those that remain popular, generation after generation.

Caution

Reinvention means changing your life, and if you can't ponder new concepts or learn new things, you can't change your life. An out-of-shape mind is no longer adept at the mental skills of creative thinking and learning. Without substantive thought, deliberate action doesn't occur. Without action, you can't reinvent yourself.

to be entertained." Sounds like a pleasant way to spend the afternoon, but the key to using reading as mental exercise is to read books that are not only pleasurable but that exercise your mind.

Classic novels fit the bill perfectly. The novels that are recognized as classics usually have interesting stories, compelling plots, and sympathetic characters— all the things that make reading any kind of fiction a pleasure. Yet, they also usually deal with significant themes such as morality, religion, or death in ways that avoid clichés and demonstrate true, original thought.

What if you were to spend the next year reading as many classic novels as you can? This is a good way to expand your mental horizons and get your mind in shape for the kind of serious thinking that accompanies personal reinvention. At the end of the year, you'll have different ideas about literature, and probably about life itself.

Many Great Choices

How do you decide which classic novels to read? Obviously, you want to choose novels that will hold your interest and be enjoyable. It seems that the older the fiction, the harder it is for most modern readers to enjoy reading it. Don't worry; you don't have to cast your net quite that far back in the seas of time to haul in a good read. The twentieth century provides more than enough good, classic fiction to last you many quiet mornings spent alone or rainy afternoons curled up on the sofa.

If you don't have Internet access at home, your local public library probably has computers you can use to get on the Internet.

Modern Library's top 100 list contains such classic novels as the following:

➤ *On the Road,* Jack Kerouac's freewheeling bohemian novel about the adventures of beatniks on the highways of postwar America

➤ *The Catcher in the Rye,* the coming-of-age novel by J. D. Salinger that seems to have been banned almost as often as it has been critically praised

➤ *The Age of Innocence,* a tale of upper-crust New York society by Edith Wharton

These and other listed novels will provide fine literary grist for your intellectual mill.

Selected by Smart Readers Everywhere

Modern Library also solicited votes from the reading public for what they thought the top 100 English-language novels of the twentieth century should be. The readers' list, which is displayed on the same Web page as *Modern Library*'s official list, includes books like *The Lord of the Rings,* the fantasy classic by J.R.R. Tolkien; *A Prayer for Owen Meany,* John Irving's quirky story about a tiny boy with a big voice and a fixation on God; and *Beloved,* the searing novel of the aftermath of slavery by Toni Morrison, winner of the Nobel Prize for Literature.

Here are other ways to generate lists of worthwhile books:

➤ Seek the lists of classic novels in some bookstores or on the Internet by doing a search on "classic novels."

➤ Reference librarians are wonderful people to ask for suggestions on which classic novels to read.

➤ Bookstore owners, managers, and staff are often well-read and can be another source of good suggestions.

➤ Friends who have college degrees in English or who have taken literature classes can also provide good recommendations.

Tip

A good place to start looking for classic novels to read is *Modern Library*'s list of the 100 best fiction books of the twentieth century in the English language. The *Modern Library* list can be found on the Internet at www.randomhouse.com/modernlibrary/100best/novels.html

Caution

Some of the books on the readers' list don't qualify as mental exercise. You can tell rather easily which do and which do not. (I shan't name names!)

Starting a Good Routine

Once you have a list of classic novels from which to choose, set yourself up a reading schedule of sorts. This could mean you're reading as many as one or two books a week, or it could be as few as one or two books a month, depending on such variables as your personal schedule, how fast you read, and the length of the books.

A slower reader, or someone who doesn't have much time to read, may want to choose 12 books to read (one a month). Someone who is a fast reader, or who has more time, may want to pick 24 or 36 books to read, or even more. If you finish your list before a year is up, don't rest on your laurels. Pick out some more classic novels and keep reading until the year is through.

Reinvento Observes

By the end of your year spent reading the classics, you'll probably have developed some opinions about the kind of classic fiction you like best, authors you prefer, and periods you want to seek out or avoid. Going forward, you can make the reading of classic and modern classic novels a regular part of your intellectual life.

Word Power

Book clubs are relatively informal groups where everyone reads a book and then meets to discuss it.

Tip

Remember, you want to exercise your mind, so seek out a book club that will be reading books that fit the bill.

Most classic novels are easily obtained through bookstores or public libraries. If a bookstore doesn't have the book you want on the shelves, they can usually order it for you. If your public library doesn't have the books for which you're looking, try a college library. Many college libraries will let nonstudent members of the community have limited borrowing privileges.

Read and Discuss

To develop a regular reading habit, join a local book discussion club. *Book clubs* are a great way to meet other book readers. Many people find that they learn more from a book when they hear other people's points of view on it.

Most book clubs read and discuss one book per month. Book clubs are organized by all sorts of people, such as groups of friends and acquaintances, co-workers, and members of neighborhood associations. Some book clubs are devoted to specific themes, such as religion, politics, or genre fiction.

Book clubs that are seeking new members will usually take out ads in the classified sections of local newspapers. Also, be sure to look in monthly, weekly, and semiweekly papers as well as the daily paper. Other good places to look are public-notice boards at libraries and bookstores, or any place where flyers are posted. Once again, reference librarians and bookstore employees are good people to ask about book clubs in your area.

Journal Writing

All this reading may give you the itch to do a little writing. Keeping a personal *journal* is an excellent way to probe the reaches of your mind and keep the mental wheels turning. It's also a useful tool for working on personal growth and getting in touch with your inner self. The self-knowledge you gain through keeping a journal will prove highly valuable in reinventing yourself.

Me and My Journal

What does it mean to keep a journal? First, obtain the kind of writing material that you prefer, such as a spiral notebook, a blank book, a three-ring binder with loose-leaf paper, or a composition book. Suit yourself; it's your journal and it should please you to write in it. Then, be sure to have a good supply of pens, pencils, or crayons—whatever you prefer to write with.

There Are No Rules

There's no formula for what journal writing is "supposed" to be. Don't let preconceived notions about journal writing deter you from starting and maintaining one. You may think a journal is for people who are more artistic or emotional than you. Indeed, a journal can be extremely artistic or emotional, if the person keeping the journal wants it to be that way. A journal can also be funny, pious, raunchy, quirky, or coldly rational (or any combination thereof).

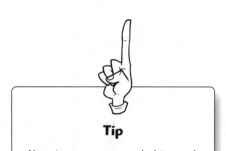

Tip

Keeping a tape-recorded journal is riskier than keeping a written one. If your recorder goes on the fritz, the power goes out, or you run out of batteries, there goes your journal. Paper and writing utensils are cheap and easy to obtain and keep on hand. And if the power goes out, you can still write by candlelight!

Word Power

For most people, a **journal** is simply a record of their everyday experiences and/or their thoughts and feelings. Most journals consist of some combination of these elements. Let's say one day you had a job interview. In your journal, you could write about how the interview went; you could expand on that by writing about what you think you did right in the interview or what you think your strengths are as a candidate.

Forming the Habit

If you've tried to start an exercise routine, you know that part of the secret to sticking with it over the long term is simply making it a habit. And because journal writing is a form of mental exercise, the same principle applies.

Reinvento Observes

A journal can be whatever you want it to be. It is simply a written reflection of who you are. It's your journal and it will be whatever you make of it. It doesn't matter what your journal ends up being; what matters is what *you* end up being.

Word Power

A **memoir** is basically your life story or some part of it.

Regardless of when it is, find at least 10 minutes out of your day when you have the opportunity to sit down by yourself and write in your journal. If you can write in your journal on a regular basis at this time for seven consecutive days—long enough to convince yourself and other people in your life, that this particular time of day is "journal-writing time" for you—then you've laid the foundation for the habit of keeping a journal.

Writing Your Memoir

Your experiences with keeping a journal may lead you to consider writing a memoir. A *memoir* is similar to a journal, because it's also a record of your experiences, thoughts, and feelings. But a memoir is usually a longer work that covers your entire life in sequential order from sometime around your birth until the present day (or whenever you choose to end it).

You may have read or heard of *Angela's Ashes*, Frank McCourt's memoir of his childhood in Ireland. This book, winner of a Pulitzer Prize in 1999, is an excellent example of a memoir.

Why do people write memoirs? Some do so out of a desire to remember and honor their lives and what they've been through. Others write memoirs to give future generations a look at life as it once was. If you let family members read your memoir, it can foster a new closeness among you. Many have said the act of writing a memoir is a healing experience that brings new insight into their present lives. Also, it's a lot of fun to sift through old memories and set them down on paper.

From When You Were Small

If you decide to write a memoir, a simple way to get started is to begin with the facts of your birth and move forward from there. Also, memoir-writing classes are offered in many communities for those of you who want more structure or instruction in your efforts.

Building Educational Muscles

If you've done any creative writing, you've likely experienced the feeling of groping for just the right word. Mark Twain said, "The difference between the right word and the nearly right word is the difference between lightning and a lightning bug." The search for the right word can lead you to another great way to exercise your mind: building your vocabulary.

Increasing Your Vocabulary

Reading all those classic novels, you'll probably run into words you don't know! This presents the perfect opportunity to work on your vocabulary. First, you'll need to have a good, useful dictionary on hand. This means something larger than a typical pocket dictionary, which usually has 50,000 entries or less. The English language has more than 450,000 words!

Concurrently, you'll never use most of the words in massive dictionaries. They exist primarily to meet the needs of specialists (usually academicians) and to serve as records of the English language at a given point in time. Invest in a dictionary in the middle of that range—something that includes around 100,000 to 150,000 words.

Looking It Up

When you come across a word you don't know, either look it up right then, or write it down and look it up later. The more you read, the more likely it is that you'll encounter these words and the faster you'll build your vocabulary. You can take your vocabulary-building efforts a step further by giving yourself vocabulary tests. Once you've accumulated 20 new words, write their definitions.

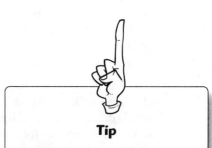

Tip

To form your journal-writing habit, choose a time of day that will usually be a good time for you to write. It could be the morning, while everyone else is asleep; lunchtime, when you have half an hour or more to yourself; or after dinner, when you might otherwise be watching television.

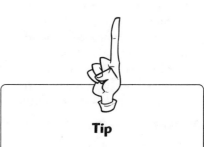

Tip

The only standard your memoir has to meet is the one you set. You certainly don't have to worry about pleasing other people with your memoir or trying to get it published. Simply writing it is achievement enough.

Finding Your Learning Niche

Everyone has different learning styles. While some people prefer self-guided learning, others find that they learn more effectively within some sort of structured educational program. If you're one of those people, then going to college or going back to college—whether or not you already have a degree—may be a great way for you to exercise your mind.

What does college offer that you may want? You can take noncredit continuing education courses, such as "How to Write a Novel" or "Landscaping for Beginners." You can enroll in courses for credit in an area in which you're interested, such as history or a foreign language, without enrolling as a degree-seeking student. You can enroll in a certification program to gain a new skill, as phlebotomists and paralegals do.

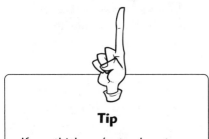

Tip

If you think you're too busy to take any classes, keep in mind that more and more colleges are offering programs geared toward nontraditional students. Most schools (especially community colleges) offer night courses to fit the schedules of working students.

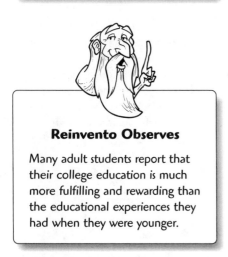

Reinvento Observes

Many adult students report that their college education is much more fulfilling and rewarding than the educational experiences they had when they were younger.

Going Back to College

You can enroll in a typical undergraduate or graduate degree program. If you're at all interested in taking college courses of any kind, don't hesitate to get in touch with your local institutions of higher education. Virtually all of them have Web sites, which have a complete list of programs and course offerings. Learn what options are available to you and determine whether or not any of them spark your interest.

Some schools have adult degree programs that offer flexible scheduling, distance learning, and individualized curriculum, designed to accommodate the needs and abilities of adult learners. More colleges are offering courses online, and increasingly schools are offering entire undergraduate and graduate degree programs over the Internet. Going back to school (or going for the first time) may be much easier than you think.

Older students typically are more responsible and mature, which usually makes them better students. They often are more diligent in their schoolwork, resulting in less perceived pressure and better grades. They also may find that, because they're closer in age, they can relate to their instructors more easily than younger students.

Most people who go back to school or who begin at a later age are glad they did, because now they are wise enough to make the most out of it!

The Least You Need to Know

➤ A year spent reading classics will limber up your brain and broaden your horizons.

➤ Joining a book discussion club will help cement the habit of reading and give you a chance to participate in stimulating discussions and meet other readers.

➤ Writing a memoir provides many writing-related benefits and fixes your place in history.

➤ Going to college provides the intellectual growth that only higher education can.

Chapter 9

For Advanced Intellects

In This Chapter

➤ Finding out about yourself by researching your family

➤ The aid of religion

➤ Talking it out

➤ Learning a foreign language

Have you ever dug around in an old shoebox, looking for a bank statement or a sales receipt, when you ran across a letter that someone sent you 10 or 20 years ago? This kind of unexpected discovery can lead to time spent reliving your past while kneeling in a closet. Or maybe you've found old family memorabilia locked away in a trunk when you went looking for a blanket. Sometimes such searches accidentally open a new world of discovery—the world of the past. These explorations of the past don't have to be accidental, however. You can give shape and structure to this kind of exploration by tracing your ancestry.

All in the Family

One of the best ways to learn more about yourself is to learn more about family members. After all, they did have an impact on who you have become.

The Aid of Your Ancestors

Probably the most famous book ever written about genealogy was *Roots,* by Alex Haley. This best-selling account of one African-American man's search for his

Reinvento Observes

Alex Haley's search for his roots was an experience of transformation that demonstrated the profound satisfaction to be found in establishing a connection with one's personal heritage.

Caution

It's important to get as much of your own knowledge down on paper as you can. After all, memories, including your own, are fallible. The longer you wait to begin your search, the greater the risk that you'll forget a vital fact or remember it incorrectly.

ancestors was made into an award-winning TV miniseries in 1977 and spurred a tremendous surge of interest in genealogy. Haley overcame tremendous odds to trace his ancestry all the way back to Western Africa, where his ancestor, Kunta Kinte, was kidnapped and sold into slavery hundreds of years ago.

He used a wide variety of research methods to retrace the steps of his ancestors—a trail of steps that eventually led him across the Atlantic Ocean to Africa and the source of his ancestry.

How do you begin your genealogical research? Start with yourself and what you know. Write down everything you know or can remember about your ancestry. If some of your recollections are hazy or unsure, write them down anyway and note that you're unsure of them. You can prove or disprove them later.

Then, scour your home for documentary-type information on your family (and include yourself as family). Examples of this information can include the following:

➤ Birth and death certificates

➤ Marriage licenses

➤ Family Bibles

➤ Letters

➤ High school yearbooks

➤ Photographs

➤ Diplomas and degree certificates

➤ Diaries

➤ Newspaper clippings

Talking to Family Members and Friends of the Family

Ask everyone you can to give you all the information they have about your family. You may already possess much (or all) of the information your relatives have, but you never know when one of them will be able to produce some random anecdote or fact that could make all the difference in your research.

Focus especially on your older relatives. They are the most likely to have truly valuable information.

Using Outside Sources

Now you've laid the foundation for your genealogical research and you're ready to move on to other sources, which happen to be plentiful. Sources available to the public, among dozens, include the following:

➤ The Social Security death index

➤ Census records

➤ Military records

➤ Obituaries

➤ Immigration and naturalization records

➤ Real estate records

➤ Marriage records

➤ Birth announcements

If you want instruction in tracing your ancestry, many colleges offer courses in genealogical research. Hundreds of local genealogical societies exist throughout North America; check your local telephone listings or visit a Web search engine to determine whether one is located near you.

Many books are also available on genealogy. Here are a few titles to help you get started on your research:

➤ Rose, Christine. *The Complete Idiot's Guide to Genealogy.* Indianapolis: Alpha Books, 1997.

➤ Greene, Bob, and D. G. Fulford, *To Our Children's Children: Preserving Family Histories for Generations to Come.* New York: Doubleday, 1998.

➤ Taylor, Maureen. *Through the Eyes of Your Ancestors: A Step-by-Step Guide to Uncovering Your Family History.* Boston: Houghton Mifflin Company, 1999.

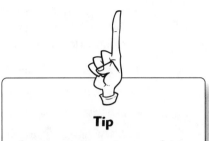

Tip

As soon as you start accumulating information, begin keeping a record of all your research activity. This will make it possible for you to document your genealogical discoveries. It will also enable you to remember where you got a specific piece of information, which may come in handy at a later stage in your research.

Caution

Obviously you want to get the information that older relatives have before they pass away and their knowledge of your family history passes away with them.

Using Technology

Computerized databases have vastly simplified the task of searching for old records. The Internet makes it possible to conduct genealogical research without even leaving your house. Here are some of the most prominent sites for tracing your ancestry:

➤ www.ancestralquest.com

➤ www.ancestry.com

➤ www.cyndislist.com

➤ www.ngs.genealogy.org

➤ www.polaris.net/~legend/mainsite.htm

➤ www.rootsweb.com

These sites typically contain links to outside databases that offer exactly the kind of information you'll be seeking. They also contain expert articles and tutorials on how to trace your ancestry.

Reinvento Observes

If you decide you want to undertake the rich and rewarding endeavor of tracing your genealogy, you have available all the information you need to make it a success.

Letting Religion Be Your Guide

Most people say they believe in a Supreme Being. The twin topics of religion and spirituality—both your own religion (if you have one) and others'—can be endlessly fascinating areas of study and can serve as an avenue toward spiritual renewal, if you want them to.

Even agnostics or atheists can benefit from studying religion because the spiritual or religious impulse, regarded by sociologists as one of the true universals of the human experience, speaks volumes about human nature.

Beginning with Your Own Faith

Reinvento Observes

The study of religion and spirituality can be a powerful tool for reinventing your life.

The percentage of American adults who attend religious services regularly dropped from 49 percent in 1991 to 36 percent in 1996. These numbers are taken from public opinion polls; when the number of attendees is actually counted in small geographic areas, church attendance is shown to be about half of the above figures. It seems that some people give the pollsters the "right" answer, rather than the true one. Nevertheless, the easiest place to begin a study of religion is with your own religious tradition.

Some 85 percent of adults in the United States identify themselves as Christian, according to www.religioustolerance.org, a Web site dedicated to disseminating information on all the world's religions. So, suppose you're from North America, and the faith in which you were raised is Christianity.

To begin a study of Christianity, attend a house of worship regularly, if you don't already. Or, study the history of Christianity, which is filled with stories.

Reinvento Observes

The renowned psychoanalyst Carl Jung recommended that his clients actively explore the faith in which they were raised as an integral part of their analysis.

Narrowing Your Focus

You could also focus your studies on one of the many different strands of Christianity, such as Roman Catholicism, the AME Zion Church, the Society of Friends (Quakers), and the Church of Jesus Christ of Latter-day Saints (Mormons). Greek Orthodox Christians practice a form of Christianity older than Roman Catholicism; Coptic Christians in Africa practice a form even older than that.

Consider becoming involved in one of the many ideological camps active in Christianity. Evangelical Protestants are issuing a call for a return to what they see as the fundamentals of Christianity, and for Christians to become active in politics. Liberal Christians, however, stand squarely opposed to the evangelicals on many issues.

You may also focus on the *Creation Spirituality* movement.

Word Power

Creation Spirituality is a recent religious movement that seeks to return Christianity to what are purported to be its early, pre-patriarchal roots by emphasizing grace, blessing, and creation rather than sin, judgment, and death.

So Many Other Options

There are many other religions to learn about:

➤ Hinduism, one of the world's oldest religions, is linked strongly to the nation of India and was the primary religion of Mahatma Gandhi.

➤ Buddhism was founded by the Buddha in what is now Nepal and quickly spread all over the East, becoming particularly popular in China and Japan.

➤ Judaism is the religion out of which Christianity sprang. Of all the religions, it probably has the greatest influence relative to its numbers.

➤ Islam was founded in the seventh century C.E. by the prophet Muhammad. Followers of the Islamic faith regard it as the culmination and fulfillment of the truth taught first by Judaism and then by Christianity.

There are other spiritual traditions you might prefer to study. The New Age movement is a loosely defined spiritual movement that synthesizes elements of many religious and spiritual belief systems in countless different ways. It is often characterized by a belief in paranormal phenomena (such as prophecy, psychic phenomena, divination, or angels) but usually without a rigidly structured worldview or belief system.

The neo-pagan movement, including Wicca, paganism, and druidism, seeks to excavate the pre-Christian, earth-centered spiritual traditions of ancient Europe and rejuvenate them for modern use. There are many other spiritual and religious groups—far too many to mention here. Suffice it to say that the study of religion promises an unparalleled opportunity to learn, to expand your mind, and to grow.

Here are some books to aid you in your study of religion:

➤ Elkins, D. N. *Beyond Religion: A Personal Program for Building a Spiritual Life Outside the Walls of Traditional Religion.* Wheaton, IL: Theosophical Pub. House, 1998.

➤ Gallagher, Winifred. *Working on God.* New York: Random House, 1999.

➤ Sharma, Arvind, ed. *Our Religions.* New York: HarperCollins, 1993.

Talking It Out

You may have heard the old saw that religion and politics should never be discussed in polite company because of the controversy they generate. Yet, to refrain from discussing these or other volatile topics is to miss out on one of the best ways there is to broaden your horizons and help reinvent your life. These kinds of discussions or debates give us a chance to try our ideas out on other people. We can learn a lot from other people's ideas, whether or not we agree with them.

How do you go about generating these kinds of discussions? Do you currently associate with people who like to learn new things and discuss what they learn? If so, then you're already perfectly set up to instigate stimulating conversations about everything you're learning as you reinvent yourself.

Starting with Friends

Ask your friends what they think about a classic novel you've read, a religion you're studying, or a piece of nutritional advice you've heard. Your friend replies, and the dialogue is born—not a lecture or a speech, but a relatively equal exchange of two people's ideas. As long as the information keeps flowing back and forth in a give-and-take, you'll derive the fullest benefit from your conversation.

You don't necessarily want to avoid controversy, but you do want to make sure neither one of you feels attacked or denigrated. It's easy for discussions to become heated when the topic is controversial, and many people interpret that heat as an attack, even when it isn't meant that way. You don't want to sacrifice a friendship for the sake of a stimulating conversation!

Widening Your Circle

Consider all the friends, acquaintances, and relatives that you have. Perhaps some of them would be willing to have those kinds of discussions with you, but you may not know that about them.

Give them a try! Trot out a film, a book, or an idea and see what they have to say. You might be surprised. Then, broaden your scope to look for discussion groups in your area (see Chapter 8, "Exercising Your Mind"). There are many different kinds of discussion groups that focus on a wide variety of topics, such as politics, sexuality, religion, and philosophy, to name a few. Look for notices for these groups in the classified ads of your local newspapers, as well as on notice boards at markets, bookstores, and colleges.

There are countless discussion groups on the Internet as well. The most rudimentary search on almost any topic will instantly bring a host of groups to light. Internet groups conduct discussions either via e-mail postings or a chat interface. You can also start your own discussion group in any of these areas.

As you get better at formulating your ideas, you may find that strong ideas are a solid foundation for reinventing your life.

Caution

You don't want to water down your opinion to keep the peace; that would be dishonest. Yet, it's possible to express one's opinion honestly, and even to disagree, without generating personal animosity. Compassion is the key.

Reinvento Observes

After you've been having this kind of discussion for a while, you'll probably notice two changes in yourself. First, you'll be better at having these discussions or debates. Second, you'll be more skillful at both expressing and defending your ideas, as well as analyzing and discussing the ideas of others.

Learning a Foreign Language

Thoughtful discussions and debates force you to cast your ideas in the form of language, as opposed to letting your thoughts dwell in the relatively nebulous world of unspoken thought. Language itself helps give shape to your ideas.

Reinvento Observes

The ability to read, write, and understand a foreign language vastly broadens your mental and experiential horizons.

Imagine, then, what happens when you cast your ideas into a different language. A different set of rules applies; a different logical order prevails. If you can learn to express yourself in two (or more) languages, you will know how to step in and out of different logic systems, which will enhance both your powers of expression and your powers of thought. This is only the beginning of the many benefits of learning a foreign language.

Ain't No Mountain High Enough

Consider all the books, periodicals, films, and music created in the English language. It seems like quite a mountain, doesn't it? Now add the books, periodicals, films, and music created in modern French. The mountain just got a lot bigger! The plays of Molière, the philosophy of Foucault, the novels of Camus, the music of Edith Piaf, and the politics of Napoleon and Robespierre do not even scratch the surface.

Caution

It is true that English translations exist for much of this material, but keep in mind one important fact about translations: They are almost never 100 percent accurate, and often far less than 100 percent, as when poetry (such as that of Baudelaire) is involved.

If you've ever seen a foreign film with subtitles, you know that the subtitles did not always offer an accurate rendition of what the characters were saying. The best way to hear or read the words the author intended you to hear or read is to learn the author's language.

Broadening Your Scope

Being able to speak a foreign language widens your possibilities for social interaction, especially if you live in an area with an influx of people whose first language is not English. The United States, for example, has 28 million people whose first language is Spanish and is the fifth-largest Spanish-speaking country in the world (behind Spain, Mexico, Argentina, and Colombia).

By the year 2010, one in every four U.S. citizens will be Hispanic. Hispanics are projected to be the nation's largest ethnic minority group by the year 2025. Clearly, command of the Spanish language is going to be an increasingly important skill in the near future.

Traveling with Greater Ease

Knowing a foreign language comes in handy whenever you travel to a foreign country. Many Americans rely on the widespread use of English to get them by when they travel, but this doesn't always work. Many Americans can tell you horror stories about lost luggage, missed trains, stolen money, and other mishaps that have resulted directly from the language barrier.

Also, the locals usually appreciate it when you demonstrate that you've made an effort to learn their language. It shows them that you have respect for their country and customs.

Language Instruction

If you're planning on a two-week trip to Europe where you'll visit two or three countries that speak languages you don't use much at home, then a private *language school* may be the best approach for you.

If you plan to spend several months or a year overseas, or you live near an ethnic community with which you want to be able to communicate, then seek more in-depth instruction. This kind of instruction is offered by some private schools, such as those operated by organizations that are devoted to promoting a specific language, but is more often offered at colleges. College language courses emphasize both conversation and grammar.

Students in these courses do a lot of listening, speaking, reading, and writing in the language. This instruction takes much longer to complete than the instruction businesspeople usually take, but the student gets a much deeper and broader grounding in the language.

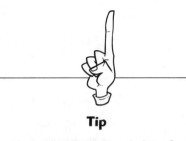

Tip

Having your own knowledge of the language enables you to get off the beaten path or away from a tour group and to spend more time interacting with local people and really learning about the country on a more substantive and intimate level.

Word Power

Language schools usually offer courses that focus more on conversation and "survival skills" than on the finer points of grammar. The course of instruction is relatively short and focuses on achieving concrete results.

In-depth techniques for reinventing your life, such as tracing your genealogy, studying religion, debating ideas, and learning a foreign language, often result in more fundamental changes in your outlook. Apply yourself to these areas, and watch your life change before your eyes.

The Least You Need to Know

➤ Tracing your ancestry enables you to establish a deeper connection with your past and to place the present in a richer context.

➤ The study of religion poses some of the largest questions humans have ever asked.

➤ Debating your ideas with others will help you become better at thinking and expressing yourself.

➤ Learning a foreign language sharpens the mind while exposing you to the wit and wisdom of other cultures.

Part 3

Reinventing Your Body

When you're insufficiently rested, you're severely tested on a daily basis. Everything requires more effort, and you tend to seek salvation through excess: eating too much, drinking too much, staying up too late, watching too much television. And excess takes its toll on your body.

In Part 3, we'll take a look at what it means to get proper rest, and what it will do for you. We'll look at working out versus spreading out, and reinventing the inner and outer you by changing what you buy at the supermarket—starting with your very next trip.

We'll also examine the concept of changing the shape of your body—literally—through physical feats of wonder, manipulation by trained specialists, and by medical and cosmetic procedures. Hey, that's a form of reinvention, too, even if all you do is pay your money and lie there!

Chapter 10

Above All,
Get Balanced

In This Chapter

➤ How to stay balanced

➤ Balance at work

➤ Avoiding overwork

➤ How to let go of controlling behavior

Everybody talks about achieving balance these days, but how many are actually doing it? If your life is about meeting deadlines, chauffeuring others, constantly competing, and racing around the clock, with nary a moment for yourself, chances are that you're going to be out of balance in a hurry. Without balance, you can't properly attend to the different aspects of your life, and, often, taking care of your body becomes low priority. Finding balance enables you to discover the time you need to get more rested and further reinvent your life.

Keeping Your Life in Balance

It's easy to get caught up in worrying about the future, rather than experiencing the here and now. Buddhist philosopher Thick Nhat Hanh puts it this way:

> "If I am incapable of washing dishes joyfully, if I want to finish them quickly so I can go and have dessert, I will be equally incapable of enjoying my dessert. With the fork in my hand, I will be thinking about what to do next, and the

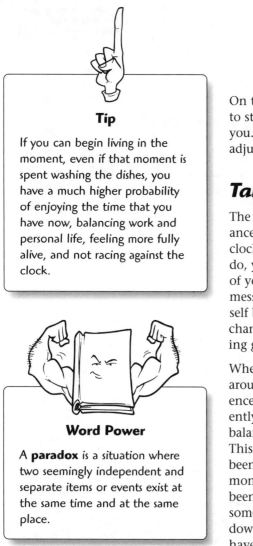

texture and flavor of the dessert, together with the pleasure of eating it, will be lost. I will always be dragged into the future, never able to live in the present moment."

On the road to living in the moment, it makes sense to step back and evaluate what's most important to you. This could lead to anything from making small adjustments to making major life renovations!

Taking Time to Take Stock

The great paradox of getting your life back into balance is that if you're stressed out, racing around the clock, and feeling as if you always have too much to do, your inclination is to avoid taking some time out of your day to plot a strategy for getting out of your mess. In other words, you create a catch-22 for yourself by believing that you don't have the time to change your life. Please, let that kind of archaic thinking go the way of the woolly mammoth.

When speaking at conferences and conventions around the United States, I frequently tell my audiences that one of the *paradoxes* of living in our apparently sped-up society is that sometimes, to achieve balance, the first thing you need to do is slow down. This doesn't always feel so great. After all, if you've been racing along week after week, month after month, year after year, and everyone around you has been doing the same, slowing down feels as if you're somehow admitting defeat. "My goodness, if I slow down, I may find out how exhausted I am and never have the energy to get started again."

You know, however, that you have many times throughout the week when you could take 30 to 60 minutes to work on the big picture of balancing your work and personal life. May I suggest watching one less television show?

Prioritize Life

To put some life back into your life, first make a list of all the activities you enjoy or want to know more about. As you review this list, consider the last time that you actually engaged in these activities, or even took a step toward finding out more about one. If you're honest with yourself, it has probably been weeks, months, or worse! Now, rearrange the list in the order of what you want to accomplish first, descending to the least important.

Next, consider all the daily and weekly responsibilities, chores, and obligations that you face—the things that you can't put off. Of all the things you "have to do," how many could you perhaps tackle another way? For example, could you start taking advantage of delivery services, rather than making trips yourself?

Looking for Alternatives

Can you hire part-time help, high school students, or others in your immediate vicinity to handle some of the domestic chores you don't need to be doing? Can you shop by mail, flipping through catalogs or browsing the Internet, and have products shipped to your door? Of course you can!

At work, are there company-sponsored childcare programs or other available low-cost forms of childcare? Can you swap childcare services with another parent in your neighborhood so you at least have some time free?

First Things Come First

Author and family balance guru Dr. Steven Covey stresses the importance of doing "first things first." Covey contends that if you pay homage to the most important things in your life, as you've identified them, you begin to find ways to make it all work. He uses the analogy of filling a glass jar with rocks, pebbles, and sand.

Suppose the rocks represent your highest priority items, the pebbles represent secondary items, and the grains of sand, tertiary items. When you deal with the rocks, i.e., primary items, first, a magical thing happens: You still find room for the secondary and tertiary items. They fit in and around the spaces available. If you attempt to do it the other way around, too often you end up giving short shrift to what is truly important in your life, and, instead, dissipating your energy and efforts on the minutiae of life.

Reinvento Observes

Get creative about approaching your responsibilities and obligations. Often, alternatives show up that you could not, or would not, have even contemplated before you slowed down and took a look at the big picture of balancing your life.

Caution

If you begin to fill the jar with the pebbles and sand, you run the risk of not being able to get all the rocks into the jar. Now suppose you put the rocks in first, followed by some of the smaller pebbles, and then sprinkle in the sand. Voilà! Everything fits into the jar.

Okay, So What's Important to You?

Here's an exercise on finding out what you value most in life, which will help you focus on the areas that need the most reinvention. Draw a pie chart in which wedges are proportioned according to how you spend your time now.

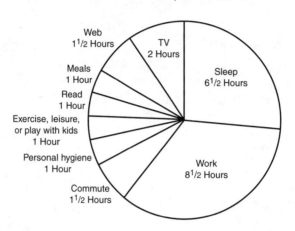

Time Spent Actual

Draw a second pie chart in which wedges are sized based on how you *want* to spend your time.

Time Spent Ideal

In examining the two charts, do you see any dramatic differences? You probably do, and the difference is the degree to which you probably feel out of balance in your life.

So, how can you adjust the first chart—that is, eliminate or change items—to achieve the ideal balance and match the second chart? This takes mental and emotional strength, because undoubtedly you're going to have to give up some time-worn, personal customs in favor of new behaviors.

It's important to have realistic expectations; you simply can't do everything at once. Indeed, gradual change is a much more desirable approach than radical upheaval.

Reallocating Your Time for What's Important

It's prudent to plan for some personal time each day, even if it's as little as 15 minutes. If you don't plan some personal time, chances are that you won't have any, and this can contribute to the feeling of being out of balance.

For some people, the very beginning of the day is a wonderful time to keep for themselves. Some people get up extra early in the morning so they can have that quiet time to themselves, before their spouse and family awaken. Whether you're married and have a family, or are single, an extra 30 minutes in the morning can change your entire outlook—not just for the day, but for your life.

Caution

Any time you undertake a change that is too radical, too upsetting, "too much too soon," you're in danger of springing back to exactly where you were. Keep working, though, and soon the balance will come.

Thirty Minutes Can Make a Huge Difference

In the quest for balance, 30 minutes a day can mean a lot. Still, the prospect of getting up 30 minutes earlier may seem out of the question. What if you went to bed 30 minutes earlier? What if you perused one less meaningless magazine, or watched one less sitcom, and instead gave your body the gift of an earlier-than-usual bedtime? When you get up early in the morning, say 30 minutes earlier than usual, strange and wonderful things happen:

➤ You may actually see the sun rise. It's glorious; it happens every morning, and hardly anyone is aware of it.

➤ You get to hear birds chirp.

➤ You see delivery people making their rounds.

➤ Maybe you're up before the newspaper's delivered.

In any case, there's vibrancy, energy, and excitement that permeates the air. Another day on earth, and another day in your life, is about to start. What could be more titillating than that?

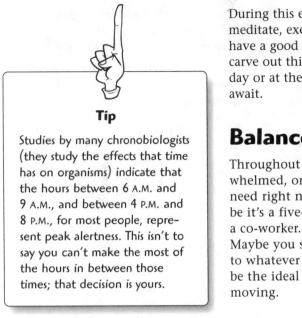

Tip

Studies by many chronobiologists (they study the effects that time has on organisms) indicate that the hours between 6 A.M. and 9 A.M., and between 4 P.M. and 8 P.M., for most people, represent peak alertness. This isn't to say you can't make the most of the hours in between those times; that decision is yours.

During this early morning time, you may choose to meditate, exercise, have a slow and leisurely shower, have a good breakfast, and so forth. If you choose to carve out this time for yourself sometime during the day or at the end of the day, many of the same gifts await.

Balance at a Desk Job

Throughout the day, if you feel a little weary, overwhelmed, or short of energy, ask yourself what you need right now to feel more on top of things. Maybe it's a five-minute walk. Maybe you need to talk to a co-worker. Maybe you need to munch on a carrot. Maybe you simply need a drink of water. Pay heed to whatever answer your body gives you. It may not be the ideal solution, but at least it will get you moving.

Time Out for Adults

If you're feeling down, in a bad mood, or otherwise having things "not go your way," give yourself what school children today call a "time out." Take a five-minute walk; splash some water on your face; log on to the Internet and visit your favorite Web site; give yourself a pep talk. Engage in any type of activity that will take you away from your current mood.

For some people, time out means listening to a favorite song. For others, it's taking deep breaths. For others, it's reading an inspiring poem. You can do this in your office, during the work day, as foul moods besiege you, or you can do it on the way home, so that you don't bring your ill feelings into the house. Sit in your car, if you have to, until you feel more at ease, relaxed, and positive.

Time Out When Arriving Home

If you face a highly stressful time at work (and who doesn't?), talk with your family so that they can help create an environment that's supportive of you when you first come home. Perhaps for the first 15 minutes after your arrival, you get to change your clothes, have a beverage, rearrange things, and get settled. Once out of the "work" mood, you'll be far more receptive to your spouse and kids than otherwise.

Contrast this peaceful arrival with the working parent who, as soon as he or she walks through the door, gets hit with questions, problems, and tasks that need to be done, and situations that need to be resolved. Is this the road to balance?

Periodically, step out of your evening routine and do something new and exhilarating. Now and then, have dinner delivered, or stop off and get a massage before coming home. On occasion, have dinner without the kids, or have the kids serve you dinner. Whatever the method, cut yourself some slack.

Staying in Balance on the Road

All of what's been discussed thus far presumes that you maintain a fairly regular, in-town schedule, and therefore have the opportunity to regain balance, and reinvent yourself, within that context. What if you travel frequently for business? In that case, you face an even greater challenge in balancing your work and personal life. Obviously you can use (and hopefully not abuse) the tool of technology to stay in touch with your loved ones.

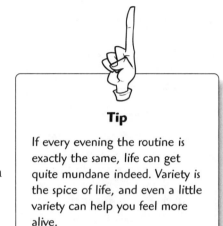

Tip

If every evening the routine is exactly the same, life can get quite mundane indeed. Variety is the spice of life, and even a little variety can help you feel more alive.

Travel Smart and Less

It's wise to meet with your family or partner to discuss how much travel is actually reasonable. You might be surprised to find that the amount you're traveling now is not acceptable at all for your spouse or children. Talk to the powers that be and show them that you can still be effective if you rearrange your schedule or duties so that you can travel less.

Plan around sacred family days, such as birthdays, anniversaries, kids' functions, and so forth. This can help you avoid lots of problems. It can also help your significant other feel as if you're there when it's important to be there.

If weekends are important in your household—and I'm betting that they are—try to schedule as much of your work as you can on Tuesdays, Wednesdays, or Thursdays, so that you aren't gone on the weekends. Weekends can be a long and lonely time for your partner and/or children, especially if they had fun things planned to do with you!

Recreating as You Travel

Perhaps you can turn business travel into a mini vacation by bringing your family along. If you only have to work on a Thursday or Friday, then you can spend the rest of the weekend with your family.

Reinvento Observes

Business Traveler magazine reports that in the last year, the number of traveling executives who brought family members along actually increased.

When it's just you, and you're on the road, be sure to take at least 30 minutes each day to "renew thyself." Take a swim if you're at a hotel that has a pool. Take a long walk or visit an interesting store.

Caution

Try not to plop down in front of the hotel room television set with the remote and stuff your face with food. This is only likely to further drain you of energy and make you less vibrant upon your return.

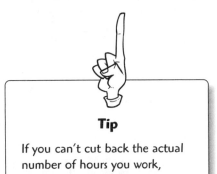

Tip

If you can't cut back the actual number of hours you work, maybe you can lobby for working more of your hours at home.

Communication Routines

Establish a routine so that you contact your partner and/or kids at the same time each day that you're gone. Also, leave nice notes and little gifts for them to find during your absence—perhaps putting something under the pillow of a child on the day you depart, or sticking something under your spouse's magazine so that he or she will see it within a day or two.

Upon your return, make it your number-one priority to listen to family members about what happened while you were gone. They've got lots of things to tell you, and if they keep them bottled up, they'll feel frustrated. Only when they're done should you share your adventures.

Avoiding Overwork

Let's explore the profound and hairy notion of cutting back the number of hours you actually work. If you work over 40 hours, you may want to cut back to 40. If you feel stressed at 40, then cut back even more. In either case, prepare and present a proposal to your boss. Cover every detail. For example, how will you handle your present duties if you're going to be working fewer hours, or will you be working from home or some other location? Here are some other questions to consider:

➤ How will you handle emergencies?

➤ What do you think is fair compensation?

➤ What represents a fair benefits package?

Do You Need to Cut Back Temporarily?

Perhaps you want to have reduced hours for a finite period of time, as little as one month or as long as half a year. In your plan, spell out when you'll return to your original status. Also, elaborate on how the organization benefits from your plan. For example …

➤ They will retain a high-performing, experienced worker who comes back with more energy and new insights (see Chapter 20, "Taking a Sabbatical").

➤ They'll spend less time and money than they would searching for a replacement.

➤ You may incur fewer sick days.

➤ You'll be loyal and grateful (this is important to state).

➤ You might even develop new skills in delegating from afar, planning, setting priorities, and delivering on projects.

Depending on your situation, you may want to call your state department of labor to see if you're covered by laws that prohibit discrimination against part-time employees. Some bosses may pose the argument that it will be too tough to reach you if you work part-time. Yet, full-timers are often only partially available when you consider the trips they take, the meetings they're involved in, the training sessions they attend, and so on.

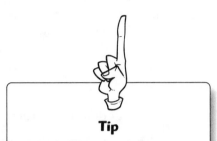

Tip

If you spell out your plan for staying in touch through phone calls, voicemail, fax, e-mail, beepers, and regularly scheduled activity reports, as well as attendance at staff meetings, you can make a sound argument indeed.

Flex Time

You may also wish to examine scheduling options such as working a half-day every day, two-and-a-half full days a week, two full days one week and three full days the next week, two days in the office and then one at home, one full week on and one full week off, and so on. These types of alternative hour arrangements are limited only by your imagination and what you can persuade your boss to consider.

Once you do reach an agreement on any type of reduced or *flexible hour* working arrangement, get it all down on paper, sign it, and have your supervisor sign it. Detail your hours, responsibilities, pay, benefits, and any other expectations. Somewhere in the plan, also include a provision that indicates when you will reevaluate the agreement (for example, in one month, three months, six months, and so on).

Word Power

A **flexible time schedule** is a schedule that varies from the usual eight hours a day, five days a week. Flex time can be used by either full- or part-time employees.

All the while, it's your responsibility to keep abreast of developments in your field, particularly in your organization and the division or department in which you're employed. It's also your responsibility to keep up with any new training to learn new programs, systems, and so on, and to stay in touch with mentors and network members so that if and when you want to resume full-time status, your skills and awareness levels are commensurate with the position. If you regain your sense of balance, it will all be worth it!

The Least You Need to Know

➤ It's difficult to achieve happiness and well-being without balance.

➤ Sometimes, to achieve balance, the first thing you need to do is slow down.

➤ Talk with your family about creating an environment that's supportive of you when you first come home from work.

➤ If you travel as part of your job, meet with your family or partner to discuss how much travel is reasonable.

➤ Be honest with yourself: You may need to cut back the number of hours you actually work.

Chapter 11

Working Out Versus Spreading Out

In This Chapter

➤ The need to drop those extra pounds

➤ The importance of physicals

➤ How to make time for exercise

➤ Small changes, big results

Exercising gives us more energy and makes us healthier, not to mention that looking better is sure to make you feel better. Yet, over the last several decades, an increasing percentage of Americans, now a staggering 61 percent, and others from industrialized nations have become overweight, if not obese. What better way to reinvent yourself than to drop those extra pounds and get in shape?

Bloating Isn't Pretty

Weight Watchers International, a company with a vested interest in having people lose weight, and which also knows a lot about *obesity*, reports that an astounding one third of the American population today is obese. "Research shows that obesity increases the risk for disabling and life-threatening chronic diseases including diabetes, hypertension, heart disease, and some cancers," says Linda Webb Carilli, General Manager, Corporate Affairs, Weight Watchers International. "There is overwhelming scientific consensus that achieving and maintaining a healthy weight, or at a minimum preventing further weight gain, should be a national public-health priority."

The Bare Facts About Obesity

Less than a quarter of American adults are getting the amount of exercise they need each day. Most of us, 60 percent, exercise only occasionally, and 25 percent don't exercise at all! This inactivity is harmful to your health, because it can cause coronary heart disease, adult-onset diabetes, colon cancer, osteoporosis, and high blood pressure.

The prevalence of obesity has drastically increased in the last nine years, by more than 9 percent within most races and each gender. The number of overweight children has more than doubled in the last 20 years, according to a report from the American Heart Association. "Twenty years ago, 15 percent of children, ages 5 to 14, were overweight. Today 32 percent are overweight."

Word Power

Obesity is currently defined as being 30 percent or more over the norm for one's weight and body type.

A Weighty Topic

Here's a good indicator of how overweight we're becoming: When old sports stadiums around the country are refurbished with new seats, there are often fewer of the new seats per row because Americans are more obese now than they used to be. These days, seat manufacturers are replacing 17-inch seats with 23-inch seats, to accommodate the increased obesity of the average American.

Paradoxically, just when we're at our most obese, we venerate thinness like never before. Society tells women, and girls in particular, that their innate worth is directly tied to their physical appearance—and their physical appearance is not acceptable unless they're thin.

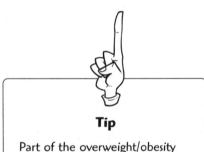

Tip

Part of the overweight/obesity problem is a sedentary lifestyle. Computers and TV are taking a toll. Turn off the electronics. Shoot some hoops with your kid tonight.

Fashion models, television and movie stars, those representatives of the ideal body image, are quite thin. This brutal insistence on "perfection" through thinness has resulted in the tragic widespread prevalence of various eating disorders. Perhaps if we could leave aside all the societal issues surrounding weight and focus instead on the health issues, we could make some headway.

A Valid Measurement Tool

The National Heart, Lung, and Blood Institute, a part of the federal government's National Institutes of Health, has developed a measurement of obesity called the *body mass index (BMI)*.

If you want to figure out your own BMI, but you don't want to do the math, you can use the NHLBI's automatic BMI calculator on the Internet at www.nhlbi.nih.gov. Don't worry about the metric measurements. The BMI calculator asks you to enter your height and weight in standard measurements, and it makes the conversion for you.

The NHLBI states that a BMI of 25 to 29.9 is overweight, and a BMI of 30 or above is obese. The NHLBI reached this determination by performing a meta-analysis of hundreds of weight-related studies on many thousands of subjects to determine the ideal BMI from a health standpoint.

Some people believe mistakenly that the BMI doesn't take into account muscle mass versus fat mass, and that this can make for misleading results. They point to very muscular people who weigh a lot for their size. Fear not—alternative BMI calculations can take into account chest and waist size so that the there are no "false" readings.

Word Power

The **body mass index** (**BMI**) is a number derived by dividing body weight in kilograms by height in meters squared. For instance, a woman who is 5'2" tall and weighs 150 pounds would have a BMI of 27.4. A man who is 6' tall and weighs 225 pounds would have a BMI of 30.5.

How High Is Your BMI?

The Institute found that people who had BMIs higher than 25 were at substantially higher risk of death from hypertension; type-2 diabetes; coronary heart disease; stroke; gallbladder disease; osteoarthritis; sleep apnea and respiratory problems; and endometrial, breast, prostate, and colon cancers. The higher your BMI is above 25, the greater your risk from a statistical standpoint.

After calculating your BMI, if you're at all concerned about your weight, don't hesitate to address the issue. You'll be glad you did—and so will the people who care about you.

Reinvento Observes

BMI measurement offers an objective, scientifically validated way to determine whether your weight is healthy for you. Hence, you can evaluate your weight and decide what to do about it without buying into what society says about body weight.

Weight Loss vs. Weight Maintenance

Diets usually work in the short term and not in the long term. This is because most diets are structured around weight loss, not weight maintenance. Weight loss gets the pounds off; weight maintenance is what keeps them off. Weight loss and weight maintenance are two different processes.

People who are able to maintain a given weight have made two decisions on a very deep level:

1. They've decided they want to be at a given weight over the long term.

2. They're committed and have chosen to do what it takes to achieve and maintain that weight.

Caution

Weight loss is easier to achieve because it's a short-term, intensive activity with a precise, often short-term goal in sight. Weight maintenance is a long-term, recurring activity without a more arduous long-term goal.

Reinvento Observes

If you haven't made the two fundamental decisions about weight, there is not a diet, book, tape, seminar, group, pill, powder, shake, herb, wrap, exercise, therapy, or surgery in the world that will work for you over the long term. If you do make these decisions, it doesn't matter what technique you use. You'll get the weight off and keep it off.

These decisions come about as the end result of an internal process, usually entailing self-examination, self-discovery, and personal growth.

Starting with a Doctor Visit

The road back to health and fitness starts with a doctor visit and a complete physical. Yet, a recent Harris Survey commissioned by the Commonwealth Fund found that nearly "a quarter of men had not seen a doctor in the previous year ... 8 percent of women had not." Four out of five women have a regular doctor; only two of three men do.

Let's Get a Physical

David Knoepfler, M.D., offers a definition of a physical exam on the Eastside Primary Care Web site, www.ePrimarycare.net. He says, "In the course of a complete physical exam, issues regarding personal habits are addressed, medications reviewed, and family history detailed. Screening tests are also usually performed. The purpose of these steps is to assure your continued health and determine what changes can be instituted to maintain long-term health."

He suggests checking with your insurance company prior to your physical to see if it covers the expense. In addition to regular check-ups, here are other exams that should be conducted regularly:

➤ Dental exam—every year

➤ Eye exam—every three to five years (if you have no vision problems)

➤ Blood pressure—every two years

After having a physical, discuss a safe and realistic exercise program with your doctor, which may involve activity in and around your home and/or joining a health club.

Joining a Gym

If you opt to join a health club, make the most of it. If you already belong to or have access to a health club, then, of course, you have many fitness tools at your disposal. The treadmills and bike machines are great for warm-ups, because in each case you can start at slow speeds.

Break a vicious cycle. When you work out vigorously for too long, as so many people you see in a health club do, you fall into a cycle that's hard to undo. The cycle is as follows:

➤ Dehydration, so you fill up on water

➤ Hunger, so you fill up on food

➤ Weariness, so you need more sleep, or drag yourself around all day

Then, you wake up the next day hungry and thirsty again. You can end up overeating as a result of your vigorous workouts. It helps in reinventing your weight to join a health club, but use the facilities wisely.

Reinvento Observes

If the health club facility has mirrors along the walls, use them while you exercise because they help you maintain proper form. Mirrors may also prompt you to stay on the bike or other exercise machine longer, or do more repetitions.

Setting Fitness and Health Goals

How many people actually determine what they want their waistline to be one year from now, two years from now, and so on? What would you like your blood pressure to be six months from now?

On average, how many hours of each night do you want to be sleeping in a given week, starting, for example, one week from now? What size would you like your waistline to be? If this sounds like something that's outside your control, think again. You once had a slim, trim waistline (maybe it was as far back as age 18 or 20, but you had it). Chances are that you're not taller than you were when you were 20.

While your frame may have widened a bit, you could have a far trimmer waistline than you might

Caution

If the health club facility has a sauna, steam-room, or whirlpool bath, feel free to use them, but don't overdo it. Prolonged stays in any of these can actually end up draining energy from you.

think. Consistently losing one pound a week is no easy feat. That would mean four pounds in a month and eight pounds in two months.

Those who do crash-course weight loss are most susceptible to putting weight back on just as quickly. People who have lost 40 or 50 pounds often turn around months later and add 60 or 70 pounds.

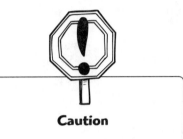

Caution

Don't be fooled by the infomercials, advertisements, and just plain come-ons. When you see a parade of people claim that they lost eight pounds in the first four days or six pounds in the first week, switch the channel. Most of this loss is water. It is not healthful or desirable to lose weight too fast.

Reinvento Observes

Author Edwin Bliss once said, "If you're too busy to stay fit, you're too busy." Truer words were never spoken!

Setting Workout Goals

If you've got the bucks, it helps to have an experienced coach work with you in your weight-loss and workout programs. If you don't have someone else to help you, however, you can often be an excellent coach yourself. Set different goals for yourself:

➤ **Long-term goals:** Give yourself a goal for the next three to six months. Make sure that your long-term goals are realistic—lose eight pounds in 16 weeks or walk one mile in under 15 minutes, for example.

➤ **Short-term goals:** To stay motivated, you need to feel a sense of accomplishment along the way. Set short-term goals for one week to one month. Examples include making it all the way through step-aerobics class without stopping, or improving last week's one-mile walk time by 10 seconds.

➤ **Immediate goals:** These goals are for each day or each workout. Examples may be spending a full 10 minutes stretching at the end of a workout, running two miles, or bicycling on a hilly course.

In Just Minutes Per Day

Regardless of what you face at home or at work, there's no excuse to let your body go to pot. Here's an ingenious method for maintaining regular exercise: It seems that this guy rigged up his television set to his exercise bike, such that the TV would only stay on as long as he was pedaling. What a country!

If you find exercise videos to be invigorating, then go for it. Many people will pop them in for a while, but after a few sessions, lose interest. If you have cable or satellite link television service, undoubtedly you can find an exercise channel, or an exercise program of some sort, at any time during the day. If no such programming is available, then find some show to sustain your interest while you work out.

Exercising on the Fly

Here are small ways to build exercise into your day:

➤ Take the stairs in your office building whenever you go down, and when you're going up only one or two flights.

➤ Park a little farther from the mall the next time you go shopping.

➤ Use the inside of shopping malls as your exercise track. Even after shopping, you can spend an extra 5 to 10 minutes going to the far end of the mall and back.

Develop the habit as well, of taking a stroll after dinner. Even a light, 10- to 15-minute walk, can make all the difference in how you feel, in your energy level the next morning, and in your ability to maintain your current weight.

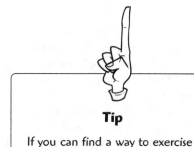

Tip

If you can find a way to exercise in a manner that does not seem laborious to you, you're much more likely to exercise regularly. Maybe it's doing calisthenics or aerobics in front of your favorite program or the nightly news. Perhaps it's joining a group of others who exercise each morning, each evening, or even during the middle of the day.

Opportunities Abound

You have various opportunities, throughout each day, to exercise and stay in shape. It can even be fun, if you're creative. Take advantage of nature, while getting a workout, by walking in the woods, doing the backstroke in a tranquil lake, or inline skating through the park. Here are some other ideas:

➤ Look for little ways all day long to engage in a few moments of exercise. For example, park your car a block or two from your job.

➤ Get in the habit of taking a walk before and after each meal, even if it's for a couple minutes. You'll feel the difference, and after a while, begin to notice the difference. I find that walking after dinner, in particular, enables me to enjoy the rest of the evening and, surprisingly, helps diminish my appetite for anything else.

➤ Enroll in an exercise course with a friend. That way, you reinforce each other, attend more regularly, and stay for the entire session.

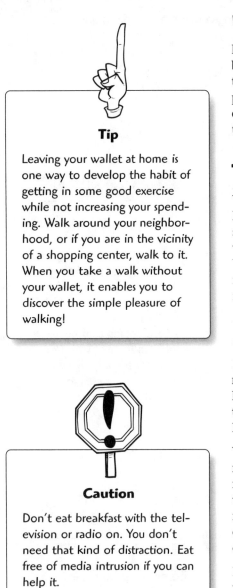

Watching How You Eat

It is important that your diet contains enough vegetables, legumes, fruits, and fiber. Researchers are finding that a highly nutritious, low-calorie, low-fat, moderate protein diet, similar to the traditional Mediterranean diet, is very healthy. Yet, it's not entirely what you eat that may need to change.

The Deal on Meals

When you continually short-change the time you have to eat properly, you may be back on the job sooner, but your overall energy level and productivity are bound to suffer (see Chapter 12, "You Are What You Eat [Sort Of]"). Here are suggestions for making the time to correctly eat the three major meals of the day.

Breakfast of Champions

Breakfast is the meal that people in America skip most often. If they do have breakfast, it's a cinnamon Danish or honey-glazed doughnut. I suppose they do this so they'll have enough of a jolt to get to work. But the nutritional value is next to nothing.

You say you don't have time for breakfast in the morning? Then I say go to bed 15 minutes earlier the night before. If preparing a hot meal for breakfast is too much trouble for you, even with the advent of the microwave, perhaps your best bet is to stay with the cold cereals. Many manufacturers make high-nutrient cereals, such as Total and Special K.

I keep my cupboard stocked with oats, some type of wheat, and a variety of other cereal foods. On any given morning, I might sprinkle two or three different grains into the cereal bowl, so that I get a good variety of nutrients early on.

Joining a Lunch Bunch

Have you fallen prey to the lunch-at-your desk syndrome? You may need the exercise and the perspective of being out and about, away from your desk. Here are some strategies for making sure you eat a good lunch, away from your desk:

➤ Make a goal of trying every restaurant in the area over the next couple of weeks. Just be sure you eat at healthful restaurants, not fast-food eateries.

➤ Eat lunch with friends.

➤ Pick a different destination for lunch each day, such as a park bench one day, the rooftop terrace another.

➤ If you live close enough, go home and eat there occasionally.

Supping Light on Most Nights

The great nutritional myth is that you should eat three square meals a day. It could actually be two square meals a day with some nutritional snack. Of the meals you could miss, dinner carries the fewest penalties.

The earlier you eat dinner, the better. If you can eat before 7 P.M., you should. Before 6 P.M. is even better—your body has more time to digest food before you retire for the evening.

One of the most important ways to reinvent yourself as a person is to reinvent your methods of exercise and eating. By doing so, you'll become healthier and gain motivation. Simple, everyday changes to your fitness regime are sure to make you more content.

Reinvento Observes

Ben Franklin once suggested that you eat a heavy breakfast, a less heavy lunch, and "sup light."

The Least You Need to Know

➤ Statistics show that Americans are becoming more and more obese, which is dangerous to us as individuals, as well as a society.

➤ The road back to health and fitness starts with a doctor visit and a complete physical. Getting regular physicals is a vital part of staying healthy and staying in shape.

➤ Those who do crash–course weight loss are most susceptible to putting the weight back on just as quickly.

➤ Throughout the day, small changes to your usual habits could add a large amount of exercise, and you'll feel better as a result.

➤ Of the meals you could miss, dinner carries the fewest penalties.

Chapter 12

You Are What You Eat (Sort Of)

In This Chapter

➤ A closer look at unhealthy eating habits

➤ Re-examining your diet

➤ More facts about weight

➤ How to get started

Imagine waking up in the morning feeling well rested and happy instead of tired and anxious. Imagine eating a breakfast that's healthy and satisfying, not one that's unhealthy and hurried. Imagine feeling good about what you eat, instead of ignoring your food or regarding meals as a chore to be completed. Imagine feeling good because of what you eat, not in spite of it.

Sound like a fantasy? It doesn't have to be. You can convert your eating habits so that every meal you eat—every morsel you put in your mouth—is part of the overall project of reinventing yourself. You can bring the same energy and sense of purpose to your meals that you bring to exercise, career changes, or any other aspect of reinventing your life.

So, What Does That Make You?

The saying "You are what you eat" has become a cliché, but like many clichés, there's a kernel of truth in it. Almost every piece of matter in your body originated in the form of food or drink you ingested. We transform the things we eat into blood, skin, teeth, bones, and organ tissue. This doesn't mean that you turn into a chicken if you eat one, but it does mean your food choices have a wide-ranging impact on the quality and, eventually, the length of your life.

What types of food choices do most people make these days?

Unhealthy Eating Habits

According to the NPD Group, a research firm based in Port Washington, New York, the number of breakfasts carried from home (to one's car or on one's commute) has doubled since 1984. The number of Americans who get their breakfast from quick-service restaurants (did somebody say McDonald's?!!) has jumped 28 percent since 1995, according to the Washington, D.C.–based National Restaurant Association.

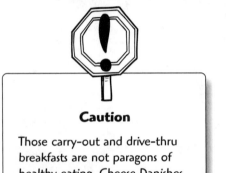

Caution

Those carry-out and drive-thru breakfasts are not paragons of healthy eating. Cheese Danishes, sausage biscuits, and dough-nuts are just what the doctor ordered—ordered you to avoid, that is.

Tip

McDonald's stopped calling their shakes "milkshakes" years ago when consumer groups vehemently pointed out that the drink contains no milk whatsoever and is primarily a concoction based on fat and calorie-laden coconut oil.

Lunch often isn't much better. For many, lunch amounts to swinging by another fast-food restaurant or getting the same kind of food at a company cafeteria or convenience store.

Let's say you go to McDonald's for lunch and you get a Quarter-Pounder with Cheese, a medium order of French fries, and a small soft drink. Your moderately sized lunch has given you 1,130 calories and a whopping 52 grams of fat! If you decide to splurge a little and have a small shake with your lunch, you can add another 360 calories and 9 grams of fat, for a truly grand total of 1,490 calories and 61 grams of fat—equal to half of the calories and more than all the fat an adult normally requires in a day. Not bad for a meal that takes most people a mere half an hour to eat.

Dinner, which is the largest meal of the day for most Americans, usually brings on even more calories, fat, and cholesterol. And don't even mention those extra-high-fat premium ice creams for dessert.

Indigestion after dinner? What a surprise. Most people just pop an antacid and hope it works. Consumer-spending on both over-the-counter drugs and prescription drugs is at an all-time high. If that antacid doesn't work and you have a restless night, don't worry. You can get up in the morning and slug back some coffee to wake you up as you dash out the door and start the whole cycle over again.

Record Levels of Nutritional Abuse

Obesity (see Chapter 11, "Working Out Versus Spreading Out") and cardiovascular disease are at record-high levels. Not only does this increase in obesity affect individuals by deteriorating their health, which may also cause them to miss work, but it's also taking a toll on the earth itself. Thomas Samaras, author of *The Truth About Your Height,* observes that "In nature, when the average size of a species grows larger, the size of the population declines to offset the additional food needs and resources required. Humans are violating this rule in that we are growing bigger in both size and numbers." He goes on to say this:

> "This trend places much greater demands on the earth. More food, water, resources, and energy are needed to support us in our current lifestyle. In addition, we produce more air and ocean pollution, destroy rainforests faster, and reduce biodiversity."

Is it far-fetched to suggest that contemporary dietary practices might have something to do with all this?

Becoming Something Better

It's time to inject sanity into this process! Start with some information about your nutritional needs from the United States Department of Agriculture. Remember the old basic four food groups? They've been replaced by the USDA Food Guide Pyramid, known by many but heeded by few. Instead of four food groups that are given equal weight, the new Pyramid delineates six food groups that you need in different amounts.

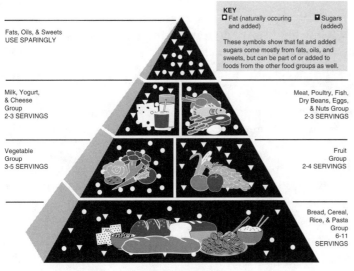

Food Guide Pyramid.

KEY

☐ Fat (naturally occuring and added)   ■ Sugars (added)

These symbols show that fat and added sugars come mostly from fats, oils, and sweets, but can be part of or added to foods from the other food groups as well.

Fats, Oils, & Sweets
USE SPARINGLY

Milk, Yogurt, & Cheese Group
2-3 SERVINGS

Meat, Poultry, Fish, Dry Beans, Eggs, & Nuts Group
2-3 SERVINGS

Vegetable Group
3-5 SERVINGS

Fruit Group
2-4 SERVINGS

Bread, Cereal, Rice, & Pasta Group
6-11 SERVINGS

Source: U.S. Department of Agriculture - U.S. Department of Health and Human Services

The USDA recommends that you get 6 to 11 servings daily from the bread and rice group, 3 to 5 servings from the vegetable group, 2 to 4 servings from the fruit group, 2 to 3 servings from the milk, yogurt, and cheese group, and 2 to 3 servings from the meat, poultry, fish, beans, nuts, and eggs group. ("Servings," as used here, mean only a few ounces.) The USDA also advises that you use fats, oils, and sweets sparingly.

The more you can move your diet away from the typical American diet and toward the USDA Food Guide Pyramid, the better off you'll be. For example, a salad can be fun to make and nutritious to eat.

The Importance of Vitamins

As discussed in Chapter 11, vitamins serve many purposes, all of which make you a healthier person. Everybody has different metabolic and nutritional needs, and you may have specific issues that a multivitamin doesn't address. In that case, you should supplement your multivitamin with additional amounts of the vitamins for which you have a particular need.

Listed below are the functions of the most important vitamins and minerals, so you can decide which ones you need the most. Make sure the multivitamin you choose contains 100 percent of the Recommended Daily Allowance (RDA):

➤ Vitamin A promotes better vision, strengthens the immune system, and enhances the growth and maintenance of bones and skin.

➤ Vitamins B1 and B2 help regulate your appetite and your energy metabolism.

➤ Vitamin B3 aids in metabolic functions, supports healthy skin, and plays a role in the smooth functioning of the digestive and nervous systems. Vitamin B3 is actually made by the body, so the RDA is only an estimate.

➤ Vitamin B6 helps you think more clearly, boosts the immune system, and supports hormone activity. Alcohol consumption inhibits B6 activity, so drinkers should be especially careful about their B6 levels.

➤ Vitamin B12 ensures the proper functioning of your nervous system and helps support bone growth and metabolism.

➤ Folate is essential for new cell development. Pregnant women should take folic acid during the first trimester of pregnancy to help prevent birth defects in their newborns.

➤ Vitamin C performs a host of functions. It protects against disease and infection, promotes the body's absorption of iron, helps bones grow, aids in the formation of scar tissue, and strengthens blood vessels. Smokers are in extra need of vitamin C.

➤ Vitamin D strengthens bones and helps maintain the brain, pancreas, skin, muscles, reproductive organs, and immune system, among other functions. Vitamin

D can be ingested via food or as a supplement, but the body is capable of synthesizing it through exposure to sunlight.

➤ Vitamin E keeps skin healthy, helps scars heal, and protects the lungs from air pollutants.

➤ Others: Calcium is best known for keeping your bones strong. Copper helps you absorb iron. Chromium helps the body maintain its balance of glucose. Iron is necessary for the transport of oxygen throughout the body. Selenium enhances the functions of vitamin E and may help prevent cancer. Zinc helps support your sense of taste, plays a role in the manufacturing of sperm, heals wounds, and aids in manufacturing genetic material and proteins. Your multivitamin also should provide at least 10 percent of the RDA for magnesium.

Re-Examining Your Nutritional Intake

Let's say you've made some dietary changes to your breakfast: You're having old-fashioned oats instead of a sausage biscuit, and a piece of fruit instead of a doughnut. What are you using to wash down your morning vitamins? If you're getting enough rest, the importance of which we discussed in Chapter 10, "Above All, Get Balanced," then you won't need that morning cup of java just to crank your eyelids open.

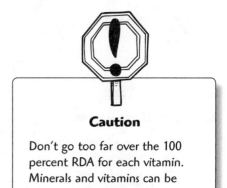

Caution

Don't go too far over the 100 percent RDA for each vitamin. Minerals and vitamins can be toxic at high dosages.

Have Some Juice

The National Cancer Institute, the American Dietetic Association, and the American Heart Association all say that incorporating fruit and vegetable juices into a healthy diet is one way to maintain and possibly improve health.

If you still want the comfort of a hot drink in the morning, consider drinking herbal teas. True herbal teas are caffeine-free and can give you a boost. For instance, some blends of Chinese herbal teas are noted for their energy-enhancing properties, as well as for lowering cholesterol, counteracting the effects of stress, combating allergies, and possibly even fighting cancer.

Caution

While moderate caffeine consumption is not associated with any health risk, excessive caffeine intake can lead to a fast heart rate, *diuresis*, nausea and vomiting, restlessness, anxiety, depression, tremors, and difficulty in sleeping.

For example, peppermint tea can be used to soothe an upset stomach; chamomile relaxes you and counteracts the effects of stress.

Go Organic

You've got a vast array of dietary options from which to choose. Vegetarianism, macrobiotic diets, food-combining regimens, ethnic cuisines—there are too many dietary reinvention options to be enumerated here.

As you're trying out new dietary options, keep in mind that there is one option you could pursue that would probably have a greater positive impact on your overall diet than any other dietary decision you could make: buying and eating organic foods.

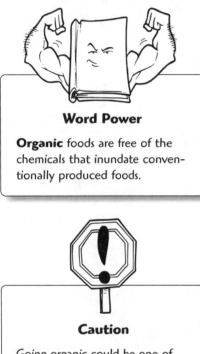

Word Power

Organic foods are free of the chemicals that inundate conventionally produced foods.

Caution

Going organic could be one of the best things you'll ever do for your health. While the federal government has determined that the chemicals used are safe in food production, proponents of organic foods disagree. They point to ever-increasing cancer rates across the country as evidence of widespread environmental contamination by chemicals.

So, What's "Organic"?

For fruits and vegetables to carry an *organic* label, no pesticides, herbicides, or preservatives can be used in their growing, production, or processing. Organic meats come from animals that do not receive antibiotics and are allowed to roam outdoors instead of being confined to feeding areas ("free-range" animals).

Many large-chain supermarkets now carry organic produce, either in a separate organic section of the produce area or scattered throughout the conventionally grown produce. But beware—a campaign of disinformation is underway to try to discredit organic foods and the organic foods industry.

You can find organic processed foods (such as breakfast cereals, canned vegetables, and soups) in health-food stores, upscale markets, or the healthfood section of a supermarket.

So They Cost a Little More

Organic foods sometimes cost more than conventional foods, often because organic foods are produced and distributed in smaller quantities. This means that the prices of organic foods don't benefit from the same economies of scale available to food production giants like General Mills and RJR Nabisco.

Boosters of organic food say it's well worth the higher prices when you consider how much money you could be saving in healthcare costs down the road!

Not Eating?

How about not eating? More and more health professionals are recommending limited, structured *fasting* as a way to promote overall systemic healing of the body. While uncommon in the United States, fasting is widely practiced in Europe. Most European countries even have clinics that administer therapeutic fasting programs.

Fasting is particularly popular in Sweden. Many ancient cultures, including some from Asia, India, and the Americas, have long regarded fasting as a dependable curative. Modern health practitioners in the United States are starting to agree.

Word Power

Fasting is abstaining from all or certain foods.

Proponents of fasting hold that aging and disease are exacerbated by the fact that the cells of the body never have a chance to clean out all their wastes and toxins, because they're constantly processing nutritive material. Fasting gives your cells the breathing space they need and very well could prolong life as a result.

Different Ways to Starve Yourself

There are generally two kinds of therapeutic fasting. A water fast means the only thing you ingest is … water! This kind of fast induces rapid internal purification, but it's also a shock to the system.

In a juice fast, which is less of a systemic shock, you drink natural fruit and vegetable juices to provide a few calories to keep your engine running, essential vitamins to maintain metabolism, and minerals to help your body remove wastes and toxins. Ideally, you would drink at least two quarts of liquid per day, either water or juices, during any therapeutic fast (and preferably more, up to a gallon) to help your body eliminate wastes and toxins.

It's common after a fast for practitioners to report that they feel renewed mentally, emotionally, and spiritually, in addition to the physical benefits.

How long should you fast? Most therapeutic fasts generally last between three and seven days. However, always pay attention to the way your body and mind feel during a fast. If you start getting

Reinvento Observes

Fasting allows the organs to empty and rest. This resting period conserves energy and promotes the elimination of wastes and accumulated toxins, which makes the ongoing task of cell regeneration much more efficient.

signals to stop (besides hunger, that is), then stop! Many books, courses, and Web sites are devoted to fasting, so be sure to find a safe, reputable fasting program to follow before you abstain.

Get Help and Check Credentials

You have a vast—some would say bewildering—array of dietary choices open to you. How do you know what your vitamin needs are? Does green tea really fight cancer? Is a vegetarian diet right for you? Is your fasting program safe? If you want answers to these or any other dietary questions, you may wish to consult a dietitian or a nutritionist.

Caution

Most Americans lack the proper reserve nutrients necessary for a healthy and safe water fast.

Dietitians and nutritionists are trained professionals who are experts in counseling individuals and organizations about nutritional issues. They have at least a Bachelor's degree in dietetics, foods and nutrition, food-service systems management, or a related area. Twenty-seven of the 41 states with laws governing dietetics require a license, 13 require certification, and one requires registration.

Check Credentials

The Commission on Dietetic Registration of the American Dietetic Association (ADA) awards a Registered Dietitian credential to those who pass a certification exam after completing the required academic course work and supervised practice experience.

You can find dietitians and nutritionists by looking under each classification in the Yellow Pages of your local telephone directory. You can also go to the ADA Web site at www.eatright.org and use the ADA's referral service to find a registered dietitian in your area. Here are other Web sites that should prove useful in your efforts to achieve a healthier diet:

Reinvento Observes

Many religious traditions, including all the world's major religions, have encouraged fasting for a variety of reasons, including penitence, preparation for ceremony, purification, mourning, sacrifice, union with the Divine, and enhancement of the faster's knowledge and powers.

➤ **American Cancer Society:** www.cancer.org

➤ **American Council on Science and Health:** www.acsh.org

➤ **American Diabetes Association:** www.diabetes.org

➤ **American Heart Association:** www.amhrt.org

➤ **Center for Science in the Public Interest:** www.cspinet.org

➤ Food Allergy Network: www.foodallergy.org

➤ International Food Information Council: www.ificinfo.health.org

➤ Tufts University Nutrition Navigator: www.navigator.tufts.edu

➤ USDA Nutrient Database: www.nal.usda.gov/fnic/cgi-bin/nut_search.pl

➤ U.S. Food and Drug Administration: www.fda.gov

Ask your doctor for a referral to a good dietitian or nutritionist. Ask your friends and acquaintances if they know of anyone you can retain.

Now Is the Time

Now is the time to sketch out a nutrition road map for yourself. Start thinking more about diet and nutrition. Do some research, both in books and on the Internet. Educate yourself. Hang out in health food stores; they're wonderful places to learn about nutrition. Discuss nutritional issues with your friends. Seek professional advice or guidance when you think it's necessary. Develop a plan and stick to it.

Measure your progress, congratulate yourself for your successes, and forgive yourself when you stumble. Above all, stay focused.

From Junk Bonds to Education: He'll Always Be Rich!

Michael Milken is the poster boy for greed in the 1980s. He is often called the "Junk Bond King," and for many common people, the words "insider trading" still ring a bell. Because of his involvement in the insider trading scandals of the 1980s, Milken was prohibited from trading in securities for the rest of his life.

Yet, the Michael Milken that the media has given us is not the total Michael Milken at all. Milken has become one of the most generous philanthropists in the world and an established author. Most of all, he is a man with a stake in the education of our children.

The Story Behind the Headlines

Working for Drexel Burnham Lambert, a modestly sized investment-banking firm, Milken created a market for bonds issued by companies which previously would not have been creditworthy to get a bank loan. By 1987, the value of these bonds, what we call "junk bonds," had soared to the figure of $200 billion.

At that point the U.S. Government started to investigate—an increase from nothing to $200 billion activates a lot of alarms. Investigations in Milken's operations and subsequent charges led to his pleading to six breaches of securities law. He was ordered to pay over $1 billion and was sent to prison for several years.

Overcoming Life-Size Obstacles

After being released from prison, Milken learned that he had prostate cancer and could only expect to live for 18 months. He ultimately conquered his prostate cancer, which he attributes to a healthy diet and meditation. Still extremely wealthy, to help those men who are in the same predicament, Milken wrote a book titled *The Taste for Living Cookbook: Mike Milken's Favorite Recipes for Fighting Cancer*. In it, he offers fat-free and meat-free recipes to help the body fight cancers.

A Different Direction

Banned from returning to the securities business, Milken turned his focus elsewhere. Besides writing and philanthropy, he serves as the chairman of Knowledge Universe, founded in 1997 by Milken's younger brother, Lowell, and Larry Ellison, the CEO of Oracle software company. Knowledge Universe develops and invests in companies that help individuals reach their full potential.

The more than 40 Knowledge Universe companies operate in one of two groups: Knowledge Universe Business Group (KUGB) or Knowledge Universe Learning Group (KULG). In particular, companies within KULG seek to enhance the learning process from birth to graduate school. They supply a range of products and services, including interactive education products.

Milken has survived the humiliation of being sentenced to prison and the perils of prostate cancer. He has managed to make the best of these setbacks and even use them as springboards into business and social ventures. He is now heavily investing in cancer research so that men, someday, will not have to face what he did. Most important, he is investing in America's future by giving children and their parents the tools necessary for true education.

The Least You Need to Know

➤ Americans in general have unhealthy eating habits, so don't follow the norm!

➤ If you're not consistently eating balanced meals, vitamins can help enormously.

➤ To make a simple change in your diet, start drinking natural fruit and vegetable juice.

➤ Fasting, although it isn't for everybody, can be a healthy way to lose weight, clean out your system, and feel healthier.

➤ Visit www.eatright.org and use the ADA's referral service to find a registered dietitian in your area.

Chapter 13

Physical Feats of Wonder

In This Chapter

➤ Ways to get in shape while having fun

➤ The usefulness of exercise videos and home equipment

➤ Health clubs

➤ Lifestyle overhaul

People who don't get enough physical activity are more likely to develop a wide range of physical problems that can seriously reduce both the quality and the length of their lives. These *diseases of affluence,* as they are sometimes called, include stroke, high blood pressure, and heart attacks, to name a few.

Get Moving

Physical activity yields many benefits. An adequate level of regular physical activity can do the following:

➤ Strengthen your heart, lungs, muscles, and bones

➤ Lower your chance of heart attack or heart disease

➤ Help you manage your weight and blood pressure

➤ Give you more energy and strength

➤ Help you sleep well

Word Power

Diseases of affluence are illnesses that are common to Western industrialized societies that have rich diets and sedentary lifestyles.

Reinvento Observes

Physically fit people are not fundamentally different from the rest of us. Anybody can get in better shape at any time.

➤ Make it easier for you to handle stress

➤ Help you feel generally positive about life

If you're concerned about the quality of your life, then you, as a physical being, need to be concerned about the health and fitness of your body. Exercise is one of the best things you can do to help your body realize its maximum potential and become a vital part of your life.

While there's no denying that natural talent plays a role in determining who wins gold medals, talent isn't a necessary component for the humble goal of increasing your own fitness level. Consistent effort is all it takes to transform your body from that of a couch potato into a healthy, thriving organism. You may not wind up in the Major Leagues or the Olympics, but you can reinvent your body through exercise so that it's healthier, more capable, and more responsive to your needs and desires.

Becoming Part of a Team

One good way to begin making physical activity a bigger part of your life is to start playing a team sport, such as basketball, soccer, or hockey. Team sports provide many advantages as a form of exercise. For instance, many people find it easier to exercise if they have partners in the endeavor. When you play a team sport, everyone on the team is your partner.

Most team sports have established traditions. To begin playing one of these sports is, in a sense, to join the community of players. Usually, a jargon is associated with the sport to be learned. The newcomer learns about publications and programs devoted to the sport. This process of investment in and identification with the sport serves to bolster a sense of commitment to it and, thus, to exercise.

Have Ball, Will Play

Common team sports that most of us learned how to play in grade school include basketball, football, soccer, softball, volleyball, and hockey or field hockey. Basketball, football, and soccer are the easiest of these sports to play, requiring the least in terms of equipment and facilities. A ball, a field (or a ball, a court, and a hoop) and some friends are all you need to play. The others are also quite easy to begin playing.

Playing Against an Opponent

If team sports don't spark your interest, perhaps an opponent sport would be better suited for you. These sports pit one person against another, or sometimes two against two. Well-known opponent sports include tennis, racquetball, handball, squash, and fencing.

These sports have the advantages of team sports, in that you have a partner and you develop a commitment to the sport, but opponent sports typically appeal to people who prefer to function independently and would rather not coordinate their actions with other players on a team. These sports may also be faster-paced and more demanding aerobically, so they're ideal for people seeking that kind of activity.

Many health clubs, country clubs, YWCAs, YMCAs, and community centers offer tennis lessons, and it's easy to find private tennis instructors in most areas. Fencing instruction is a little less common, but most universities have fencing clubs or offer fencing lessons that anyone in the community can take.

Local gyms should offer ample opportunities for you to engage in these and other rewarding opponent sports.

Individual Sports

There is no shortage of individual sports for you to explore. Running and swimming are sports that you can do either in the climate-controlled comfort of a health club or in the great outdoors, and they both provide excellent aerobic benefits. Those who enjoy being outside and who live in a coastal area may be drawn to a sport such as surfing, provided the seas in your area have good waves. Here are a few other individual sports to consider:

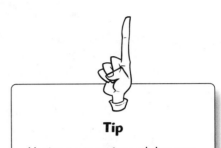

Tip

Having partners is good, because it's harder to find excuses for not exercising when other people are counting on you to show up. Also, having company while you're exercising can make it more pleasant, because the social interaction is fun in its own right, and it can serve to distract you from the physical exertion (an added bonus for out-of-shape beginners).

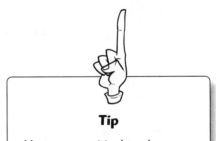

Tip

Most communities have leagues for more common sports; check with your local YWCA or YMCA for information about league play in your area.

➤ Inline skating is a great sport for people who like to be outside and who live in urban areas.

➤ Scuba diving, wind-surfing, and kayaking require more of an up-front investment in equipment—and scuba diving also requires you to pass a diving certification course—but they repay more in terms of variety and excitement.

➤ Hiking is a wonderful activity for people who enjoy being in natural settings, but don't want to take too many risks or get too exhausted.

➤ Rock-climbing is one of the riskier individual sports, but some thrill-seekers wouldn't have it any other way. With the advent of indoor climbing walls, rock-climbing is another sport that can be performed outdoors or indoors.

If you like to hike, find a group of like-minded friends who can go with you. Runners often run with regular partners. Rock-climbers, kayakers, and scuba divers virtually always go out in pairs for simple safety reasons. If you have a partner with whom you can exercise, it's a lot more likely that you'll stick with your program.

Here is some information to help you find personal trainers if the spirit so moves you:

National Federation of Professional Trainers
PO Box 4579
Lafayette, IN 47903-4579
Phone: 1-800-729-6378
Fax: 765-447-3648
E-mail: info@nfpt.com

National Academy of Sports Medicine
123 Hodencamp Drive, Suite 204
Thousand Oaks, CA 91360
Phone: 1-800-656-2739
Fax: 805-449-1370
Web site: www.nasm.org/

The American College of Sports Medicine
401 W. Michigan Street
Indianapolis, IN 46202-3233
Phone: 317-637-9200
Fax: 317-634-7817
Web site: www.acsm.org/

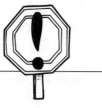

Caution

Opponent sports tend to be more technique-dependent than most team sports, so some degree of coaching, training, or education is often necessary in order to play the sport with a satisfactory degree of competence. This is particularly true of tennis and fencing.

Caution

Individual sports often require more discipline. If you're not part of a team or competing against someone else, it may be easier to call off your exercise session when you don't feel like doing it.

Dancing the Night Away

There are other ways besides sports to engage in the physical activity your body needs. Ballroom dancing, also called social dancing, is a good example. Social dance is a fun activity that enables you to listen to good music while you participate. It also gives you a chance to meet people who share your interests.

Classes in various kinds of social dance, such as the waltz, tango, fox trot, and swing, are quite popular and easy to find these days. And it's a workout! An added benefit is the fact that the concentration it takes to learn to do the dance takes your mind off the physical exertion, making the whole experience more enjoyable.

Martial Your Arts

The martial arts are another worthy form of exercise. These disciplines, such as karate, tae-kwon-do, and aikido, have provided beneficial exercise for centuries upon centuries.

Practicing the martial arts increases strength and flexibility and can provide aerobic conditioning. The martial arts also engender greater self-awareness of the body, which leads to an expansion of overall personal self-awareness. Having a better relationship with your body means having a better relationship with yourself.

Here are two other forms of exercise you might want to explore:

Reinvento Observes

The primary purpose of these arts is to teach self-defense techniques. They are effective for this purpose when well taught and well applied, but beneficial side effects are great exercise and increased focus of the mind.

➤ **T'ai Chi.** T'ai Chi is an ancient Chinese practice that originated as a martial art form but has mutated over time to become a more health-oriented activity. If you've ever seen groups of people performing slow, stylized movements in unison in a park or on a beach, this was probably a T'ai Chi group. T'ai Chi focuses on using natural movements to provide healthful, low-impact exercise that stimulates relaxation. This exercise is especially well suited for older people or those who have injuries or other special issues that preclude more vigorous forms of exercise.

➤ **Yoga.** *Yoga,* the oldest known exercise system, was developed thousands of years ago in India. Yoga is often identified with the Hindu religion, but it actually predates Hinduism. There are eight different kinds of yoga; the kind most commonly practiced in the West is called hatha yoga. This form consists of three elements: physical postures, controlled breathing, and meditation.

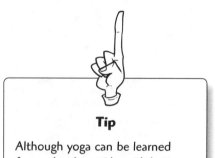

The postures range from basic to complex and from the easily accomplished to the challenging. While yoga movements tend to be slow and controlled, they still provide invigorating exercise. Yoga exercises are designed to ease tense muscles, tone up internal organs, and improve flexibility. A yoga workout can range from easy to difficult or anywhere in between.

An estimated six million Americans now practice hatha yoga. Increasingly, the medical community is embracing yoga for its positive benefits, both physically and mentally. The oldest exercise system of all is also one of the best for you.

In the Comfort of Your Own Home

Workout videos provide a great way for you to get plenty of exercise without having to join a club, buy equipment, meet people, or even leave the house. You don't even have to spend money on the video; some video stores have a free rental section of public service videos, and workout videos can often be found in this section. Some libraries have them as well.

Workout Videos

Some workout videos are notable because they were created by a skilled or famous instructor. Those by fitness guru Richard Simmons are probably the most prominent example of this kind of video. Jane Fonda's workout videos also generated a lot of attention when they were initially released back in the 1980s. Fonda then branched out into yoga videos in the 1990s.

Other videos promote a specific exercise technique or system, such as the Tae Bo videos by martial arts expert Billy Blanks. Tae Bo combines self-defense, dance, and boxing for an overall exercise program. Some videos, such as *Buns of Steel* or *Abs of Steel,* focus on a certain body part.

Home Exercise Equipment

If the idea of getting a workout without leaving the house sounds good to you, but you still want to perform the more elaborate kinds of exercise that are usually done on gym equipment, consider buying your own home exercise equipment.

You can buy equipment that provides resistance exercise to build muscular strength, or you can buy machines that enable you to do aerobic exercises. Some kinds of equipment, such as indoor rowing machines or skiing machines, don't take up much room and are easily stowed under a bed, behind a sofa, or in a closet. Others, such as stair machines or treadmills, take up more room and usually have to stay in one place all the time, like in the corner of a larger room.

Home workout machines range in cost from relatively cheap to quite expensive, but they can be a good value, depending on your exercise needs. For instance, if you want to work out with sophisticated weight-training equipment, you'll have to either join a gym or buy home equipment. You may be better off buying home equipment, if weight machines would be the primary reason you would join a gym and you wouldn't really use the gym's other services and amenities.

Carefully evaluate your fitness priorities before plunking down the money for a home workout machine. Be honest with yourself, and don't buy a machine unless you're sure that you'll use it on a regular and ongoing basis. That machine won't do you a bit of good if you don't use it.

Caution

Most weight-training machines are the biggest home exercise machines you can buy and often require most or all of a room in your house.

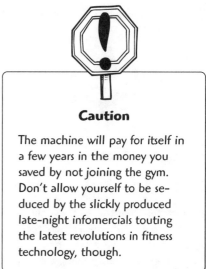

Caution

The machine will pay for itself in a few years in the money you saved by not joining the gym. Don't allow yourself to be seduced by the slickly produced late-night infomercials touting the latest revolutions in fitness technology, though.

Health Clubs: To Join or Not To Join?

Health clubs can provide a universe of wonderful ways to get in shape. They offer classes in aerobics, dancing, self-defense, and yoga. They provide stationary bicycles, treadmills, stair machines, running tracks, swimming pools, and other means of aerobic conditioning. They have dozens of weight machines for exercising virtually every muscle in the body. They've got enough free weights to sink a small yacht.

Investigating Before You Invest

Health clubs are often expensive to join, but for the people who use them frequently and regularly, they're well worth the money. Unfortunately, most of us have also known people who bought a membership to a health club and never used it. Just like that stair machine gathering dust in the garage, a health club membership won't do a thing for you if you don't use it. Many people find it difficult to make time to go to the club on a regular basis.

Some people have found that health clubs are snobby or intimidating, with members competing to see who looks best in the mirror while working out. In short, health clubs aren't for everybody.

As with the decision to purchase home workout equipment, you should carefully evaluate your own fitness needs and priorities before you spend the money on a club membership. Don't buy an expensive membership to a ritzy new health club if all you really need is a stair machine and a workout partner!

Conversely, don't buy that home weight machine if you'll be seeking aerobics classes, too. Consider your decision well before you sign the check (or the credit card slip). Your health depends on it.

Changing Your Lifestyle

Remember, a sedentary lifestyle is the chief culprit behind the lack of physical activity in our culture. You can get more activity in your life on an ongoing basis, completely separate from your exercise program, by changing your overall lifestyle so that you become less sedentary.

Your exercise is boosting your health, but your lifestyle may be dragging you down. Imagine how much better the results of your exercise would be if you had an overall lifestyle that supported your health instead of hampering it.

The TV and PC Are the Culprits

What do I mean by a sedentary lifestyle? TV watching is a good example. Your body doesn't care what you're watching. It could be a documentary about the Crusades or WWF Smackdown. Either way, it's just as sedentary. If you want to get in shape, chances are, you'll have to cut down on the amount of TV you watch.

Tip

Most clubs have fitness advisors and certified personal trainers who can guide you through your fitness journey. The larger health clubs also usually have healthy restaurants or cafes where you can relax and hang out with other fitness-minded people.

Caution

Most clubs, especially those in large cities, also experience a busy period in the early evening, after most of their members get off work. If you've ever tried to work out in a club during this after-work rush hour, you know how difficult it can be to find a parking space or to get the machine you want.

The same holds true for computer use. Web surfing has become the hobby—and sometimes the obsession—of millions of people, with new converts added every day. Both TV and the Internet have brought and will continue to bring benefits to society. But for many of us who can't seem to find time to exercise, computer use is one area where we could easily cut out a chunk.

Taking the Stairs

To offset the effect of sitting in front of a TV or PC, look around the rest of your life. How often do you take the elevator when you could be taking the stairs instead? Yes, it's true that climbing stairs can feel like drudgery, especially compared to the ease and convenience of elevators.

When increased amounts of stair climbing are combined with other means of increasing the amount of physical activity in your normal daily routines, such as walking more, driving less, and parking farther away from the stores you're going to shop in, you can achieve health benefits comparable to those enjoyed by people who have regular workout regimens! This fact was proven in a study that was recently published in *Journal of the American Medical Association* (1999; 281:327–334).

Leaving the Keys

Americans have more cars per capita than anybody in the world. While it's not likely that you'll ditch your car entirely, it may be possible to reduce your dependence on it. How often have you hopped into the car to drive around the corner or a block or two away?

Too many people drive at times when they could be walking, and every time they do this, they're missing out on potential health benefits. Plain and simple walking is an excellent form of exercise.

The lifestyle is the key. Adopt a healthy lifestyle, and you'll witness a cascading series of benefits that build upon one another to create an overall

Caution

If you add an exercise program to a sedentary lifestyle, that's better than not adding the exercise, but your lifestyle is still sedentary. In effect, your lifestyle and your exercise are pulling in opposite directions.

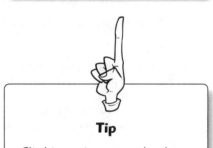

Tip

Climbing stairs may not be the most fun activity known to humankind, but it's better than letting your body deteriorate through inactivity.

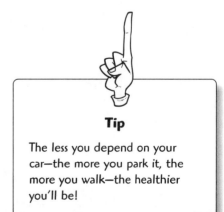

Tip

The less you depend on your car—the more you park it, the more you walk—the healthier you'll be!

healthy body and healthy life. Here are some Web sites that can keep you tuned in to a life of exercise:

➤ www.fitnesslink.com

➤ www.dietsmart.com

➤ www.gymamerica.com

➤ www.asimba.com

The Least You Need to Know

➤ Playing sports, whether with teams, opponents, or on your own, is a great way to get moving.

➤ Alternatives to sports, including dancing and martial arts, are equally effective ways to get you moving.

➤ Workout videos and home exercise equipment can be wonderful tools—if you use them.

➤ Health clubs are usually expensive to join, but for the people who use them frequently and regularly, they're well worth the money.

➤ To offset the effect of sitting in front of a TV or PC, look around the rest of your life for light exercise opportunities.

Chapter 14

Redesigning Your Outer Shell

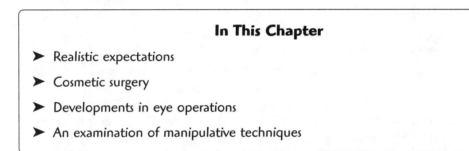

In This Chapter

➤ Realistic expectations

➤ Cosmetic surgery

➤ Developments in eye operations

➤ An examination of manipulative techniques

The techniques for bodily reinvention that we've presented so far, such as exercise, healthy food choices, and vitamin therapy, represent what you can do for your inner self. In this chapter, we'll examine ways to redesign your outer shell with the help of professionals in the art of bodily reinvention.

Getting It Fixed

As cosmetic surgery procedures continue to improve and proliferate, more and more people are availing themselves of this method of changing the body. The field is continually improving due to ongoing research and development of ever more sophisticated techniques.

Sometimes it seems there is little a skilled plastic surgeon cannot accomplish. Yet, any plastic surgeon worth his or her salt will be the first to tell you there is much that cosmetic surgery cannot do. For example ...

➤ Cosmetic surgery can't make you happy. Too many people opt for cosmetic surgery with the expectation that it will somehow fix everything that is wrong with their lives. This is too much to ask of any surgical procedure.

Caution

Cosmetic surgery is a surgical procedure—nothing more, nothing less. The way cosmetic surgery makes you look is the surgeon's responsibility; the way it makes you feel is your responsibility.

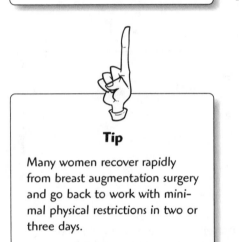

Tip

Many women recover rapidly from breast augmentation surgery and go back to work with minimal physical restrictions in two or three days.

➤ Cosmetic surgery can't make you younger. Many people seek cosmetic surgery to counteract the effects of aging, and a facelift may make you look younger. But your joints are going to feel exactly the same when you get out of bed every morning.

What Do You Want to Have Fixed?

You have an ever-widening array of elective cosmetic surgery procedures to choose from. Here is a partial list:

➤ Abdominoplasty repairs muscles of the abdominal wall that may be weakened from childbirth or previous surgery. Skin, subcutaneous tissue, and fat are removed. Recovery takes up to eight weeks.

➤ Breast augmentation is intended to enhance women's appearance by increasing their breast size through the use of soft implants. Gel implants, the source of much controversy, are not currently available except through physicians who are participating in Food and Drug Administration clinical trials to test the implants' safety. Saline implants are now the most commonly used.

➤ Botox injection is a procedure for removing wrinkles. Botox is the name of a solution that is injected underneath the skin to paralyze the facial muscles, giving a smoother appearance to the overlying skin. Its active ingredient is a bacterial toxin derived from the bacterium that causes botulism (botulinum + toxin = Botox).

➤ Collagen injection is another procedure for reducing wrinkles. Collegen is the protein element of connective tissue and serves as the foundation of skin. Plastic surgeons inject collagen into the skin as a filler to smooth wrinkles. It is not administered to pregnant women, patients who are allergic to lidocaine or bovine products, or patients with autoimmune deficiencies.

➤ Eyelid lifts are designed to remove excess skin and fat pads from the upper and lower eyelids. Recovery time for this outpatient procedure is rapid. Makeup can be worn in public 5 to 10 days after the procedure.

➤ Facelifts are intended to improve facial appearance by giving the recipient a more rested and youthful appearance. A facelift is often performed in conjunction with an eyelid lift, a forehead lift, or work on the neck to give a younger overall appearance.

➤ Liposuction removes excess fat from the body by using suction to pull the fat out. This popular procedure has some risks, such as bleeding, infection, and incomplete removal of fat. Bruising and swelling are common and may take several weeks to clear up.

➤ Rhinoplasty is designed to change the nose's appearance.

➤ Reduction mammoplasty is more commonly known as breast reduction. Many patients express great satisfaction with this procedure.

➤ Skin resurfacing minimizes sun damage, superficial wrinkles, and other irregularities of facial skin. This very new laser procedure uses a carbon dioxide laser to remove the outer layers of the skin. New, softer skin is created during the healing process, which takes 7 to 14 days. Redness of the skin may linger for as long as 12 weeks.

Great Expectations

If you're considering cosmetic surgery, do some soul-searching to determine whether the procedure you want is really right for you. Ask yourself these questions:

➤ Why do I want this procedure at this time?

➤ What results do I expect the procedure to have?

➤ Am I willing to take the risks inherent in cosmetic surgery?

You must be brutally honest with yourself. Above all, ask yourself if your expectations of the surgery are realistic. Unrealistic expectations are a recipe for grave disappointment, regardless of the clinical results of your surgery.

Reinvento Observes

A study published in the *Annals of Plastic Surgery* (09/93 31(3): 193–208) found that patient satisfaction with plastic surgery had more to do with the patient's personality type than with objective assessments of surgical outcomes.

As Always, Get a Recommendation

Cosmetic surgery, if undertaken prudently, generally can give you greater satisfaction with your physical appearance. If you choose to have cosmetic surgery, find a friend or acquaintance to recommend a plastic surgeon. You can also ask your family doctor for a recommendation. Make sure your plastic surgeon is board-certified, which means the surgeon has met the requirements of a certifying board to prove that he or she is a capable and safe, expert, plastic surgeon.

Now I See

If you have nearsightedness (myopia) or farsightedness (hyperopia), you may be a candidate for surgery to correct your vision. PRK (photorefractive keratectomy) and LASIK (laser-assisted intrastromal in-situ keratomileusis) procedures are the most common kinds of corrective eye surgery.

PRK

With PRK the surgeon uses an excimer laser to shave off a very small amount of the exterior of the cornea. This way, the cornea retains most of its strength, which makes it less vulnerable to trauma or progressive flattening.

Variations of PRK can be used to treat myopia, hyperopia, and astigmatism (an irregularity in lens curvature that prevents light from focusing sharply and precisely).

Risks of PRK include visual haze, corneal scarring, over-correction or under-correction, and development of astigmatism. Long-term side effects are not yet known. Many medical professionals still consider PRK to be experimental.

LASIK

LASIK was developed in 1996. A surgeon performing LASIK uses a device called a microkeratome to slice into the cornea from the side, producing a flap. The microkeratome flattens the cornea during the incision, which ensures that the flap created is of uniform thickness. This results in a uniformly thick flap with a "hinge" on one side.

The surgeon uses the hinge to roll the flap back and expose the cornea's inner structures. Then the surgeon uses a laser to make the necessary refractive correction on the inner layer of the cornea. When this portion of the procedure is finished, the flap is returned to its original position and the LASIK procedure is complete.

Patients report less postoperative pain with LASIK than with other procedures, as well as a lower incidence of complications. LASIK's healing time is faster as well.

Keep in mind that *presbyopia* is not currently treatable by surgery, so don't throw away those reading glasses just yet.

The biggest risk of LASIK procedures is induced astigmatism. Patients with severe myopia or thinner corneas will not be candidates for LASIK, but may be candidates for PRK.

If you're a good candidate for one of these surgeries, you could soon be seeing your world better than ever.

Word Power

Presbyopia is farsightedness caused by the advance of middle age, in which the lens becomes less elastic.

Manipulation Could Be the Cure

How about some gentler, less invasive techniques of readjusting the body? Bodywork systems (or modalities, as they are often called), when administered by trained professionals, can address chronic bodily problems and bring about genuine long-term healing that you can feel every day.

Rolfing

Rolfing is a bodywork system that uses deep muscular manipulation to correct the structural effects of aging and injury on the body. It was created by Ida P. Rolf, who earned a doctorate in biophysics in the 1920s and started to develop Rolfing in the 1930s.

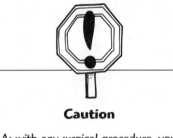

Caution

As with any surgical procedure, you should undergo surgery to correct your vision only after careful thought about the chances of success and the consequences of any risks. Your vision is too important for you to make this decision lightly! Consult a reputable physician well in advance.

How does Rolfing work? Suppose you injure your right knee while skiing and you have to walk with a limp for a month. Your limp affects the way you walk, obviously, but this also means your weight is distributed differently. That means your hips now have a different alignment when you walk.

Your hips transmit this different alignment to your spine, which tweaks the alignment of your shoulders and your neck. Your whole body is affected by an injury to one knee! (The head bone really is connected to the neck bone—and everything else!) The body, as a whole, is no longer in good structural alignment.

This misalignment (which can also occur as a result of aging) often does not resolve when the injury heals, because the body can get stuck in its unhealthy structural

pattern. This happens due to the effect of gravity on a deep tissue in the body called *fascia*. If the body is misaligned overall, the fascia is misaligned, too.

Gravity acts as a constant reinforcement of this incorrect alignment. If the misalignment is severe enough or lasts long enough, the fascia will eventually adjust to the new, incorrect alignment and can permanently exert an unhealthy structural pattern throughout the body. This can cause all sorts of physical problems, chief among them chronic pain. Rolfers use deep tissue massage to manipulate the fascia in order to bring the whole body back into patterns of harmonious alignment.

The Trager Approach

The Trager Approach is a dual-method modality that relies on both gentle manipulations and movement education to induce deep relaxation throughout the body as well as the mind. Milton Trager, M.D., gradually developed his modality over many years.

When Trager was a young man, he accidentally discovered that he had the capacity to induce significant healing responses in other people by manipulating their bodies. He worked as a physical therapist, and then as a medical doctor, and continued to refine his home-grown bodywork techniques. He didn't begin teaching his approach to others until the 1970s and later founded the Trager Institute.

The Trager Approach is intended to help you relinquish the rigidity of your muscles, freeing your body from tightness, tension, and pain. The Trager practitioner uses light strokes on the skin and gentle rocking of the body to tell the mind it can let go of all the tension it's holding in the body. When the mind lets go, a fundamental blockage in the mind-body connection is removed. The body is more relaxed, the mind is more at peace, and the body and mind are better integrated.

The Feldenkrais Method

The Feldenkrais Method is a system of body education that teaches clients how to move through the world in a more harmonious and efficient manner. Moshe Feldenkrais developed this method in response to a crippling knee injury he suffered.

He used his prodigious education to discern the role that the nervous system plays in musculoskeletal functioning. After much study and experimentation, his newly developed methods enabled him to regain full function in his knee.

The Feldenkrais Method can be taught either in private one-on-one sessions or in groups. The Feldenkrais teacher observes the student's movements and analyzes them to find problematic movement patterns. Then the teacher recommends correct, efficient ways for the student to move.

The student can practice these new movements on an ongoing basis to help him or her form new, healthier movement habits. As the student begins to move more efficiently, energy is freed up because the body requires less energy to perform its tasks. The student also has a reduction in tension and pain. Greater fluidity and grace of movement is yet another benefit of the Feldenkrais Method.

Chiropractics

Chiropractics, a popular form of manual joint manipulation, was developed by Daniel Palmer in 1895. Joint manipulations have been performed throughout the history of medicine, going all the way back to Hippocrates, but Palmer performed the first known chiropractic adjustment when he restored a deaf man's hearing by means of a careful adjustment to the neck. Palmer went on to found the first chiropractic college later that year.

Chiropractic's basic philosophy is that when vertebrae in the spine become misaligned, these misalignments (called subluxations) irritate the nerves. This nerve irritation leads, in turn, to exaggerated nerve activity, which causes poor posture, chronic pain, and limited range of motion, among other symptoms.

Reinvento Observes

The Feldenkrais Method holds that bad movement habits, such as poor posture, originate in childhood, as we unconsciously imitate parents and other adults who have bad movement habits. These bad habits continue into adulthood, causing chronic pain and functional restriction. The Feldenkrais Method teaches the client where his or her inefficient habits of movement are and how to remedy them.

Word Power

Chiropractics is a method of treating disease through the manipulation of body joints, especially of the spine.

Chiropractors aim to alleviate these symptoms by manual manipulation of the spine. When the spine is properly manipulated, the subluxation is relieved. Nerve irritation then subsides and normal functioning is restored.

A chiropractic session usually begins with a diagnosis of the patient's spinal alignment in order to determine whether the patient has any subluxations, and if so, where they are located on the spine. The chiropractor then uses manual manipulation to relieve each subluxation. At the end of the treatment session, the patient's spinal alignment is checked once again to verify that the subluxations were indeed relieved.

Chiropractors do not routinely prescribe medicine or perform surgery; manual manipulation is the primary technique used. When patients begin a course of chiropractic treatment, most chiropractors prescribe frequent treatments at first, perhaps three to five per week. Treatments then taper off until patients come in once a week or once every other week. Common benefits of chiropractic are reduced pain in specific areas and increased range of motion and functionality.

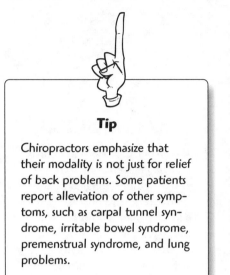

Tip

Chiropractors emphasize that their modality is not just for relief of back problems. Some patients report alleviation of other symptoms, such as carpal tunnel syndrome, irritable bowel syndrome, premenstrual syndrome, and lung problems.

The Alexander Technique

The Alexander Technique is a body education method that focuses on helping clients use their bodies effectively. Frederick Alexander, an Australian actor whose career was endangered when he developed serious voice problems, designed this technique to treat himself. He decided to attack the problem on his own after doctors proved no help.

Reinvento Observes

The technique is based on the assumption that we habitually misuse our bodies, which results in a fundamental misalignment of our entire body. This perpetual misalignment causes such problems as chronic neck, back, and shoulder pain; vocal problems; and low energy.

Alexander devoted years to a detailed examination of his bodily posture and movement patterns. The remedies he invented and implemented on himself resulted in a resolution of his vocal problems. He soon formalized his technique and began teaching it to others. His system was particularly popular among performing artists, and remains so today.

The technique consists of an Alexander teacher giving a series of Alexander Lessons. At the beginning of the series, the teacher analyzes the student's movement habits in order to pinpoint areas that need attention. Then the teacher works with the student to devise better ways for the student to move. Once the student has been taught healthier movement patterns, it's up to the student to integrate those patterns into his or her life.

The body education process focuses particular attention on the normal activities the student performs in daily life. If the student is a farmer, for instance, the teacher will help the student learn better ways to perform daily chores.

Benefits of the Alexander Technique include …

➤ More grace in movement.

➤ Better vocal projection.

➤ A reduction of body tension.

➤ Decreased pain (particularly chronic back pain).

➤ Increased self-awareness and self-confidence.

➤ Relief from symptoms like headaches, TMJ syndrome, and sciatica.

Shiatsu

Shiatsu is a form of Oriental bodywork that promotes health by inducing *homeostasis*. This balance is achieved by manipulating the body's vital energy through specific applications of finger pressure at certain points on the body.

Shiatsu originated in the nineteenth century in Japan, but its roots reach back five millennia to the basic principles of Chinese medicine, which focuses on chi, the body's vital energy.

The Shiatsu practitioner first performs an assessment of the client's health needs and problems. Once the practitioner decides on a course of treatment, he or she applies finger pressure at specific points along bodily energy pathways called meridians. These meridians, which were mapped out on the human body long ago by the earliest shiatsu masters, are paths along which vital energy flows.

The practitioner uses finger pressure on the body to manipulate the energy within the meridians. This manipulation can remove blockages in the energy, harmonize energy flow, and correct energetic imbalances. When the body's energy is once again flowing freely and harmoniously, the overall function of the body is enhanced.

Word Power

Homeostasis is the state of balance and harmonious function characterizing all healthy living organisms.

Reinvento Observes

Shiatsu practitioners believe that the harmonious flow of your vital energy is necessary for good bodily health. If your energy is drained, blocked, or imbalanced, you will be susceptible to ill health. Shiatsu works with the body's energy to promote energetic harmony and to restore homeostasis.

Many people who receive shiatsu experience improved function of the immune system, which results in greater resistance to contagious illnesses. People also report cessation of headaches, sinus conditions, and even arthritic pain. Shiatsu also commonly induces greater relaxation and an increased feeling of personal vitality. Shiatsu has helped many people to enlist their own vital energy in the cause of health promotion, and chances are it can help you, too.

Your Responsibility

This chapter has described commonly sought methods to help you redesign your outer shell. Whether you choose surgery or bodywork modalities, your body is no one's responsibility but your own. You can get just as much satisfaction out of your body as you're willing to receive. The rewards awaiting you are within your reach.

The Least You Need to Know

➤ Cosmetic surgery is becoming a more popular solution to correcting outer flaws.

➤ New eye surgeries can change the way you look at things—literally.

➤ Many body manipulations, including Rolfing, the Trager Approach, the Feldenkrais Method, Chiropractics, the Alexander Technique, and Shiatsu, are nonsurgical approaches to changing the way you look and feel.

➤ Whether you choose surgery or bodywork modalities, your body is no one's responsibility but your own.

Part 4

Reinventing Your Career

Reinventing yourself professionally doesn't necessarily mean changing jobs or changing industries. You can make strategic moves from right where you are. In Part 4, we'll look at the important concepts of managing your career, learning to live with and even thrive in the digital world, enhancing your verbal (which also includes written) communication skills, aspiring to leadership, and communicating effectively with others.

We'll also look at more progressive strategies for reinventing your career, including several ways you can take action that is incongruent with your past, and even taking weeks and months off in the form of sabbatical. I bet you hadn't considered that one before.

Let's begin with the eye-opening look at how to make all the right moves, right where you are, right in your own cubical.

Chapter 15

All the Right Moves

> **In This Chapter**
>
> ➤ Success is subjective and personal
>
> ➤ Exhibiting self-sufficiency in the workplace
>
> ➤ Your career is entirely up to you
>
> ➤ Networking provides vital connections

Improving the way you manage your career can change the way you feel about yourself and your life. In this chapter, we'll look at how you can reinvent your life through your career.

This Job, This Company, at This Time?

Do you feel stuck? Are you headed down the wrong path? Are you climbing the career ladder, but somehow still feel left behind? All of these are common problems in today's changing work environment. The real question here is this: What do you want to do in your career and where do you want to be?

Ask 10 people to define success, and you'll get 10 different answers. One of my favorite responses comes from South Carolina's Al Walker, a humorist and speaker, who says that success is "making the most of the best that is within you every day by having a goal, being committed to it, and underscoring it with enthusiasm."

Reinvento Observes

As you proceed in your career, measure yourself by your own definition of success, not by someone else's.

Some other definitions of success that I have heard include these:

➤ Enjoying what you do, being good at what you do, and getting to do it often.

➤ Being content in love and life.

➤ Being able to make a difference in this world and getting satisfaction from it.

➤ Achieving a state of prosperity or fame.

➤ Health and happiness, prosperity and charity.

➤ Consistently doing that which makes you and others happy.

➤ Accomplishing your intended purpose.

➤ Getting what you want most of the time.

You don't have to be the CEO of your organization, or even an executive, to feel successful. You only have to be happy with where you are, the work that you do, what you're learning, and what you're accomplishing. Perhaps you're an up-and-coming rookie who's doing a great job, an effective team leader, or simply someone others can consistently count on.

More Is Always Required

Whatever your field of endeavor, each step up the ladder predictably means more responsibility, longer hours, and often, more stress. It also means more visibility for what you're able to achieve and for any mistakes you make. Build on what you know and your career will keep growing and developing through your knowledge.

Word Power

An **entrepreneur** is a person who works for him- or herself, taking risks in pursuit of a profit.

Thinking Like an Entrepreneur

Whether you're in your first position or are a veteran in the workplace, it's time to start thinking like an *entrepreneur*. For most of the second part of the twentieth century, the paternalistic organization predominated. Employees could count on a paycheck, benefits, and some semblance of a career path. Today, not even employers expect employees to feel that way.

Thinking like an entrepreneur means studying trends to identify opportunities for your organization. It means doing a good job for your organization, but maintaining the highest degree of loyalty to yourself and your own career development. As any person working for him or herself, you consider every job as if it were, in a way, temporary.

Reinvento Observes

Successful entrepreneurs are self-starters, customer oriented, highly motivated, committed, and well organized. They're conscious of dollars and time spent. They're willing to move away from what's familiar and comfortable because they understand the inherent trap in sticking with the familiar and the comfortable. Every day, they're constantly on the lookout for ways to do their job better.

Continually Seek Feedback

If you question where you are in your career, turn to those closest to you in the workplace. A boss who has observed you at close range and has taken some personal interest in you and your career development can tell you more about yourself than even your own mother—at least in terms of your professional life!

If you work for a large organization, your boss can offer ideas about how to go after the next job within your organization. After all, you'll need to ask him or her for permission to interview for it anyway. Your boss can also tell you about unproductive work habits or personal blind spots that may be inhibiting your success.

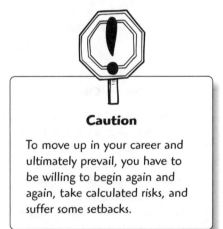

Caution

To move up in your career and ultimately prevail, you have to be willing to begin again and again, take calculated risks, and suffer some setbacks.

Don't be afraid to receive candid feedback. It can only help you in the long run. There's no use burying your head in the sand and pretending you don't have any shortcomings (see Chapter 18, "The Makings of a Leader").

Moving Up in a New Job

If you've recently gotten out of college or graduate school and are working in your first full-time career position, you may need to change your mindset. Stop thinking of yourself as a student if you haven't already, and assume the mantle of a young career professional who is widely regarded as a self-starter—someone who is self-motivated and maintains a "can-do," take-charge attitude. Remember, it's never too early to start seriously building your career.

There's something invigorating about working with someone who has confidence, whose hand doesn't need to be held, and who has the knowledge, or is willing to acquire it, to tackle project after project.

Tip

You don't have to wait for a monthly, quarterly, or annual performance review to discuss your progress and your career goals.

Reinvento Observes

The best way to prove yourself in the workplace is to be self-sufficient. Get started on assignments at once, without waiting for others, particularly your boss, to push you along. Both bosses and co-workers appreciate working with self-starters.

Faster and Smarter

In a new position or an old one, no matter how you presently do a task, or how it has traditionally been done in your organization or industry, with the rapid advances in communication and technology today, new ways of doing things will undoubtedly emerge. Continually assess how you're accomplishing a particular task, while considering alternative and superior ways to complete it. Talk to others who do what you do to gain insights as to how they proceed.

Professor Albert Bandura, who teaches psychology at Stanford University, conducted research on self-esteem and concluded that self-esteem "affects neither personal goals nor performance." Tests of academic skills of elementary students in the United States, China, Japan, and Taiwan revealed that while Asian students outperformed American students, American students felt better about themselves and their work. Whoopie!

It's wonderful if you feel good about yourself, both in your career and outside of work. It's even better for your career if you feel good about yourself and are constantly working to do your job more productively.

Making the Most of Wherever You Are

You are the only person who will ever accompany yourself along every step on your career path. Therefore, you're the only person responsible for ensuring your success or failure.

Asking Questions

It if helps, ask to observe or work with others in positions comparable to yours. Get as much accelerated experience as you can after you land that new position, so that you're "up to speed" in short order and ready, once again, to demonstrate your value to all concerned.

Some people, in the quest not to appear foolish or uninformed, don't ask critical questions that would solidify their understanding of how to approach a task. If you "sit on" questions for fear of asking them, you could end up being inefficient, or doing something entirely wrong. That means you'll have to do it over again, and potentially incur the displeasure of others, namely your boss.

It only takes a couple of times of getting projects wrong, and boom—all of a sudden, you're being micromanaged, forced to report on every little aspect of what you're doing. This is no way to proceed! Ask questions early, and earn the confidence of your boss and co-workers.

Most important, when adjusting to a new job, don't let the fear of failure keep you from taking risks. Who says that this new position is your last? Keep pushing ahead and learning and building. Some people are so risk-averse that they settle for mundane positions in mundane careers, and 10 or 15 years later find that they've hardly moved at all.

Moving On

Sometimes, for whatever reason, your current situation simply won't suffice. You're not gaining the skills or experience that you need, or you've repeatedly been denied the raise that you know you deserve. Perhaps you've hit a plateau. The job openings above you are limited, and you feel restless and bored. Unfortunately, plateaus are becoming more common as companies eliminate middle-management jobs.

Caution

Too many employees today have a skewed view of their own value to their organization. Some are stopped in their tracks when they discover that their boss or co-workers don't necessarily hold them in the same light that they hold themselves. Others are caught up in the feel-good notion that "if I feel good about myself, then I must be doing a good job."

Reinvento Observes

Along the way, you're going to make mistakes. Most of the mistakes you make will not be fatal to your career; indeed, most of them will pass, leaving no scars. Own up to your mistakes, and do your best to correct them. Assure your boss that you've learned from whatever *faux pas* you've made and move on.

The following situations necessitate making a move:

➤ There are no opportunities for advancement.

➤ Opportunities for learning are limited.

➤ No positions appeal to you.

➤ You feel stagnant in your job.

➤ You've asked for and been denied a raise, promotion, or lateral move.

➤ You're at the top of your salary range and no other position appeals to you.

➤ Your career has been blocked because someone wants to retain you where you are.

➤ Your organization is about to downsize and your department or position might be on the cutting block.

Looking Before You Switch

Before actually switching jobs, consider the long-term horizon. Undoubtedly, you'll peruse the classified ads and the top career sites on the Web. The latest development in Web sites can make your career development a whole lot easier. Web sites like www.Monster.com, www.careerbuilder.com, www.jobobtions.com, www.jobtrak.com, www.careershop.com, and www.hotjobs.com let you go online and create a resumé in an online database. You can look at offerings in your career field and post your resumé for other companies or employers to check out.

Even if you're feeling satisfied in your current job, go ahead and explore. Don't worry, many of these sites allow you to put a block on your resumé so that your current employer can't access it and won't get suspicious of your innocent online browsing.

Moving On Carries No Stigma

If you do decide to move, rest assured that there's little or no stigma associated with moving from job to job. Denise Rousseau, Ph.D., a professor of organizational behavior at Carnegie Mellon University, contends that disloyalty probably is rewarded more often now than loyalty is. Dr. Rousseau says, "People will say, getting a better job offer is the only way I can get my pay raise and my work noticed." This is unfortunate, but sometimes all too true.

Staying Aware of Your Current Position

At all times, keep current on your marketability. You can read about what your position entails in general throughout your industry, through such publications as *The Occupational Outlook Handbook,* published by the U.S. Department of Labor and generally available in the reference section of any city or college library. Whenever you attend a specialized training session, complete a course, or what have you, continually update your resumé.

Use industry terminology on your resumé (and know what it means) so that you reflect the best of your knowledge. If it helps, list at least five things about yourself that make you stand out in the career marketplace, and work these into your resumé as well. Also list any computer skills and Internet skills that you have. Increasingly, these will become mandatory for moving up within any organization.

Here's a quick checklist of key skills to develop. After developing them, ensure that they appear someplace within your resumé:

❏ Planning, organizing, scheduling

❏ Oral and written communication

❏ Decision making, leadership

❏ Critical thinking, problem solving, conflict resolution

❏ Teamwork, team building, working with others

❏ Ethics, tolerance, diversity awareness

❏ Management skills, delegation, giving feedback

Whenever you receive a letter of praise from someone within your company, or someone outside the company, file it carefully, along with these:

➤ Letters of recommendation

➤ Samples of work from successful projects

➤ Company awards

➤ Performance reviews

➤ Published articles

➤ Certificates of completion from training courses and seminars

➤ Transcripts of courses taken

➤ Materials from past jobs

➤ Anything that represents evidence of your accomplishments

➤ Anything that represents the esteem with which others regard you

163

All of these are fodder for your campaign to move up either within your present organization, or with another. Don't be afraid to ask for letters of recommendation from customers or business associates for whom you have done good work.

Co-Workers Plus

Develop a reputation as a helpful, resourceful co-worker. Banish "That's not my job" from your vocabulary, and pitch in whenever it will help the group.

Caution

Even though these are fodder in your campaign to move up, you aren't necessarily free to share all of them with interviewers or people in your network. Be careful not to use anything that is confidential or that belongs not to you but to the organization.

Do good deeds and practice random acts of kindness throughout the organization. Continually accept in-house volunteer assignments. If you have to, straighten the office library; plan the office party; make some extra phone calls; pitch in when some project team is otherwise going to miss its deadline; pass on information to others that might be helpful.

Some rare individuals understand that working longer and harder in and of itself doesn't guarantee that they'll move up. In and around the office, they get to know staff on a personal basis, including individuals' concerns, goals, ideas, strengths, and weaknesses. They know the importance of communicating regularly with their staff. As a manager, they keep a file on each staff member, including what they've accomplished, what training and seminars they've taken, and what their individual goals and aspirations are.

Strategic Networking

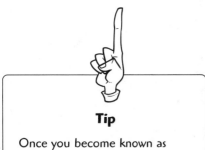

Tip

Once you become known as someone who goes the extra mile, you've set your career advancement in motion.

The adage "It's all about who you know" holds true in the professional career market. If you want to move up in your field or make a transition into another type of job, *networking* can provide you with the connections that will open up the opportunities for you to achieve your goals. Networking often appears daunting to some individuals, but with good communication skills and a clear understanding of your accomplishments and goals, this tool can lead you to further success.

Mastering the Art

Entrepreneurs, and career achievers in general, understand the value of a well-developed, current network of people. They know that networking accelerates one's career or business horizons, reveals new opportunities, and exposes one to a variety of new ideas.

Rather than networking with anyone and everyone, focused networkers meet people in key professional and alumni associations, via Internet newsgroups and list serves, within the organization, and elsewhere.

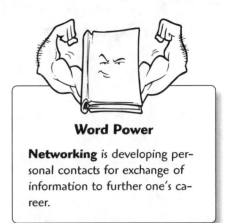

Word Power

Networking is developing personal contacts for exchange of information to further one's career.

➤ They're willing to get in touch with people they admire, whom they see in the magazines or newspapers.

➤ They naturally connect with the movers and shakers in their industry.

➤ They're ready on a moment's notice to network when it appears they're in the vicinity of someone who has valuable information and insights to impart. Hence, they are often taking people to lunch, even offering to pick up the tab, while not being afraid to state what they're seeking.

Becoming a Champion

If you've already decided that you're going to become a champion networker, here are some tips to see you through:

➤ Always carry your business cards, and even notes and information on some of your current achievements.

➤ Set up a system either on your computer, in a three-ring notebook, or on a Rolodex or some other manual system that enables you to easily organize the contacts you've made, update your records when you have additional contacts, and get in touch with them at a moment's notice.

➤ Recognize that you can only take as much as you give, and, therefore, give as much as you take.

➤ Don't expect favors out of people that you just met or from people with whom you've lost touch. Relationships build up over time, and while there are shortcuts on occasion, don't count on them.

➤ Use a personal touch to stay connected to your network. Make a phone call, or send a chatty e-mail, a fax, or a nice note at least quarterly.

165

Think Expansion

Proactively seek to expand your career opportunities. As often as is practical, ask to be included in important meetings and projects related to your work. You don't need to wait for others to invite you. Continually look to expand your position by assuming new responsibilities. If your organization has a suggestion box, feed it regularly. Don't wait until you're asked; constantly be on the lookout for ways to improve the organization and other peoples' lives.

Here's a quick list of other ways to proactively keep your career on an upward trajectory:

➤ Join professional organizations in your industry. Most of them are listed in *The Encyclopedia of Associations* or *National Trade and Professional Associations*.

➤ Enlist a career coach or counselor to help you with your career plans.

➤ Join your college alumni association, particularly if it's strong in your area.

➤ Volunteer to serve on outside organizations, particularly when it improves skills that will be noticeable back on the job.

➤ Continually seek feedback on your performance, not just from your current supervisor, but also from peers, new employees, former supervisors, and so on.

➤ Visit Internet sites that are chock full of information useful to your career and your organization. Bookmark them and visit often.

The Least You Need to Know

➤ Continually ask yourself: What do you want to do in your career and where do you want to be?

➤ Continually seek feedback. Don't be afraid to receive candid feedback about your job performance, because it can only help you in the long run.

➤ Even if you're feeling satisfied in your current job, go ahead and explore. Before actually switching jobs, consider the long-term horizon.

➤ Networking is about proactively seeking and creating new opportunities for yourself and others.

➤ Networking accelerates one's career or business horizons, reveals new opportunities, and exposes one to a variety of new ideas.

Chapter 16

Advancing Your Career in the Electronic Age

In This Chapter

➤ Learning for a lifetime

➤ Informal versus formal learning

➤ Long-distance learning

➤ A continuing opportunity, not a burden

It once was possible for one skill to carry you through your income-producing years. Today, such good fortune is not possible for anyone in any profession. Wherever you are in your career, in whatever industry, you must continually learn new skills, many of them related to the computer and the Internet, to help you move from where you are to where you want to be, or to simply maintain your present position.

As each technological advance comes down the pike (see the accompanying figure), as worldwide competition in every industry increases, as consumer demand shifts, and as your own company or organization looks for innovative ways to reduce costs yet re- main competitive, such developments all but ensure that there's no "coasting" for anyone, anywhere, anymore.

Technology Rules

1453: Movable type—Johannes Gutenberg

1470: First printing press—William Claxton

1502: Wrist watch—Peter Henlein of Nuremburg

1642: Mechanical adding machine—Blaise Pascal

1690: First American newspaper, *Publick Occurrences*—Benjamin Harris

1787: Weaving machine—Edmund Cartwright

1793: Cotton gin—Eli Whitney

1803: Steam engine—Robert Fulton

1834: Analytical engine (Early Computer)—Charles Babbidge

1835: Lightning presses and the Industrial Revolution

1844: First telegraph transmission (from Washington, D.C., to other newspapers)

1866: Transatlantic cable

1876: Telephone—Alexander Graham Bell

1903: Powered flight—Wilbur and Orville Wright

1911: Automobile electric ignition system—Charles Kettering

1920: First commercial radio broadcast (KDKA in Pittsburgh)

1942: Automated computer ENIAC—U.S. Army

1950: Television newscasts begin

1956: GE produces industrial diamonds

1958: Pan Am commercial jet service begins with flight from New York to Paris

1958: Integrated circuit—Jack Kilby at Texas Instruments and Robert Noyce at Fairchild

1959: Plain paper copier by Haloid Xerox

1962: Telstar, first communications satellite, AT&T

1962: *Silent Spring* sounds alarm over pesticides—Rachel Carson

1967: Counter-top microwave oven, Amana

1969: Arpanet, seed of the Internet, connects scientists at four U.S. universities

1970: Pan Am inaugurates wide-body jet service from New York to London

1971: Intel introduces microprocessor

1972: Britain's EMI introduces cat scanner

1972: Color TV sets outnumber black & white sets for the first time

1973: Sharp introduces calculators with liquid crystal displays

1974: Intel's second-generation microprocessor makes the PC possible

1975: First personal computer with workable hardware and software—Steve Wozniak

1978: Genentech clones first recombinant DNA product, human insulin

1980: Satellite and cable TV yield more than 300 stations

1981: User-friendly Apple computer—Steven Jobs and Steven Wozniak

1981: Graphical user interface (Windows), Xerox Parc

1983: Fiber-optic system from Corning and Siecor, MCI

1983: Ameritech receives FCC's first cellular phone license

1983: Compact discs become available for retail sale

1988: Fax machines sell more than one million units in U.S.

1989: Notes groupware, Lotus

1991: Compact discs outsell cassettes

1993: Mosaic, Netscape Internet browsers perfected

1995: FCC auctions broadband spectrum licenses for personal communication services

1995–2000: Critical mass for laptops, palm tops, cell phones, pagers, Intranets, Realplayer, MCP-3, Web TV, DirecTV, Tivo, and dozens of other technologies

Primary Source: Fortune Magazine, *May 15, 1995*

A Brave New Techno-World

In this brave, new, electronic world, each of us faces the need to develop new skills, which actually increases opportunities for reinvention. After all, in what previous age could an octogenarian become a Web designer?

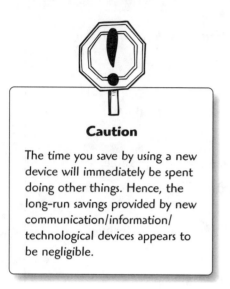

Caution

The time you save by using a new device will immediately be spent doing other things. Hence, the long-run savings provided by new communication/information/ technological devices appears to be negligible.

As time marches on, there will be a boatload of new technologies enabling you to accomplish all sorts of things. But as we've seen over and over, with the introduction of each new communication/information/ technological device comes a new set of responsibilities, instructions, time investment, and, of course, challenges. For example, once washing machines were introduced, the burden of wearing freshly cleaned clothes increased throughout society, and hence, more clothes washing ensued.

With each passing day, you'll have to make effective choices as to where to invest your time and attention, particularly on the job. Dick Tracy–like wristwatches that enable you to send and receive faxes and e-mails, check bus schedules, update your contact manager, make notes to yourself, and so on, seemingly will make you more productive. But staying competitive requires more than a wristwatch.

When you consider the growth rate in basic technology and the basic demand for online access (see the following two tables), you're likely to remain in a continual learning mode and still be striving to keep up with the latest technology.

Basic Technology Gains Have Shown Great Acceleration

Technology	Capability	Acceleration	Annual Gain
Memory chip	chip capacity	doubles in 18 months	59%
Packet switching	baud per second	doubles in 12 months	100%
Optical fiber	baud per second	doubles in 6 months	200%

Basic Demand for Online Access

	Acceleration	Annual Gain
Internet users	doubles in 12 months	100%
data bits	doubles in 7.5 months	300%
Internet core	doubles in 4 months	1,000%

Upping Your Techno-Skills

In this era, everybody must continually develop his or her skills to stay effective in the job market. The kinds of skills that you'll seek to acquire, obviously, will depend on your career situation, as well as on your immediate and long-term career goals. Fortunately, a wide variety of skill-development vehicles are available today to fit your schedule and your needs.

On-the-Job Training

On-the-job training has been around since the first time one person reported to another to get a job done. On-the-job training represents training you receive on your job day-to-day, through formal or informal processes. The training might come via your co-workers, boss, organization-sponsored training workshops and seminars, or some other form of instruction.

Job Shadowing

Job shadowing offers the opportunity to explore an occupation by observing its practitioners first-hand. In a typical situation, you would spend several hours on the job with a host who is in the position in which you're interested. By "shadowing" your host, you gain firsthand observation and understanding of what the position entails, which you would not gain by simply reading about it.

Once you get approval, you can job shadow within your own organization. This is an excellent way to gain knowledge of other positions and of the skills others bring to them.

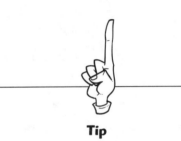

Tip

If possible, have someone show you how to use a software program. Generally speaking, it's faster and easier than grappling with an instruction manual or help files.

Tip

A technical mentor can seem like a godsend. Someone to show you how to be more effective with your PC could be your most important career ally. If you don't have a technical mentor, log on to www.barcharts.com for a list of high-powered laminated instruction sheets on everything from spreadsheets to databases to word processing to the Web.

Mentoring

A mentor, as we've discussed, is a nonpaid advisor who meets with you on a more ad-hoc basis because he or she likes you, has some type of vested interest in seeing you succeed (even if the payoff is simply emotional), and benefits from interacting with you. Mentoring usually is a one-on-one process. (See Chapter 3, "Assessing Where You Are," for more information.)

Caution

In case you think informal learn-ing has it all over formal learn-ing, think again: Formal learning offers specific outcomes, whereas informal learning may not.

Reinvento Observes

Community colleges exist in vir-tually every county in the United States and offer a variety of courses, often in the evening, to accommodate adult learning needs.

Formal vs. Informal Learning

Informal learning, such as the methods discussed above, generally is need-specific and thus tends to be more immediately relevant to you, whereas formal learning, discussed in the following sections, isn't necessarily tailored to each individual. For example, having someone show you how to cut and paste infor-mation in a document is need-specific, whereas taking a class on Microsoft Word is formal training.

Whereas formal learning is scheduled (as in classes, for example), and can sometimes delay your getting the information you need most urgently, informal learn-ing arises more spontaneously—you're more in control of the schedule. So your informal PC or Web lessons should help you significantly!

Course Offerings

You have many formal learning options to enhance and expand your technical skills. Most, such as uni-versity extension and community college courses, will be outside your organization, as are a whole network of distance learning options (see the following "Dis-tance Learning" section).

University extension courses are similar to commu-nity college courses. A major university may offer evening or weekend courses of limited duration through the auspices of its own colleges. Some univer-sity extension courses offer certificates of completion or competency, and/or what's called *continuing educa-tional units (CEUs)*.

Distance learning comes in many forms. The nature and quality of correspondence courses varies widely, and merits its own discussion.

Distance Learning

Previously, distance learning referred to correspondence schools. You paid your money and received instructional workbooks and study materials. You completed as-signments based on a predetermined schedule and submitted your work via the mail. Some distance learning programs enabled you to develop a skill that was readily mar-ketable, such as repairing radios and TVs.

In all cases, the student requires a fair amount of self-discipline. After all, with no one standing over you or insisting that you do your homework, you and you alone determine whether you complete assignments on time.

A Whole New World

Today, with the advent of the Internet and satellite transmission, distance learning has taken on a whole new dimension. Nonprofit institutions, such as some universities, and for-profit educators, such as the Arthur D. Little School, based in Boston, Massachusetts, have developed accredited programs on a wide variety of topics.

Here are two other *virtual universities:*

➤ Western Governors University offers courses by such "suppliers" as the University of Wyoming, Montana State University, Colorado Electric Community College, and for-profit Novell, Inc. In essence, Western Governors University is a degree-granting institution with an electronic course catalog, yet no campus and no onsite faculty other than course designers. WGU provides distance learning via satellite TV, video and/or audiotape, the Internet (at www.wgu.edu), and even traditional correspondence courses.

While WGU targets working adults who would have to travel great distances to attend university courses on traditional campuses, anyone who can access its Web site or participate in the other aforementioned ways can become a student.

Word Power

Continuing education units (CEUs) denotes a point system whereby professionals in an industry receive accumulating credits for courses and training they've taken, the sum of which may enable them to achieve or maintain certification or some other professional credential.

Word Power

Virtual universities are universities that offer courses online, exclusively or nearly exclusively, usually in conjunction with some real-world university.

➤ California Virtual University offers an online catalog that delineates all the online courses offered by accredited colleges and universities in the state of California. More than 700 courses at 89 campuses are referenced at www.california.edu. Once a student locates a course of interest, he or she contacts the college individually for registration, tuition, and even to design a course of study that may contribute to a university degree.

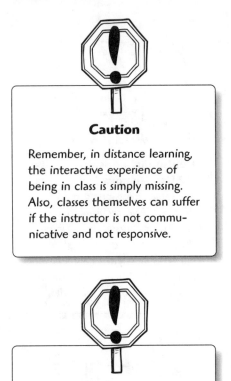

Caution

Remember, in distance learning, the interactive experience of being in class is simply missing. Also, classes themselves can suffer if the instructor is not communicative and not responsive.

Caution

The more time that passes between your skills development training and your actual application of it, the greater the risk that your skills will diminish.

Here are some other distance-learning Web-related resources:

➤ **Columbia Southern University:** www.colsouth.edu (click: Distance Education)

➤ **Distance Education Clearinghouse:** www.uwex1.edu

➤ **Southern California University:** www.scups.edu

➤ **SUNY Empire State College:** www.esc.edu

➤ **U.S. Distance Learning Association:** www.usdla.org

➤ **University of Berkley:** www.uofb.com

➤ **University of Maryland:** www.umuc.edu

Older Students Get into the Act

Distance learning is popular with older students. Mothers with children at home, for example, have the opportunity to take classes while raising their children. Career professionals with jam-packed schedules save commuting time and devote themselves to specific courses to acquire specific skills. Physically challenged students, the elderly, or otherwise housebound students all can take advantage of higher education opportunities that were not available in earlier eras.

Many Forms

While distance learning can take on many forms and combine elements of different forms, the three most common are telecourses, interactive courses, and online courses.

➤ **Telecourses** are courses in which students watch a series of lectures via cable television or videotapes.

➤ In **interactive courses,** or video conferences, students congregate in a classroom or a meeting room to watch an instructor in real time via closed-circuit television.

➤ **Online courses** are those in which students download lessons and study course materials directly from the Internet. Online courses also enable students to complete work via e-mail, ask questions, and even engage in classroom discussions at a prearranged time in chat rooms. (See Chapter 19, "Speakers Are Leaders," for more on online courses.)

Word Power

Career curriculum is that combination of on–the–job training, mentoring, job shadowing, and for-fee programs that will enable you to progress in the direction you've chosen.

If your schedule is already tight (and whose isn't these days?), chances are that telecourses and on-line courses will give you the flexibility you need to make time for learning new technical skills that may be critical to your short- and long-term career success.

There Is Always a Downside

The downside of distance learning is that students may have a difficult time staying with the courses. Many students end up missing the interpersonal connections that accrue when taking classes in a traditional classroom. If you decide to go this route, check the course outline in advance to see whether it's likely to hold your interest and encourage your continuing participation.

Reinvento Observes

Each time you complete a skills development course, a mentoring session, or any other activity that concretely adds to your technical skill base, reevaluate your self-developed "curriculum" and modify it as necessary. What training/classes/instruction do you now no longer require? What training/classes/instruction would it make best sense to acquire next?

It goes without saying that you'll have to fully research any course you see offered via the Internet. Also, once you've completed a training program, it's important to apply what you've learned as soon as possible. All psychology holds that the greatest potential for learning comes from applying what you've learned immediately after you've learned it.

Request assignments where you can apply and perfect your new technical skills. Perhaps you could make such a request before taking courses to minimize the delay between finishing the course and applying your skills.

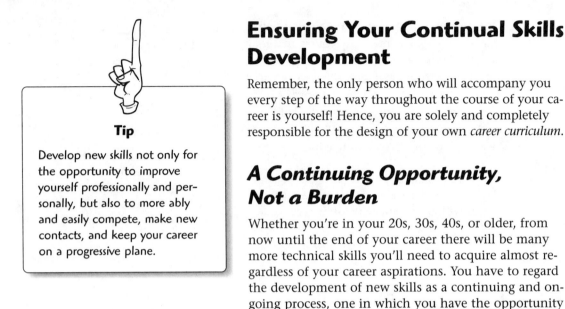

Tip

Develop new skills not only for the opportunity to improve yourself professionally and personally, but also to more ably and easily compete, make new contacts, and keep your career on a progressive plane.

Ensuring Your Continual Skills Development

Remember, the only person who will accompany you every step of the way throughout the course of your career is yourself! Hence, you are solely and completely responsible for the design of your own *career curriculum*.

A Continuing Opportunity, Not a Burden

Whether you're in your 20s, 30s, 40s, or older, from now until the end of your career there will be many more technical skills you'll need to acquire almost regardless of your career aspirations. You have to regard the development of new skills as a continuing and ongoing process, one in which you have the opportunity to continually reinvent yourself.

The Least You Need to Know

➤ No one can "coast" in his or her career anymore.

➤ Opportunities for reinvention actually increase in an electronic world where we all constantly face the demands of acquiring and developing new technical skills.

➤ The advent of the Internet and satellite transmissions means that distance and online learning will play an increasingly large role in our career advancement.

➤ The more time that passes between learning and applying a new skill, the greater the risk that the skill will diminish.

➤ Regard the acquiring of new technical skills as a continuing opportunity, not a burden.

Chapter 17

Written Tools to Transform Your Career and Your Life

Getting published can change your life; it certainly changed mine. Years ago, as an employee of a small consulting firm in Connecticut, I approached my boss during a slow period in the workweek. I asked what I could do to help the firm during this time. He suggested writing an article, an activity that would *never* have occurred to me, a B– student in English composition!

I pondered the task and, after several false starts, hit on a simple formula to help me through my first piece. The title of the article was "Ten Tips on Survival for Small Businesses." The concept was simple. I'd come up with 10 different tips, and each would be the start of a paragraph or two. I would then add opening and closing paragraphs, and that would be my whole article.

The article was easy to write. As I later found, when you attach a number to your title, such as "Eight Ways" to do something better, you finish the article with less struggle, even if you don't come up with eight ways (you might only reach six!).

Landing a Publisher

We mailed my manuscript (there was no e-mail then) to a publication that sat on it for five months and then rejected it. We then mailed it to another magazine, *The New Englander,* which sat on it for four months.

Word Power

Portable dictation equipment refers to the hand-held pocket tape recorder widely available in retail outlets that enables one to record anywhere from 30 minutes to two hours for future transcription.

One day, without advanced notice or word of any kind, a package arrived. It was thick. I opened it and found that my article had been published in the current issue of *The New Englander* magazine. As it turned out, it was the last article in the issue—the least of my concerns. The graphics and artwork that they had provided were wonderful and the article made an attractive reprint. I was so excited to have my name in print that I probably photocopied that article 500 times and sent it to everyone I knew.

No Pay but a Priceless Lesson

Although the magazine paid me nothing, the lesson I learned was priceless. Up to then I thought that only superstars and the privileged classes got their names into print. When I discovered *portable dictation equipment* a couple years later, I began dictating articles at the pace of about one per month, increasing within a year to *one per week.*

Publishing Pays Off

If writing appeals to you and you'd like to use it as a tool for reinventing your career, it's important to have realistic expectations. Publishing articles in newsletters, newspapers, and magazines certainly can accelerate your career-marketing efforts and can offer you a sense of pride. Once you've had a couple of articles published, you're better positioned for advancement than a co-worker who hasn't. Specifically, getting published …

Caution

When you distribute reprints of your published work, do so discreetly to avoid seeming egotistical.

➤ **Positions you as an expert.** Getting published means credentials for you as an expert on the article's subject area.

➤ **Leads to ever-wider acceptance.** If you concentrate on one subject area, you're likely to gain ever-wider acceptance with magazines in your field, increasing your visibility.

➤ **Makes for attractive reprints.** You can create a favorable impression by supplying clients, co-workers, and peers with reprints of an article you've had published. Most people are pleased and impressed to accept your reprint.

➤ **Supports career changes.** You can include reprints of your article with resumes when applying for a new position and with requests for raises in your present job.

➤ **Invites speaking invitations.** An article can lead to an invitation to speak before a particular group. Every article can be made into a speech, and vice versa (see Chapter 19, "Speakers Are Leaders," for more information).

➤ **Makes you and your organization visible.** Always mention your organization in your bio when you write an article. If possible, without stretching the content, you may want to mention your company's name in the body of the article.

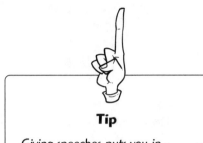

Tip

Giving speeches puts you in touch with others interested in your subject area who will help broaden your web of connections.

Caution

Some organizations are sensitive about publicity and would prefer *not* to be mentioned in connection with an employee's activities. Check out your organization's *written and unwritten* rules in this area before going ahead.

Your Own Organization's Newsletter and 'Zines

One of the best and easiest places to get published is in your organization's in-house newsletter, on-line 'zine, or other publication, or within the in-house publications of companies in your industry. Their personnel or human resources department will usually be responsible for the newsletter's publication, or will know who is.

Where to Find Publication Information

You can obtain the names, addresses, telephone numbers, editorial contents, fees paid, circulations, target audiences, and submission requirements for more than 10,000 journals and magazines by checking one of the following directories in the reference section of your library:

➤ *Bacon's Magazine Directory*

➤ *Bacon's Newspaper Directory*

➤ *Working Press of the Nation*

➤ *Writer's Market*

➤ *Oxbridge Directory of Publications*

➤ *Gebbie Press All-in-One Media Directory*

Reinvento Observes

If you have never had an article published, take heart. Each year between 800,000 and 1,000,000 people in the United States alone have their first article published in a printed publication. A multiple of that number are published on the Internet.

Many Options for Entry

When you can write articles for your organization's newsletter or online communication, you gain visibility in a hurry! Perhaps you can do interviews of top managers.

Is your organization producing any kind of videos, training films, commercials, or infomercials? Perhaps you can help write scripts, or appear in the production itself.

Learning More to Write More

As you learn more about your organization and the key players within it, continually look for ways to write about your work and link it to the overall work of the organization. Where can you find more clues about what the organization is doing? From many sources, including these:

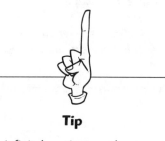

Tip

It's infinitely easier to make a lateral move within your organization and/or to get hired in another department if you're already known there, and writing articles is an excellent vehicle for becoming known.

➤ Financial statements

➤ Quarterly reports

➤ Annual reports

➤ 10k and 10q reports

➤ Organizational literature, flyers

➤ Organizational products and service descriptions

➤ President's message

➤ Posted memos

➤ Financial analysts reports

➤ Industry Web sites

➤ Search engines

Professional Magazines

Suppose you have good writing skills, enough, for instance, to fill a 1,000- to 2,000-word article. In that case, you may want to directly approach the major publications in your industry—the professional magazines and journals. It's easy enough to identify the top publications. Your boss or organization's higher-ups probably subscribe to them. One trip to the library to look through magazine directories can alert you potentially to dozens of more publications.

Doing Your Homework

Before submitting an article to a particular publication, be sure you know the editorial guidelines.

Editorial guidelines define the nature and scope of the material that the magazine publisher is seeking in order to serve the interest of the readers. Also, with each publication that you target for submission, pay close attention to the following:

➤ **The masthead.** Who publishes, edits, advertises, and circulates the publication? How often is it distributed? Who owns the publication? Is it published in affiliation with some association or other organization? The masthead provides all of this information.

➤ **Table of contents.** What kinds of articles are run? Are there regular features with each issue? What is the length of articles? In what style are they written?

➤ **The articles.** Who writes the articles and what kinds of by-lines are offered? Are articles accompanied by pictures, charts, or other artwork?

➤ **Departments.** Does the publication offer any of the following:

   ➤ Book reports
   ➤ Regulatory watch
   ➤ Trend watch
   ➤ Columnists
   ➤ Reader surveys

Reinvento Observes

Your organization's Web site or Intranet site usually offers countless opportunities for article postings. Can you assist in any way so that you gain exposure via the Net?

Tip

Those who regularly write for magazines know that most editors maintain a published set of editorial or author's guidelines. These are available to anyone who asks.

Part 4 ➤ *Reinventing Your Career*

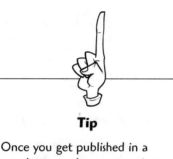

Tip

Once you get published in a newsletter, make an attractive reprint, write the words "previous publication" in the corner, and include that reprint when sending out other manuscripts to editors of larger publications.

➤ Letters to the editor

➤ "My say," opinion pieces, or guest editorials

➤ Names in the news

➤ New products and services

➤ **Classified ads.** This section, particularly if there is a job mart, is often a "giveaway" as to the needs of the industry. Yet, I bet you rarely read these even in your own industry publications!

Strategies for Breaking In

Before you get published, the task may seem as if it's beyond your grasp. Once you do get published, you begin to realize that you can do it over and over again. Take advantage of the pyramiding process when trying to get published. It's far easier to get a small column published in a newsletter than in a major, nationwide magazine serving your targeted industry.

Getting published in any publication favorably influences editors, and multiplies your chances of getting published again. When you've been published several times, you start benefiting from the *halo effect!*

Word Power

The **halo effect** is when you benefit with those with whom you associate as a result of something you've already done.

Making Each Reprint Count

Each time you write an article and have it published, make at least 20 copies of it for including with your next 20 submissions. Assuming that your writing is good and your topic is current, on the average, every 20 to 30 times that you mail out a manuscript, you will ultimately achieve one acceptance. Notice that I said "mail a manuscript"—until you get to know an editor, sending an e-mail is not likely to be effective because editors are inundated with e-mail from people they don't know. However, they still read their snail mail!

Chasing Back Your Doubts

Perhaps the greatest obstacle to breaking into print is the concern that what you have to say is not important or how you say it is unacceptable. Both of these fears are

182

unfounded. If you've done your homework, you will know what topics are most popular.

Choosing a Topic

The best topics for articles are derived from *successful work that you've already done* and that which happens to be a current topic in your industry. Examine everything you've written—including reports, papers, summaries, guides, and exhibits that you've prepared for work. Can any one of these documents be generalized and applied to a larger audience?

Here are key strategies for generating article topics:

➤ **Clip articles that stimulate you.** Every time you read the Sunday newspaper or a professional journal, save articles that strike your fancy. You might not even know how you'd use the article when you clip it. File all of the clippings by topic or subject area. Months later, review your clip file, and you'll find that what you've clipped serves as the catalyst for numerous article ideas. Freelance writers have successfully used the clip file technique for years.

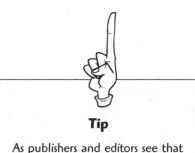

Tip

As publishers and editors see that you are well published, as a result of your including an article reprint of a previous publication, they automatically read more closely the manuscripts you send them!

➤ **Think "how to."** Think of six, eight, or more ways to do something better. The market for "how to" articles is strong as more and more people thirst for "do-it-yourself" information. By putting a number into the title of your article, such as "Seven Ways to Accomplish XYZ," you have a hook that will attract readers.

➤ **List your gripes.** A list of gripes or discomforts in connection with your work can actually contain the seeds of articles. If something bothers you, it undoubtedly bothers others. Discuss the problem in broad terms and offer suggestions for redress. By recognizing the universality of a problem that you face, you'll be creating material for an excellent article.

➤ **Remember the memorable.** An unforgettable staff member (or boss), a favorite professional experience, your biggest disappointment, or some other memorable event, can lead to some underlying lesson, something we can all use in our lives.

➤ **Focus on your potential readers.** If you concentrate for a moment on who will be reading your article and what impact it will have on them, your writing will flow more smoothly. If it helps, write the name of your target group on the top of your outline, such as "peers," "project staff," or "executives earning over $180,000 per year."

Never Start from Scratch!

Earlier in my career as a management consultant, I had to write a client report at the end of each engagement. From those reports I was frequently able to pull out five- and six-page passages that could be generalized and applied to a larger audience.

Continually be on the lookout for reports and written materials you've already developed from which articles can be extracted. Transcribe the tapes from your speaking engagements and half the job is already done.

If you've held on to your college papers, you might find one or two publishable articles from term papers and compositions that you once turned in for a letter grade. You'll be amazed to find that editors of publications are often much easier to deal with than your professors were. Also, remember that longer articles sometimes make wonderful shorter articles.

Making Your Articles Work for You

Producing spin-off articles from those you've already written is a marvelous technique for generating other articles. For example, I wrote an article entitled "How to Build a Law Practice" following a consulting engagement I had with a Washington, D.C., law firm. The article essentially followed a "14 tips" format, although I didn't use that title.

I sent the article to *Case and Comment* in Rochester, New York, which accepted it for publication. More than a year later, I was going through my files and came across the article. It dawned on me that with a little time and effort I could convert that article into "How to Build a Medical Practice." In the previous year I'd worked with a couple of doctors and dentists and was now familiar with their terminology and the differences required to restructure my earlier article.

Reinvento Observes

Think of the last time you wrote a letter to a friend or relative. Your writing task was on a one-to-one basis and your target audience was perfectly defined. Your words and ideas probably flowed freely. You can achieve the same effect when you precisely define the target group that will be reading your article.

Caution

Too many professionals who spent years writing compositions and term papers in school have been traumatized by the harsh remarks and comments of their teachers and professors. The editors who receive your manuscripts are not nearly as critical. If they like your theme, often they will help edit your manuscript!

I reworked "How to Build a Law Practice" 14 times, including versions for dentists, real estate agents, insurance agents, accountants, graphic artists, consultants, and others.

Focus on developing articles and topics that lend themselves to spin-offs, and you'll find yourself doubling, tripling, and quadrupling your publishing efforts. You'll also find yourself getting noticed, advancing in your career, and, just maybe, changing your life!

The Least You Need to Know

➤ Getting published can change your life.

➤ To gain visibility quickly, write articles for your organization's newsletter or on-line communication.

➤ Before submitting an article to a particular publication, learn their editorial guidelines.

➤ Examine reports and written materials you've already developed from which articles can be extracted.

➤ For doubling, tripling, and quadrupling your publishing efforts, focus on developing articles and topics that lend themselves to spin-offs.

Chapter 18

The Makings of a Leader

In This Chapter

➤ Success and the ability to lead others

➤ Ethical behavior attracts followers

➤ "Reading" others

➤ Corporate leaders get MBAs

Artists, inventors, chefs, and *lone rangers* might be able to reach the tops of their fields without leading others. For the rest of us, success is based, to a lesser or greater degree, on the ability to lead others. Almost magically, the act of leading others in itself becomes a transforming, reinventing process. Fortunately, leadership skills can be learned!

In this chapter, we'll focus on the nuances of what makes for effective leadership, at work, at home, and everywhere in between. The best lessons focus on the leader as a person and view the process as a makeover on the inside. Though the qualities and skills that make for a good leader do not always come easily, they can be acquired, as an advanced degree or major career promotion can, through hard work and persistence. We'll begin with two key components of leadership, among a vast sea of characteristics and capabilities: ethics and leadership.

Ethics and Leadership

In the operating room of a great hospital, a young nurse had her first day of full responsibility. "You have removed 11 sponges, Doctor," she said to the surgeon. "We used 12."

Word Power

Lone rangers are individuals who work pretty much on their own, without the need or perhaps the desire to be involved in group efforts.

"I've removed them all," the doctor declared. "We'll close the incision now."

"No," the nurse objected. "We used 12."

"I'll take the responsibility," the surgeon said grimly. "Suture!"

"You can't do that!" blazed the nurse. "Think of the patient!"

The doctor smiled, lifted his foot, and showed the nurse the twelfth sponge. "You'll do," he said. He had been testing her—and she passed.

This story, related by noted editor and author Arthur Gordon more than 60 years ago, illustrates a key component of ethical behavior and of leadership: having the courage of your convictions—sticking to your guns. Ethics is a key factor in long-term business and personal success and is the hallmark of an effective leader.

So, What Is This Thing Called Ethics?

We know ethical behavior when we see it but have trouble explaining it. Must you inform the buyer that you've substituted composition materials in a product, even when there is absolutely no disadvantage to the buyer?

Reinvento Observes

Ethics communicates to others immediately. It is being the same to all customers. It's not noble; it's not altruistic; it is a practical vehicle for success. Those who have a code of ethics seek to live by it daily.

Curiously, when it comes to the ethical practice of our competitors, we just discount it, believing that they don't ever do what's right. Paradoxically, we're quick to condemn others who display a lack of ethics, all the while overlooking or forgetting our own lapses.

Those who operate by a strict code of ethics know something that the rest of us must discover—ethical behavior, which some businesses regard as sacrifice, struggle, and nonadvantageous decision making. It actually makes operations easier, more pleasant, and more powerful.

Think about the leaders you admire most. Invariably they are the ones with a well-developed sense of ethics.

Calling All Role Models

In today's environment, we suffer from a diminishing number of effective *role models*. The tension of the moment or the focus on immediate rewards can relegate ethics to the back burner. Annually, each of us has hundreds of decisions to make in which the issue of ethics arises. Leaders, far more often than not, opt for the ethical side of the street.

Word Power

A **role model** is a person who by their position, expertise, actions, and personality serves as an example to others as to how to conduct oneself.

What effect does it have on you when the mechanic charges you less because not as much work was needed as he thought? What if the shipper paid the extra express charges on your delivery so you could get it on time? You'll go back to these vendors again and again—because of their ethics. So, too, when you encounter consistent ethical behavior from a leader in your organization, you'll find it easier and easier to follow him or her.

Reading People

No matter how high-tech the world becomes, people make deals, people make products, and people provide services. All the computers, Web sites, and technical data in the world don't make a successful company—people do. "I believe in people," explains the leader of a software firm. "This company is people."

Reinvento Observes

Leaders learn the critical elements about interacting with people that most others do not. Those at the top also realize the importance of making the people they do business with feel comfortable.

A CEO and president of a Midwest manufacturing company takes the time to establish personal contact with both the people who work for him and the people who buy his company's services. He cares, and he wants his employees to care, about their company and customers. All the sales and advertising that claim the company is a caring one mean nothing if the people behind the scenes don't truly care.

Observing Aggressively

Leaders are able to "read" others in great detail and to recognize the importance of paying attention to their needs. By "observing aggressively," anyone can learn to read people, and by reading people, work better with them.

Meeting those needs enables successful people to negotiate deals effectively, manage employees responsibly with the least amount of stress and resistance, gain information, and enlist people to support their cause. The crucial characteristic required in this process is that of "aggressive observation."

Aggressive observation, a phrase coined more than 16 years ago by Mark H. McCormack, author of *Staying Street Smart in the Internet Age,* requires working with people face-to-face whenever possible, since what you observe about them is more important than what you hear or read. When two people meet, aggressive observation requires that a person take action, carefully listening to the content of the conversation, and watching for signals in body language.

Tip

Someone may be consciously well groomed and smartly dressed, but unconsciously hesitant, evasive, or not confident, as illustrated by their closed, uncomfortable posture or by their sitting back from the edge of the meeting table. A savvy executive will understand that paying extra attention to that person and trying to make him or her more comfortable is likely to increase their contribution, adding to the likelihood of a productive meeting.

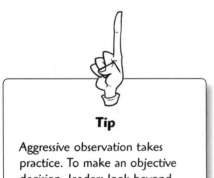

Tip

Aggressive observation takes practice. To make an objective decision, leaders look beyond the casual and superficial to take in the whole picture.

Observing with a Wider Lens

Aggressive observation involves looking at the big picture, as if through the lens of a video camera, and taking in everything at once to decipher it. Aggressive observation is not a quick sizing up, but a careful study, well worth the time spent. Since leaders understand the importance of observing people, and therefore practice it constantly, it seems to require little extra time for them.

Aggressive observation enables leaders to avoid approaching everyone in the same manner or allowing dynamic personalities to overwhelm good judgment. By observing each person in an aggressive manner and identifying behavioral types, leaders can easily and successfully work with others.

Heeding People

Warren Pelton, Ph.D., former professor of management at UCLA and a co-author of *Tough Choices,* studied the Ford Motor Company late in the twentieth century. Ford went from having one of the largest deficits in corporate history to one with the greatest profits in automotive history. Pelton attributed the turnaround to key decisions made by Don Peterson, then the company's CEO.

"Peterson assumed leadership of Ford in a highly uncertain, changing environment," says Pelton. "The major key to his strategy was a change in the way good people were used within the company." To achieve such a brilliant turnaround, Peterson asked employees how they could help and then heeded their answers. This resulted in a drastically reduced number of cars rejected at the end of the assembly line with a commensurate surge in efficiency and profitability.

The Art of Empowering Others

Empowering others means giving them the authority to make decisions. Elizabeth Jeffries, a management trainer and seminar leader based in Louisville, Kentucky, observes that many would-be leaders get up in the morning with a clear sense of where they are headed and understandably convey the same to their followers.

Reinvento Observes

Studies have shown that people would rather work with a manager with whom they disagree, but whom they respect as consistent, than with someone with whom they think they agree but perceive as inconsistent.

"I believe that most leaders really want to make a difference. They clearly define who they are and what they want to contribute to the world, to their organization, and to their staffs," says Jeffries. "Many have a deeply sensed internal need to both make a difference and to leave something of themselves in our society, before they depart."

When you have a clear understanding of what you want to accomplish, devise a mission statement to easily review and refresh your commitment.

Jeffries says that when you can communicate your mission and a plan of action explicitly to yourself, it's easier to convey it to others and to empower others in their work.

One chief executive officer of a food manufacturer said that in empowering others, his team becomes an extension of himself. In another company, which produces electrical equipment, upper management has begun to allow the people who have

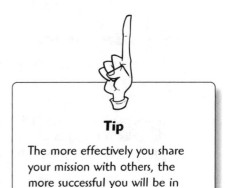

Tip

The more effectively you share your mission with others, the more successful you will be in empowering them.

direct contact with customers much more autonomy. In general, the recent focus on customer service is resulting in more companies and more business leaders shifting authority and responsibility down the line to the people who come face to face with the company's customers.

Increasing Your Perceptual Skills

Being successful as a leader requires perceiving what is happening both within one's organization and within the marketplace (or external environment). To develop and sharpen perceptual skills, you must talk with people, read the trade and daily newspapers, peruse the top industry Web sites, network with your peers, join business round-tables, and keep your "feelers" out.

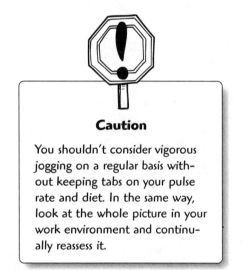

Caution

You shouldn't consider vigorous jogging on a regular basis without keeping tabs on your pulse rate and diet. In the same way, look at the whole picture in your work environment and continually reassess it.

Suppose you lead a satellite communications company that markets inter-store communication systems to nationwide department store chains. You would want to read the retailing publications that your prospective clients read. Get to know the industry and what your customers' problems and needs are.

Seeking Opportunity in Adversity

Even in the worst situations, the true leader carries on as best he or she can, and finds the good that can come of negative circumstances.

If your business failed, or you were fired, find out honestly why it happened, and what you can do to improve your odds the next time the situation arises. If the mistake was yours, learn from your error. Own up to it and work to ensure that you don't repeat it again.

Erring with Grace

Suppose you receive the news that a major deal has fallen through, and the fault lies squarely on your shoulders. Your board will learn about it eventually, so there is no pressure on you to be the "messenger of bad news."

If you're afraid to say "I was wrong," or "I erred," you are probably afraid to assume the risks of leadership. What they will remember is not that the deal fell through, but that you did not personally relay the news.

Leadership Qualities

You don't need to wait until formal leadership is yours. Take your skills and talents out into your community. Volunteer to sit on the board of an organization that houses the homeless, or spearhead a blood drive during a critical time of need. Participate in Career Day at local high schools and talk to the students. Wherever you work and live, there are always opportunities to exhibit leadership qualities.

Innovate Within Your Company

Encourage the development of a wellness program and be the first to jog around the parking lot each morning. Start an intern program, and recognize employees who oversee the interns with a special dinner or awards ceremony. Encourage research and development and reward employee achievement.

Offer No Compromise on Quality

Some of the great products and institutions of our time—Disneyworld, Siemens, Yahoo!, Hershey's Chocolate, and *U.S. News and World Report*—are known the world over. Consumers believe they can always trust that the quality of their visit, their eating enjoyment, or their reading pleasure will be consistent and unwavering. These companies' success and reputation is largely due to the leaders who run them.

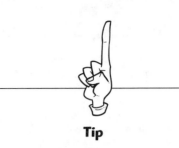

Tip

All businesses and all career professionals experience their share of losses or disappointments. An advertising agency may lose a long-standing client, despite a record of award-winning campaigns and sales increases. Don't let past setbacks limit your future or present.

Reinvento Observes

All leaders experience their share of stumbles and falls in the pursuit of goals. Unwillingness to admit mistakes betrays insecurities.

Connecting with Winners

Leaders identify the people they want to know and figure out a way to meet them. Ask yourself who at work or who in your personal life will be most able to help you reach your goals. Then orchestrate a plan to meet them. It may be a person who is already at the top, like the chairperson of the board of directors or the company's president. Titles don't matter. What does matter is these individuals' abilities to influence others or to have an effect on your future.

Handling Small Decisions Quickly

The higher up you go, the greater the need for faster decision making. You must learn to make the less-important decisions quickly and leave their execution to others, so that you can turn your attention to the larger issues. Postponing the difficult compounds the difficulty. If you procrastinate because smaller challenges or assignments are easier to tackle first, the larger challenges may become unmanageable because of your neglect (see Chapter 5, "Overcoming the Impetus of Staying Put"). Remember that hurdles often look high until you jump them. Often those large projects become a lot more manageable once you spend some time setting up your plan of attack.

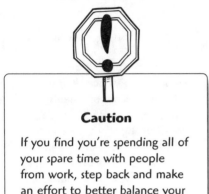

Caution

If you find you're spending all of your spare time with people from work, step back and make an effort to better balance your social schedule. You will be pleasantly surprised to discover how old friends, alumni, and acquaintances can, when you least expect it, actually contribute toward you reaching your goals.

Stepping Out of Your Field to Generate Cross Linkages

The relentless and constricting pursuit of goals can lead to tunnel vision. Life offers other interests, fascinations, and ideas. The more successful you are in business, the more you will need to know about other fields. The best leaders have contacts with people in many different industries and interest areas.

The Epitome of Entrepreneurial Leadership

Effective leadership is as important to long-term career success in the entrepreneurial company as it is in the monolithic corporation. Tom Randall (name disguised to protect the modest), with only a high school education, started in the working world as a plasterer, but along the way he acquired the self-taught equivalents of a Ph.D. in organizational behavior, another in social psychology, and an MBA. Today, as president of the Randall Companies, he epitomizes the forward-thinking, entrepreneurial leader who is dedicated to leading his employees.

From 1975 to 1998 Tom built the company's field force that is still in place today. Starting with a workforce of 145, he made the company into the southwest's largest employer in the construction field, now employing 970 people.

Tom's construction contributions are visible everywhere: several hotels, shopping centers, transit systems, and high schools among hundreds of other projects. Tom saw an industry in which leadership was an unknown concept. Essentially, no one was human resources–oriented. So, he set about to apply his knowledge. His results speak for themselves.

Tom's approach to leadership is inspiring while rooted in common sense and good business practice. Here are his observations and guidelines for effective leadership:

Leadership and Life

Regardless if you're first or last in the race, you can still do your best.

Always consider the other person's point of view.

At times, our job requires learning to say "no," "bye," or "stop."

Earning a profit involves developing people and building strong relationships with customers.

Our people are our business, so human-resource development is our most vital activity.

Excellent wage and bonus plans represent only a small part of an effective compensation system.

Effective leaders lead by example; not heavy-handedly, but gently.

Values have more impact than control.

Leadership and the MBA

In business, if you want to be a leader, do you need to have an MBA? Certainly among many start-ups today it's not entirely necessary, nor is finishing college! In the corporate ranks, however, one could make a good argument for getting an MBA. Nearly upward of a half million people, just in the United States, seek admission to MBA programs at leading universities each year. Another 1,000,000+ people, particularly college sophomores and juniors, consider getting an MBA.

Getting an MBA is no "flash in the pan" phenomenon. The three-decades-old nationwide MBA boom was supposed to have tapered off by now. Instead, annually, more people than ever are taking the graduate management admissions test (GMAT) in the hopes of getting into a top "B" school. Decreases in the degree's popularity have been predicted every year since the mid-1970s. Yet, every year a healthy number of applicants from a more diverse range of backgrounds compete fiercely for a few openings among the nation's premiere graduate business schools. The rising GMAT scores of successful candidates reflect the intensity of this competition.

At Duke University's Fuqua School of Business, for example, one MBA class averaged a 50-point increase over the year before. At UCLA, more than 10 times the number of applicants compete for the scant openings. MBA degrees remain a hot choice among women. The Occupational Outlook Quarterly of the U.S. Department of Labor shows steady increases in the number of female MBAs since 1962.

Presently, the U.S. MBA population vastly exceeds 1,000,000, with most degree holders being under age 40. Lee Iacocca once called MBAs "the green berets of business." To college students and those with but a few years in the working world, the MBA is regarded as the key that opens more doors faster, the key to riches. Many studies indicate the substantial employment and compensation advantages enjoyed by MBAs.

The Leader in You

So, what about the leader in you?

We've seen that the key components of leadership, among a vast sea of characteristics and capabilities, include soliciting and heeding a talented staff, empowering others, developing perceptual skills, seeking opportunity in adversity, and erring with grace.

Other components include exhibiting leadership even before you've been promoted to a leadership position, innovating within your organization, never compromising on quality, narrowing your strategic focus, maintaining your self-esteem, connecting with winners, continually analyzing your situation, handling small decisions quickly, and delegating appropriately.

If you believe that you're destined for leadership in your chosen field, there are many activities you can initiate right now. To develop and sharpen perceptual skills, talk with knowledgeable people in your industry, read the trade and daily newspapers, network with your peers, join business roundtables, and generally keep your "feelers" out. If you think you are a leader in the making, you're probably right.

The Least You Need to Know

➤ Leadership skills can be learned, and the most important lessons initially focus on the leader as a person. The qualities and skills that make a good leader can be acquired through hard work and persistence.

➤ If you're afraid to say "I was wrong," or "I erred," you're probably afraid to assume the risks of leadership.

➤ The more successful you are in your career, the more you need to know about other fields. The best leaders have contacts with people in different industries and interest areas.

➤ Effective leadership is just as important to long-term career success in the entrepreneurial company as it is in the monolithic corporation.

➤ Getting an MBA makes good sense because it increases one's odds of making it to the top in the corporate world.

Chapter 19

Speakers Are Leaders

The *Book of Lists* by Amy Wallace and Robert Wallacinsky cited "public speaking" as the number one adult fear. This book was so popular and so widely read that, for much of the 1960s and 1970s, it almost became gospel—"public speaking is the number one adult fear." Yet, this has always been utter nonsense. More recent surveys, such as one undertaken by the Discovery Health Channel, have shown that of 1,000 polled, the number one fear is "snakes," followed by these:

➤ Being buried alive

➤ Heights

➤ Being tied up

➤ Drowning

Public speaking is only a *social* fear. I could list dozens of activities that you would be more afraid to pursue than speaking to a group, such as driving a car without brakes down a mountain roadside, walking a tightrope between two 25-story buildings, or going into an unstable mine shaft. Nevertheless, if you're uncomfortable speaking to others but have always had a desire to be a more effective speaker, take heart—this is one aspect of your life that is prime for reinvention.

Anybody can be a good speaker, and anybody can be a better speaker than they already are. Let's examine what it would take for you to become a better speaker, and to use your new-found speaking capabilities to be more effective with people, both personally and professionally. This way you can articulately air your views whenever you choose, and use your burgeoning speaking capability to become a leader.

Word Power

Inarticulate means indistinct, garbled, or incomprehensible conversation, and a general inability to effectively communicate.

Reinvento Observes

Having a large vocabulary is synonymous with having a wide variety of linguistic tools you can draw upon in any given communication situation. People with a large vocabulary tend to be better in written communications, as well as more effective interpersonally, than those who have a lesser command of the language.

Watching Your Language

A large vocabulary is a strong predictor of career and even financial success. Those with a large vocabulary have the ability to express themselves more creatively. Undoubtedly, people are impressed by those with a large vocabulary, as opposed to those who are *inarticulate*. (See Chapter 8, "Exercising Your Mind," for more on increasing your vocabulary.)

While you don't want to use a large vocabulary to act superior to other people or browbeat others to get your way, there is nothing wrong with using your educational, verbal, and oral skills to demonstrate your intelligence, particularly in this era in which vast segments of the population are enamored with low-brow culture, tuning in to endless episodes of self-flagellating and moronic sitcoms, soap operas, and talk shows.

There's Still Room for Plain Speaking

Having a good vocabulary and using language well is not contrary to plain speaking. Harry Truman, the thirty-third President of the United States, was regarded as a master of plain speaking. Those who heard him knew exactly where he was coming from. The potential for misunderstanding was next to nothing.

Today, more than 50 years following his presidency, you often hear pundits and reporters refer to the Truman era with fondness and even nostalgia. This is because of the simple and direct manner in which he spoke, which contrasts with today's leaders whose speeches seem to meander from topic to topic.

While he was a plain speaker, Truman also had a good vocabulary and strong command of the language. So, banish any thoughts that having a large vocabulary and being a plain and direct speaker are somehow *incongruent!*

Tools at Your Disposal

As with so many aspects of reinventing yourself, you have many options available for increasing the effectiveness of your speaking. A variety of cassettes, videos, CD-ROMs, and online sources are available to help you increase your vocabulary, practice your diction, and employ powerful persuasion techniques. Many bookstores feature audio book sections where you're likely to find at least a couple of titles related to better speaking.

Likewise, your public library has an audiovisual department often stocked with programs on how to be a better speaker. The children's section of many libraries has stories recorded on cassette. Borrow one or two such programs, and listen to the diction and clarity of the speakers on these cassettes.

Using Daily Conversation

Speaking is one arena of life where emulation can work wonders. Be on the lookout for opportunities to enhance the quality of your interpersonal communications. Use daily conversation as an opportunity to improve your speech patterns.

If you have problems initiating or sustaining conversations, have a ready-made list of potential topic areas and questions that you can introduce into the conversation to keep it going. Try the following examples:

➤ Have you always lived in XYZ city?

➤ What led you to be in the XYZ business?

➤ What position did you hold before this one?

➤ To which organizations do you belong?

➤ What are your long-range career goals?

Tip

Articulation speaks for itself. One human resource specialist at a large company reports that he can tell in the first 30 seconds of conversation whether a prospective employee has a reasonable probability of success with the organization. He bases this assessment on the applicant's speech pattern, vocabulary, and interpersonal discussion capabilities.

Word Power

Incongruent means not in alignment.

➤ What is your proudest achievement?

➤ What are the two biggest issues facing your industry right now?

➤ What is the one topic that you never get tired of discussing?

Public Speaking for the Career Achiever

If you want to use your speaking ability to establish yourself as a leader, you most likely will want to do some public speaking. This means going beyond interpersonal communications and small-group presentations within your organization, to more formal presentations to larger audiences.

Public speaking is not nearly as intimidating as it might seem at first. As I discuss at length in my book *Market Your Career and Yourself* (Adams Media), you can get started easily. Begin by speaking in familiar arenas, such as at church, at a town-hall meeting, and at trade group meetings. While you may employ an outline or notes, be sure to speak directly to the group.

A Little Preparation, Please

Your first step in preparing your speech is to focus on exactly what you want your speech to convey to the group. Try describing the impact you want in one sentence. Then tackle two or three ideas at most. It's more effective to illustrate a few ideas in depth than to touch on a wide variety of topics. Examples and anecdotes will help your audience remember the main points.

Word Power

Compelling means commanding attention, as in "The audience found the speech compelling."

A strong opening is vital to holding your audience's attention. If figures can document your point, use them. Be careful, however—don't overwhelm your audience with figures throughout the speech. Your listeners will become disinterested if they hear too many numbers after the first third or so of your presentation.

The body or middle of your speech, is the meat of it. Here, you strive to be *compelling*, alluring, and insightful. If you're going to lose members of the audience, here is where it's most likely to happen. Some may nod off, others may daydream. Some may give you stares of false attention. I always take the attitude that it's not my audience's responsibility to stay interested in what I'm saying—it's my responsibility to get them and keep them interested!

Your conclusion is equally as important, if not moreso, than anything in your speech. Make it dynamic, drawing together the points you have made with a strong example or anecdote.

Perfect Practice Makes Perfect

Practice your speech using the outline, written on note cards or employing any other method that's comfortable for you. Your speech will be different each time you practice it. Don't worry about that. It will vary for each audience as well.

If you use an unfamiliar or technical word that your audience may not know, rephrase it or define it in the next sentence without being condescending.

Once you actually engage in the process of speaking to outside groups, whether it be at breakfasts, luncheons, after work, or on weekends, you will find that improvement comes rapidly. You should feel more at ease by your third or fourth presentation.

Nervous? Who? Me!!?!

While it's customary for all speakers to feel a little nervous before going on, you may find, as I did early in my career, that you actually begin to look forward to it. This ease may not come until you've made several presentations over the span of weeks or months. To ensure that you are the best that you can be when offering public speeches, here are tips to keep in mind for before, during, and after your speech:

Before

➤ Remember that each day of your life has helped prepare you for the presentation you're about to give. In other words, you are qualified to be making this presentation.

➤ Consider the purpose of the group. Why is the group meeting at all?

Tip

If no one is around, and the spirit moves you, practice emulating the sentences that you hear.

Caution

"The surest way to turn off an audience is to read a speech," says Maggie Bedrosian, author of *Speak Like a Pro*. People come to hear you speak, not to hear you read.

Tip

You can't go wrong following the adage, "Tell 'em what you're going to tell 'em, tell 'em, and then tell 'em what you told 'em."

➤ Adjust to the conditions. If your audience has had a long and terrible morning, maybe you need to be more upbeat.

➤ Never lean on the lectern and avoid touching it at all if possible. Pretend that it's hotter than a stovetop. Otherwise you dissipate your energy and look less commanding to your audience.

➤ If you have the opportunity, walk around the meeting room where you'll be speaking, especially the podium or stage, to get comfortable.

➤ As you approach the lectern, be aware of your body language. Be confident, smile, and make immediate eye contact.

➤ Request that your introduction be read word-for-word, with no ad hoc comments, and no ad libs, especially if you know your introducer from previous work or personal contacts. Otherwise you may hear comments you don't like, or worse, the connection to your opening sentence may be lost.

➤ Request that you come on immediately after the introduction is made. Much energy is lost if announcements come between your introduction and your speech.

➤ Coordinate the timing so you are ready and are four steps from the introducer the moment he or she finishes the last word.

Reinvento Observes

The secret to becoming a good speaker is the ability to turn a speech, even to a huge audience, into a two-way conversation. You modify your speech based on the energy level, intellectual understanding, enthusiasm, and many other characteristics of the audience.

During

➤ Start with a smile. If this doesn't come easily, recall a funny incident so that a smile overtakes your face.

➤ Employ a strong opening that encourages your audience's continued interest in your speech. Your first sentence, like a first impression, carries more weight than succeeding sentences.

➤ Tackle only two or three key ideas at the most.

➤ Appeal to both emotions and intellect, but primarily to emotions.

➤ To be at your influential best, stand erect with your best posture.

➤ Remember, audiences are becoming less interested in listening and more interested in interacting.

After

> ➤ Handle questions by simply saying, "First question."

> ➤ There are two great reasons to repeat what a questioner has asked: 1) to make sure that everyone heard the question, and 2) to give yourself more time to formulate the answer.

> ➤ Offer genuine appreciation of the audience for their participation.

> ➤ Offer to stay longer and handle more questions. This is more to your advantage than anyone else's.

> ➤ Close succinctly, in half a minute or less. You can even use the words, "In closing …"

> ➤ The better your last point and last sentence, the more applause you'll receive.

> ➤ Help people depart feeling good about themselves.

Reinvento Observes

Most beginning speakers don't realize that your audience *wants* you to succeed. They want to see you sail through your presentation and most are ready and willing to give you visual cues that show they're following along with you.

Using the Web

Every day a new Web site is launched that offers online training programs. These are programs and courses that you can take right at your desk, when you want, so there's no problem fitting them into your schedule. Most require some type of subscription or one-time fee. Programs may range from 10 or 15 minutes to an hour or more and be of the single-serving variety or continuing series.

I'm a member of MentorU University on the Web at www.MentorU.com. We have more than 40 founding faculty members, each offering programs in a variety of career and business areas. My programs, which are largely involved with life balance, accomplishing more with less, and advancing in your career, can be found on the Web at www.MentorU.com/Davidson.

Other founding faculty members offer presentations on improving your speaking. You can access these by visiting www.MentorU.com and then typing in the key search words "presenting" or "speaking."

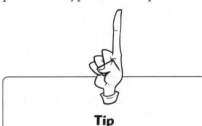

Tip

Dozens of other good online training sites also are available. These include www. OnTimeTraining.com, www.HighTechCampus.com, www.BizQuiz.com, www. iti4training.com, and www.YouAchieve.com.

And Now, at Your Desk …

The ability to improve your speaking at your desk represents a breakthrough that simply wasn't available to previous generations of career professionals. At best, it behooves you to check out the possibilities. If you've never engaged in an online training program, then, as the old expression goes, "You don't know what you're missing." Heck, as a result of taking other people's programs, you may find that you have something worth putting online.

Becoming Memorable

I once spoke to a group in Washington, D.C., called 40 Plus. I was in my early 30s at the time, and everyone else in the room was age 40 or more. The organization was specifically designed to help individuals, 40 and older, who were trying to land a new job or reenter the career world after many years away.

Before I spoke on this particular morning, a man preceded me who I will never forget. Part of 40 Plus's meeting agenda is to have a success story each morning. One of their members would get up and give a 5- to 10-minute presentation on how he or she was able to land the job they had been seeking.

The gentleman who preceded me was originally from Europe. Although I can't recall the native language, he spoke English with a heavy accent. He was short, and though he wore nice clothes, they didn't seem to "ride" him well—he was scruffy.

Caution

The mark of an effective speaker, particularly one who aspires to leadership, is to be able to influence others in a way that has a lingering effect. To do this, you have to be able to relate to your audience on an emotional plane. If you simply give them "just the facts," you're not likely to be memorable or moving.

Hearing My Story

As he stood in front of the group, he gave a heartfelt summary of what it was like when he was unemployed, how hard his search had been to find a new position, and then how he used some of the resources of the 40 Plus organization to assist him in his search. As he continued speaking, his emotions mirrored what he felt during the job search process. It just seemed to happen naturally. His body posture, his tone of voice, and his facial expressions all conveyed that he wasn't merely retelling his story, he was reliving it!

Initially feeling desperate, he moved to a state of hope and determination. Right before our eyes, he *metamorphosed* from someone vitally concerned about his career prospects to someone who was now ready to take on the world. He had only been speaking for a few minutes, but everyone was moved by his highly emotional presentation. This man was inspiring!

While English was not his native language, and he mispronounced many words and twisted many phrases, his powerful message was easily conveyed to everyone in the room: Don't give up hope; keep trying; you will find light at the end of the tunnel.

When he had finished speaking, the room burst into applause.

Word Power

Metamorphosed means changed, converted into.

A Tough Act to Follow

I had the somewhat unlucky task of having to follow him! I recognized that my rather "nuts and bolts" presentation on how to market your career would seem bland by comparison. So, I quickly shifted the focus of my presentation from that of a clever strategic plan to one in which strategy *and* feeling went hand and hand.

I began by thanking the presenter before me for inspiring everyone in the room and then interspersed some of what he said with the insights I had to offer. I knew that I would have my audience's high attention for at least the first few minutes following the preceding speaker, and chose to build on what we had all heard.

It worked! I, too, was lauded long after my presentation (and, ultimately, was invited back two more times to speak to 40 Plus chapters). When I went home that evening, I thought about the gentleman who had preceded me and how he had injected so much emotion into his presentation. Thereafter, I realized that if I was to have a higher impact on my audiences, I would have to engage them on an emotional level, too. Prior to this experience, I thought that simply doing a good job, laying out steps that were logical and actionable, would be enough.

Mere Logic Leaves Them Cold

When it comes to speaking, logic is never enough. President Jimmy Carter was one of the most intelligent people to ever hold the office of President. He would often analyze an issue at length and, when he was ready to make a presentation to Congress or the American People, certainly was well prepared. He meticulously laid out his facts and figures. The strategies that he offered for overcoming a particular problem were presented with the skill of a mathematician or logician. Perhaps a few highly intellectual types responded to such presentations, but most people did not.

Reinvento Observes

Most people want to be won over through emotion, and then will be ready to listen on a more rational plane.

In essence, when speaking to a group, head follows heart. If you don't appeal to their hearts, you are not likely to get to their heads, and you are not likely to be remembered.

Winning One for the Gipper

Carter was succeeded in office by Ronald Reagan. Initially, I cringed at the thought of having Ronald Reagan, a former "B" actor in Hollywood, as president. He seemed wholly unqualified for the job. Yet, every time he spoke, he connected with conviction and purpose in a straightforward way, right to the camera. Whether or not you were in the same room with him, you felt as if he were speaking to you.

Reagan spoke to you one to one, as if he were your father, your brother, your boss, or your friend. He used small gestures, props, good facial expressions, and a variety of other subtle tools. Reagan was not a grandstander and was not prone to bombastic speech. He offered just enough emotion to capture your attention, and then buoyed his argument with conviction. The upshot of this was that even if you didn't agree with Reagan politically, you had to like him as a speaker and as a person.

As time passes, Ronald Reagan is rated higher and higher when compared with the other presidents in U.S. history. His personal foibles, gaffes, and mishandling of issues tend to fall by the wayside. What people remember is the personal forcefulness and conviction with which he spoke.

What Works for You?

On your road to reinvention through speaking, you're likely to encounter a wide variety of recommendations that suggest flamboyant dress, flamboyant language, and flamboyant rhetoric. Forget them all. Instead, take a lesson from the gentleman who preceded me at the 40 Plus meeting and from President Ronald Reagan. Remember:

➤ Speak with emotion, but not so much that your passion gets the best of you. You don't want anything to get in the way of connecting with your audience.

➤ Speak also with conviction, never wavering from your core principles and beliefs. Even if the audience doesn't agree with you, you're likely to gain a fair measure of respect, and are more likely to be memorable. After all, if you speak to a group and no one remembers you, what was the point of speaking at all?

Fortunately, you have many opportunities in your career and your life to be a memorable speaker, and the next opportunity comes with your next presentation.

She's No "Bimbo": Donna Rice Hughes

Donna Rice Hughes (she was known as Donna Rice in 1987) was the woman who helped bring an end to Gary Hart's 1988 campaign for U.S. president.

Not-So-Innocent Mistake

Sailing on Senator Gary Hart's yacht, "Monkey Business," may have seemed like a worthwhile venture at the time. Senator Gary Hart was attractive, wealthy, and personable. And the good senator was up for the Democratic nomination to run for president. But after Rice was photographed sitting on the married Hart's lap on their sail to the Bahamas, Hart's campaign for the presidency, and political fortunes in general, went downhill. Although he was more than 20 percentage points ahead of the field, Hart lost the nomination and Governor Michael Dukakis of Massachusetts was nominated instead.

What became of Donna Rice? Hers is a true story of reinvention.

Cleaning Up the Net

Out of the media's eye for many years, Rice married and then, like Chuck Colson (see Chapter 4, "Feed Your Head"), found her calling as a born-again Christian. At age 39, Donna Rice Hughes is one of the nation's leading advocates for making the Internet safe for children.

Unknown to most people, Hughes received a Bachelor of Science Degree from the University of South Carolina and graduated Magna Cum Laude and Phi Beta Kappa. From 1994 to 1999, Hughes served as Communication Director and vice president of "Enough Is Enough," a nonprofit educational organization—a long way from sitting on the lap of the front-running candidate for the Democratic Party in the U.S. presidential election. The members of "Enough Is Enough" work to make it difficult for children and nonconsenting adults to view pornography on the Web. Their goal is nothing short of making the Internet a safe media for children and their families.

Spreading the Word

Hughes has given more than 1,700 interviews, a staggering number, on the subject of ensuring that children have a safe learning or entertainment experience on the Web. She is not against children using the Web; instead, she fights for the rights of those she feels should not be exposed to the Web's more than 40,000 porn sites.

While serving with "Enough Is Enough," Hughes developed a "tripod strategy," which involves working with the public, the technology industry, and the law in sharing responsibility to protect families from the bad parts of the Internet.

Reinvento Observes

Perhaps Donna Rice Hughes' stance against pornography on the Internet is not so surprising. Following the Gary Hart scandal, she turned down numerous offers from *Playboy, Penthouse,* and countless tabloids that would have made her exceedingly wealthy.

Hughes has taken her experiences and used them to reinvent her life in a positive way. She not only helped herself by doing so, but she is helping America's children stay safe.

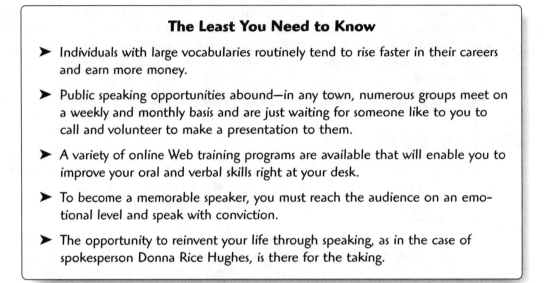

The Least You Need to Know

➤ Individuals with large vocabularies routinely tend to rise faster in their careers and earn more money.

➤ Public speaking opportunities abound—in any town, numerous groups meet on a weekly and monthly basis and are just waiting for someone like to you to call and volunteer to make a presentation to them.

➤ A variety of online Web training programs are available that will enable you to improve your oral and verbal skills right at your desk.

➤ To become a memorable speaker, you must reach the audience on an emotional level and speak with conviction.

➤ The opportunity to reinvent your life through speaking, as in the case of spokesperson Donna Rice Hughes, is there for the taking.

Chapter 20

Taking a Sabbatical

In This Chapter

➤ What is a sabbatical?

➤ How to get started

➤ What happens when it's over?

➤ Personal experiences

Perhaps you've heard the word sabbatical before, but aren't exactly sure what it is. For example, someone you know took a year-long paid sabbatical to complete a master's degree, and someone else you know took a three-month sabbatical without pay for a religious pilgrimage. Could both of these be sabbaticals?

The answer is yes. There are many definitions of sabbatical. *Webster's Dictionary* defines sabbatical simply as "a leave from work," but then adds, "especially a paid leave of absence granted for rest, study, etc."

Why a Sabbatical?

The longer you work, the greater the odds that you need time away from work. If the need to make money, to watch over Jason and Jennifer, or simply to feed Fido were not issues, could you mentally and emotionally bring yourself to the point of acknowledging that a month or three months away from work is something your inner and outer being desperately craves? Even if you can't foresee the possibility now, hold on to your hat—there may be a sabbatical in your future.

Reinvento Observes

Many companies believe that sabbaticals offer key employees a way to learn and grow and, hence, ultimately be more valuable to the firm. The probability of most people bettering themselves and bringing new skills and perspectives back to the workplace is a realistic expectation.

Caution

Most experts agree that sabbaticals should not be taken merely as time off to recover from a variety of stress-related maladies. A true sabbatical is a learning, not a recovery, experience.

Why Would a Company Offer Sabbaticals at All?

Companies sometimes provide sabbaticals as recruiting tools to attract top talent or as a reward to keep valued employees. Conversely, some companies use sabbaticals as a way to facilitate their downsizing plans. A senior public relations manager at AT&T commented that, "AT&T expects that a number of people will not return, a situation that would ease the need to downsize."

Often, companies grant sabbaticals to employees who will be engaged in job-related study or research. A lesser number of companies grant them for employees who simply seek rest or vacation, and still a slightly lesser number for nonjob-related study.

Mental Obstacles to Taking Off

On your way to achieving the mindset that you, too, can take a sabbatical, you may need to overcome some mental obstacles. The common ones are not having enough money, caring for kids, and making a smooth transition back into work. Let's mow 'em down in order:

➤ **"I don't have the money!"** Probably the majority of sabbaticals taken are unpaid. The more time you have before a sabbatical, the more time you have to plan your finances. Your daily expenses when not working are actually less than they are while working. You don't have the commute, the corporate lunch, the dry cleaning costs, and a variety of other items that add up to many dollars in the course of a week.

➤ **"What about the kids?"** Perhaps there's a neighbor, relative, grandparent, or semi-willing spouse who'll grant you the month or two months you need to get away. While it might be emotionally difficult to spend one month away from your children, ultimately it could be an enriching experience for everyone concerned. Your child may actually appreciate and respect you more upon your return!

➤ **"Won't I be out of sync at work?"** Will a couple of months away put you behind when you finally step back into the office? In many respects, the two months or so that you're away will be an advantage, because of the newfound perspectives you'll gain. You can quickly catch up on the corporate memos and scuttlebutt. That'll take half a day.

Getting Specific

After you've decided that you can go on a sabbatical, pick the actual time. It's no good to have a vague date. If you keep postponing the time when you'll take a sabbatical, the chances are it won't happen.

Making It Happen

Once you're finally committed to taking a sabbatical, here are the steps to making it happen:

1. When you pick the date, actually mark it on your calendar, and let co-workers and family members know about it.

2. Set up a savings plan.

3. Ensure that all your benefits still accrue.

4. Talk with your boss about the plans he or she has for you upon your return.

5. As the magic time approaches, start sending out a reminder of your time away to all correspondents.

6. Arrange the manner in which you want correspondence to be handled.

7. Plan a minicelebration, both at work and at home, on the day of, or a few days before, your actual sabbatical begins.

8. Get your other affairs in order, in case something out-of-the-ordinary happens to you during your time away. Update your will, pay bills in advance, ensure that certain minimum sums are in various checking and savings accounts, and so forth.

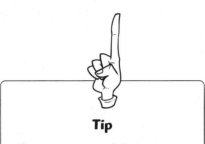

Tip

If you opt to travel during your sabbatical, use a few travelers' guides from your local library and find relatively inexpensive lodging all over the world.

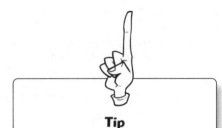

Tip

Chances are, within one week of your return, you won't feel as if you've missed out on any-thing. You're more likely to feel as if your time away was too brief, like a distant dream.

Tip

Any of the major search engines such as Yahoo!, Alta Vista, HotBot, and Excite offer a variety of Web sites at your disposal. Also, log on to dejanews.com and see what people are saying in the newsgroups about sabbaticals. You'll gain lots of insights and observations in a hurry, and these may help to improve the quality and nature of your sabbatical.

9. Install appropriate messages on your voicemail, answering machines, and e-mail.

10. Identify what you need in terms of clothing, implements, and so forth.

11. Get a complete health checkup, so that you leave with a clean bill of health.

12. If you'll be traveling by car, take your car in for a complete tune-up.

Letting the Sabbatical Begin!

On that first day, when you don't head into work and your routine is different, you'll probably feel good. Over the next couple of days, if you're at home, you may feel rested. You get to clean out the freezer, take care of the minor inconveniences that you let slide during the interim, and feel in command of your home.

If it's not a stay-at-home sabbatical, i.e., if you're on the road, almost from the opening day, you'll experience what the stay-at-home types experience by about their sixth or seventh day: "My goodness, this really is different." Here's a list of *do's* and *don'ts* to help you along during these first few impressionable days:

Do:

➤ Allow yourself to get extra sleep.

➤ Allow yourself to try new foods.

➤ Take a multi-vitamin every day.

➤ Be open and responsive to new viewpoints.

➤ Allow yourself to explore, wander, or simply do nothing.

➤ Feel free to keep a pen or pocket dictator nearby to capture the thoughts that strike you.

➤ Allow yourself the opportunity to just *be*.

Don't:

➤ Fall into the trap of trying to make every day and every moment "productive."

➤ Let your exercise routine slide.

➤ Be concerned if you feel out of sorts.

➤ Feel guilty about the work and people that you've left behind.

➤ Second-guess yourself about whether you should have taken the sabbatical.

Alternate Forms of Sabbatical

Sometimes a sabbatical might find its way to you, even when you aren't looking for it. An unexpected job loss is one example. Rather than focus on the job loss, why not focus on the time you now have to do something for yourself?

Maybe there was some special trip or journey that you always wanted to take, but for which you could never find the time. Well, now the time has been given to you. Of course, you can't ignore the fact that you need to find another job, but there is nothing wrong with taking some time for yourself first.

Exploring Your Options

Your sabbatical can consist of traveling the country or a region of the country to find out more about alternative careers. If you absolutely can't find the time to take a full-fledged sabbatical, you might consider turning your vacation into a minisabbatical, even if it's only for a week or two.

Caution

The benefits of a sabbatical may not appear for quite awhile, perhaps not even until the sabbatical is over.

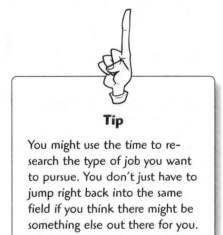

Tip

You might use the time to research the type of job you want to pursue. You don't just have to jump right back into the same field if you think there might be something else out there for you.

Perhaps there is an out-of-town event that you are taking time off to attend, such as the wedding of a family member or friend. Instead of just taking a few days off or taking a long weekend and flying to the event only to return quickly, why not take a whole week off and drive to the event? That way you can choose the route that you travel and stop in places that interest you.

What to Do, Where to Go

There are countless possibilities for where you can spend your sabbatical and what you can do. Most of the decision will depend on your personal interests and needs. In other words, no one thing is right for everyone. You will have to do your homework. Many resources are on the Internet and at your local library that can help you choose the perfect sabbatical.

Something Totally New

There are also people whose sabbaticals take the form of a spiritual *pilgrimage*. Throughout the world, certain spots are believed to be sacred, and there are stories about miracles and extraordinary things that have occurred as a result of visiting these places. This list of sacred places includes Stonehenge, Jerusalem, Mecca, and the Pyramids. People who go on pilgrimages usually do so to gain inspiration and a new or reinvented perspective on life. Here's some information about a few:

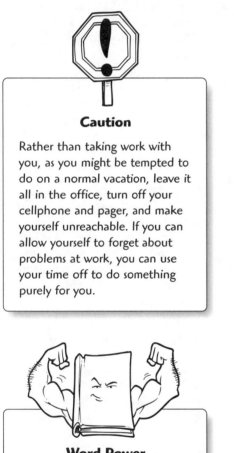

Caution

Rather than taking work with you, as you might be tempted to do on a normal vacation, leave it all in the office, turn off your cellphone and pager, and make yourself unreachable. If you can allow yourself to forget about problems at work, you can use your time off to do something purely for you.

Word Power

A **pilgrimage** is a journey, usually prompted by religious beliefs or convictions. People often travel to holy lands or lands of their ancestors to better understand their origins and religious traditions.

➤ A trip to the Dead Sea, a salt lake between Israel and Jordan, might be an enjoyable sabbatical. The Dead Sea is famous for its chemical composition, which enables people to float on the surface because of the density of particles in the water. The experience of floating on water is said to be surreal. The surrounding landscape is also captivating and includes views of the Moab Mountains in Jordan.

➤ Spend some time at a dude ranch. Montana has several dude ranches in operation. You can choose the extent to which your experience is authentic—in other words, the extent to which you choose to enjoy modern conveniences. You get to live the life of a cowboy and even learn to herd cattle if you wish. You can forget the fast-paced world that you leave behind during your sabbatical and enjoy the slow, nature-filled days of ranch living.

➤ If you enjoy being close to nature, your best bet may be to visit one or many of the country's national parks. For example, you can spend time in Rocky Mountain National Park in Colorado. The lakes are open for boating and fishing, and they have designated places for overnight camping. The park's claim to fame, however, is its extensive network of hiking trails, which experts say offers some of the world's best hiking.

Touring and More

Maybe you aren't interested in such an athletic adventure. Many other options are more geared toward relaxation—both mental and physical. You can tour various places of interest in which you're driven around in a touring vehicle. For example, you can be driven deep inside the California Wine Country to see the vineyards up close. The tours are educational and fun, especially if you have a special interest in the business.

Having an interest or a hobby can also become the inspiration for your sabbatical. Perhaps something has always intrigued you, such as trains, country music, or aviation.

Maybe you have always enjoyed classic cars. With a little research, you will find that there are classic sports car tours you can take in various areas of the United States. You get to drive a classic car while touring scenic places.

Certain highways and routes are considered classic for their unmatched beauty. Some trips will take you down the East Coast, along the Mississippi, or along the Appalachian Trail, depending on your interests. Traveling alone by car enables you to set your own pace.

If an out-of-country experience excites you, but you don't want to go so far, don't overlook Canada as an option. The major cities like Montreal and Vancouver all have their own unique attractions to offer. Canada also has numerous places to enjoy fishing, hiking, skiing, and white-water rafting.

Sabbatical Experiences

Below are scenarios of people who've taken sabbaticals, what they've experienced, and what they had to say. The names have been changed to protect the innocent, but the experiences and insights are real.

Pedal Power

In her early forties, Ellen decided to bike her way across the Midwest during her time off. She had long been a bike enthusiast, and was eager to embark on a trip that would enable her to bike for hours and days on end. Of her three months off, she biked for all but about two weeks of it.

"It was great being on the open road," she said.

> "Just me and my bike and the slimmest pack of gear and supplies I could bear to take with me. I'd stop and use hostels when I could find them, YMCAs, college dorms, and occasionally a Motel 6. In two weeks, I felt my body begin to return to my more youthful, slimmer self, although I'd never really gotten too far out of shape. The spring in my legs was amazing. I reduced my waist by an inch and a half, and other parts of me by even more.
>
> "You know, when you're biking, even for a few hours just on the weekend in the middle of your normal work life, you get to think great thoughts. When you

bike for hours on end, your mind will take you places faster and further than your wheels ever can. I started to think about all the things that I wanted to do with the rest of my life, the kind of relationships I wanted to have, the kind of work environment I wanted to create."

Back to School

Jenny had just completed her fourth year of teaching high school English. She loved her job but was longing to be back on the other side of the teacher's desk. After a lot of thought and research, she decided to go to an out-of-state college and do some work toward her Master's degree. This was a huge decision for Jenny because she had completed her undergraduate degree at a college only a few hours from home and currently lived only 20 miles from her parents.

"I just realized one day that it was the perfect time to do something different," she said. "I was not married, so I didn't have anyone to worry about but myself, and I had never been too far from home. I was happy with my job, but was ready for a break."

Jenny took a year off with the condition that her job would be waiting for her upon her return. She packed up her things and moved away to a little studio apartment near her new college's campus.

> "It was my first time living alone, without my family or a roommate. It was quite an adjustment, but I grew to love it. I was able to focus all my attention on my schoolwork and thus enjoyed the academic part of college a lot more this time around. I returned with a whole new perspective on things. I bought a house and joined some academic groups in my town. I honestly feel like I had more to offer my students after my time off, because I had renewed my connection to my own education."

She admits that she does not know how much longer she would have been a teacher if she hadn't taken the year off to reevaluate her reasons for being there.

Sacred Grounds

Jim always had a special interest in his family's ethnic heritage. In his spare time he worked on filling in the gaps of a rather detailed family tree that he made for his mother's side of the family. He always had a particular interest in their American Indian heritage because it was the hardest to find information on. After another family member wrote a book about their ancestor's tribe, Jim decided to document their heritage. He took a month off from work, bought a video camcorder, and set out to the Midwest to explore the grounds on which his Indian ancestors once lived.

Jim traveled widely, visiting sites where battles had taken place and cemeteries where ancestors were buried. He met with other descendants of the tribe who lived in the areas through which he traveled. These distant relatives offered insights about the tribe from their own research, and helped to guide Jim's journey.

"It was amazing to actually walk on the ground that they had once walked on, and to visit cemeteries where chiefs were buried," Jim commented. "I followed trails that the tribe once followed and found actual treaties and documents involving the tribe in the local libraries. It was magical."

He video recorded his entire journey and spoke about what he was taping as if he were making a documentary.

"It was important to me and I hope that it will be important to my children and to their children," he said. "Some of those landmarks might not be around in 20 or 30 years. I just felt like there needed to be some documentation of them while they were still there."

Quiet, Hemingway at Work

Marisa, like many people in the workaday world, longed to write the great American novel. But on top of everything else she was doing, she never quite found the time. Once she was able to take six months off, without pay, from her Atlanta-based employer, she knew exactly what she would do. That first day, she expected to start on her novel with a flourish. But she found herself procrastinating, sharpening pencils, adjusting the venetian blinds, and so forth.

Reinvento Observes

How about you? Are you inspired to take control of your life in a way that a small but growing number of others are beginning to discover? In any case, enjoy your time off!

After about two and a half days of fits and starts, she began writing. The words poured onto her PC screen. She wasn't concerned about the time, because she knew she had days and days and weeks and weeks to work at her craft. "There's a wellspring of creativity that opens up when you know you don't have to trudge back into work the next morning," she said. "Just me and my screen, that's all I really needed."

Returning from a Sabbatical

Depending on the length of your sabbatical, your re-entry into the workplace may be easy or difficult. If you convince yourself that it's going to be hard to go back to work, then you're probably making it even harder. If you understand that some things have probably changed while others have not, you will be more able to embrace the changes and deal with them appropriately.

Many people claim that they return from sabbatical with some insight or peace of mind that helps them deal with the obstacles of re-entering the workplace. Often-times a newfound excitement and sense of adventure accompanies individuals to their jobs after a sabbatical.

Not everyone claims to have such a successful re-entry process, but you can do things to increase the chances that yours will be successful. If you find yourself feeling nega-tive about your job once you return, remind yourself why you took the sabbatical in the first place. Also, remind yourself about the insights that you brought back with you that might have changed your perspective. Finally, keep asking yourself the ques-tion, "How can I bring the joy of my sabbatical back into my everyday life?"

The Least You Need to Know

➤ Sabbaticals come in many forms, all of which serve the purpose of enabling you to take some time off from routine living.

➤ Sometimes you have to leave everything behind to get the full benefits from a sabbatical.

➤ Your sabbatical can take place anywhere from your home to a foreign country.

➤ Sabbaticals can profoundly change the lives of those who take them.

➤ To make your sabbatical a reality, start planning for it now.

Part 5

Reinventing Your Relationships

No man (or woman) is an island—or at least that's how the expression goes. It's likely that your quest for reinvention involves others. "Others" could be your significant other (a terribly awkward term for your spouse or mate), your relatives (including those you like and those you can't stand), neighbors, friends, and anybody else around you during your time on earth.

It has been said that you can't change others; you can only work on yourself. By working on yourself, however, you change the dynamics of the relationships you have with others, and, hence, you change their relationships with you. As it turns out, that may be just enough.

So, let's get started on Chapter 21, "Improving Your Relationship with Your Significant Other."

Improving Your Relationship with Your Significant Other

In This Chapter

➤ Changing the dynamic of your relationship

➤ The efforts needed for change

➤ Achieving motivation

➤ Working together

Reinventing your relationship with your significant other, as well as with your children, is a continuing process. In the book *The Day America Told the Truth* by James Patterson and Peter Kim (Prentice Hall Press, 1990), "communication problems" were most frequently cited by survey respondents as the top reason for divorces in America.

A growing body of evidence suggests that to be an effective communicator with members of your immediate family, including your partner, you need to connect with them so that they know you're on their side. In other words, achieving the outcome you seek often involves helping your partner achieve the outcome he or she seeks.

By listening to your partner, you show that you are interested in maintaining a consistent relationship that grows each day. If you're a gung-ho, career-climbing world beater, for example, arriving home still mentally immersed in the affairs of the work day and revving at the pace of business, your family may have difficulty relating to you.

Communication Breakdown

Reinventing yourself becomes much harder without the support of those around you, especially the person with whom you spend most of your time, your partner or spouse. Imagine how much happier you would be if you not only reinvented personal aspects of yourself, but of your relationship as well!

Caution

Experts agree that the number one cause of marital discord and eventual breakdown is lack of effective communication.

In all Western industrialized societies, the most common cause of marital discord and breakdown is lack of communication. Married couples either have a difficult time communicating their feelings to each other or do not communicate at all. Yet, to be truly satisfied in any relationship, you have to be willing to communicate your feelings, thoughts, and opinions.

The relationship between a husband and wife requires excellent communication, because of the ongoing close proximity of the couple. Compounded with the daily worries of life—money, work, and children—a couple with poor communication skills could end up not being a couple at all. Do you know anyone in that category?

Changing the Dynamic

What can you do to avoid this common pitfall in marriage? The key to saving (or maintaining) a marriage is to first recognize what type of marriage you have. Three main types exist: conflicted, worn-out, and growing. Each marriage functions as its name suggests:

➤ In the conflicted marriage, the couple argues frequently.

➤ Couples in worn-out marriages have lost their excitement and have become half-hearted participants.

Reinvento Observes

Even if you are not currently in a growing relationship, developing one is possible.

➤ A growing marriage is the most desirable type. Here, the couple continues to build on their initial relationship by working through their problems as a unit.

Love Ebbs and Flows

When you examine the lives of Elizabeth Taylor, Johnny Carson, Mickey Rooney, and Larry King, as well as legions of noncelebrities who have had five to seven or more marriages, you realize that for these people, unfortunately, little learning and little growth is occurring. It wouldn't matter if they were married 15 times. If they're simply treading down the same paths, they will continue to miscommunicate with and misunderstand their partners or drive new partners away.

So, too, those who marry and abruptly part more than likely failed to communicate effectively before and during the marriage.

Some of the All-Time Shortest Marriages Among Celebrities

Celebrity	Length of Marriage	Year
Joe DiMaggio* and Marilyn Monroe	273 days	1954
James DeBarge and Janet Jackson	212 days	1984
Charlie Sheen and Donna Peele	147 days	1995
James Woods and Sarah Owens	128 days	1989
Bruce Hasselberg and Loni Anderson	91 days	1964
James Thomas and Drew Barrymore	50 days	1994
Ernest Borgnine and Ethel Merman	38 days	1964
Michael Tell and Patty Duke	13 days	1970
Dennis Hopper and Michelle Phillips	8 days	1970
Rudolph Valentino and Jean Acker	.5 day	1919

Kept in touch with her constantly up to her death in 1962
Source: Joe Dziemianowicz in Marie Claire, *12/97*

How does any couple expect to have a healthy, lifelong partnership if they cannot even discuss the simple things in life? Maybe our basic ideas and expectations are what we need to change, starting with the definition of love. Researchers at the University of Tennessee observe that "the feeling that we sometimes call love comes and goes." A working definition of love could be "a commitment to continued growth with your partner." Defined this way, a committed relationship such as marriage means being true to your commitment even when negative feelings arise.

Caution

Although most marriages still begin based on strong feelings of love, divorce continues to claim half within seven years. So, maybe the love these couples thought would hold them together wasn't all that was needed to do so.

Acknowledging What Is and What's Needed

Nobody is perfect. Not you and not your partner. It is how one handles disappointments and setbacks, not avoids them, that keeps a relationship healthy and strong. Presumably, everyone wants a growing relationship. All growing relationships have certain things in common. Both partners …

➤ Are committed to a strong relationship.

➤ Continue to find ways to solve problems.

➤ Cooperate to build their relationship together.

Once you and your partner decide that you want to have a happy, healthy relationship and open the lines of communication, make sure that you continue that commitment.

Creating the Climate

Therapists will tell you that opening the lines of communication is usually the boost needed to rejuvenate a relationship. Over time, if partners have begun to withdraw and not express their needs, they begin to expect the other person to know what they need. This almost ensures that they won't get what they want, because no one can read minds.

Reinvento Observes

Partners in a successful marriage continually choose to and are willing to do the work required to develop a growing relationship.

In their book, *Active Listening,* Carl Rogers and Richard E. Parson say:

"Active listening carries a strong element of personal risk. To sense deeply the feelings of another person, to understand the meaning that certain experiences have for him or her, to see the world as he or she sees it, we risk being changed ourselves. It is threatening to give up, even momentarily, what we believe and start thinking in someone else's terms. It takes a great deal of inner security and courage to be able to risk one's self in understanding another."

Practicing the Platinum Rule

To create a climate in which the lines of communication are open and helping to reinvent your relationship, remember the Platinum Rule: Treat others the way they want to be treated. Do you want to be heard? Then learn to listen to and understand your partner; get to know his or her point of view.

Don't allow your partner's suggestions to fall on deaf ears. If you possibly can, fulfill the requests to show your commitment to the marriage.

Your Turn

After listening to their suggestions, give some of your own. Ask your partner to do things that he or she can do and will probably be willing to do. Be sure that your partner understands your requests. A request may seem self-explanatory to you, but it may mean something totally different to your partner or spouse.

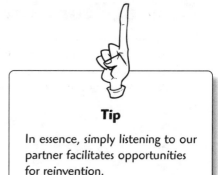

Tip

In essence, simply listening to our partner facilitates opportunities for reinvention.

Dropping Back and Punting

After both of you have listened, made suggestions, and fulfilled requests, learn to let some things go. There are times to argue and there are times to be silent. The end of the day, when you are irritable and hungry after work, is not the time to discuss your partner's lack of cooperation in caring for the family dog. Despite our individuality, we all basically react the same way during stressful situations. Eat, rest, and then make the small, specific suggestion that your partner help take care of the dog.

Even if you and your spouse have had an argument, certain behaviors and techniques help reduce anger. These include the following:

Caution

Don't belittle or hurt your partner if he or she suggests something that you do not want to do. The point of opening the lines of communication is to keep them open, not to shut them down on the first attempt.

➤ Contemplating how he or she might view the issue you're about to discuss.

➤ Minimizing any negative feelings you have before speaking.

➤ Eliminating the notion that your partner "should have done this" or "could've done that."

➤ Letting go of feelings of omniscience or superiority.

➤ Realizing that your way may be the way this time, but it's not always so.

➤ Looking for the good in your partner.

➤ Considering things to appreciate rather than issues to analyze.

The challenging part of marriage, or any relationship, is resolving conflict and continually sharing. While everyone may want to have his or her own way, *compromise* and communication are the stepping stones to a happy marriage.

Tools at Your Disposal

Despite a 50 percent divorce rate in society, most couples do nothing special to improve their odds of staying successfully married for the long term. Too many think that their love is so special that they'll make it. They don't realize that the survival of marriage is not about love, but about *skills*.

Word Power

A **compromise** is a settlement in which both sides make concessions, or a solution that is midway between two alternatives.

We go to school to learn a profession, or Home Depot to learn how to tile our kitchen floors, but where do we go to learn how to become good spouses? Most of us weren't given the tools to be good partners, even if our parents were superb examples and stayed happily married. Obviously the world has changed, and so has marriage. Take advantage of resources such as marriage classes to help you have a great marriage.

Different Approaches

One type of "marriage" class involves compassion training, in which one partner is asked to see things from the other partner's perspective. This type of course emphasizes *empathy*—empathic listening and empathic responding. The best and most knowledgeable purveyor of such ideas is marital counselor Harville Hendrix in his book *How to Keep the Love You Find*.

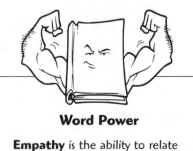

Word Power

Empathy is the ability to relate to another person's situation in a way that conveys some sense of caring.

While some courses focus on making it possible to identify with your partner, others emphasize the differences between partners. These courses see arguments as inevitable and attempt to make the arguing more productive. Hence, you not only learn how to argue, you learn how to listen through the rules imposed in these structured "fights." Such courses also may emphasize the importance of communication after an argument. An argument is seen as a natural occurrence, and the couple needs to believe and expect that they can resolve their problems by accepting the differences and coming to a compromise.

Any good courses place high value on effective communication. If you take a course, and you don't perceive results immediately, don't give up. As long as both you and your partner are committed to making your relationship work, you have an excellent chance of making it work.

Keeping Your Relationship Vital

In my book, *The Joy of Simple Living,* I asked readers a question that is worth asking here: When is the last time you felt supremely happy being with the mate you once tried so hard to woo (and won!)? Here are some ideas to pump life back into your relationship.

Give a Caring Caress

People apparently have a specific pathway of nerves that sends pleasure signals to the brain when the skin is gently stroked. Allegedly, the pathway helps infants distinguish comfort from discomfort. It's been known for a while that human beings have separate nerve networks for detecting pain, temperature, and touch. Touch means much—have you hugged your partner today?

Trade Weekends

One weekend your spouse does everything that he or she wants to do, and the next weekend it's your turn. Or pick one weekend day to do everything that your partner wants, and the other day to do everything that you want. Attend to your partner's every desire, without crabbing or cutting corners. You both will feel renewed and in control.

Make Love Longer

The next time you're together, spend an hour or more building up to you-know-what. Give yourselves the gift of peace and serenity with no thought about the clock. If you do this only once a month, it will still be a boost to your relationship.

Keep the Relationship Vibrant

Hug together under a blanket while watching a video. Buy something together that you've long discussed but have not yet acquired. Disclose three secrets each. Rediscover your photo album and reflect!

Reinvento Observes

From the experience of seeing life from your partner's perspective, it becomes possible to identify with your partner. Differences between partners are lessened because of this process of identification.

Declare Your Intentions

On separate sheets of paper, both you and your mate list your career, family, and other goals. Also list any goals specific to your partnership. Then exchange sheets. If you both feel comfortable in terms of supporting one another on most of what each has written, great! If there is some lack of support with regard to some of the goals, then at least you know where to focus your attention and resulting discussion.

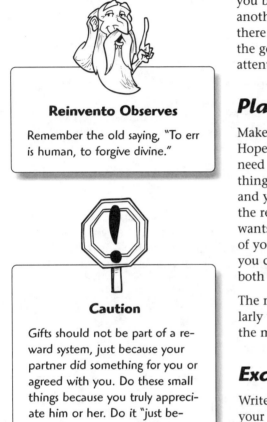

Reinvento Observes

Remember the old saying, "To err is human, to forgive divine."

Caution

Gifts should not be part of a reward system, just because your partner did something for you or agreed with you. Do these small things because you truly appreciate him or her. Do it "just because."

Play the Match Game

Make a list of goals *specifically* for your relationship. Hopefully, you match up well here. If you don't, no need for alarm, necessarily. Perhaps some of the things your partner listed represent good ideas to you, and you'd be willing to add them to your list. Perhaps the reverse is true as well. For example, if one of you wants to live as a retired couple earlier in life, but one of you wants to remain active in a career, together you can come up with ideas that seem palatable to both of you.

The more items that make both of your lists, particularly when it comes to your partner-oriented goals, the more solid your future together is likely to be.

Exchange Lists

Write down all the times you wished you had told your mate "I'm sorry." Then exchange lists. The longer the list, the greater your potential to receive forgiveness!

All Motivation Is from Within

Once you've begun to experience positive changes in your marriage, don't let up! Marriage requires constant growing and learning on the part of both spouses. You and your partner are both ever-changing individuals, so be willing to change with one another.

Remember the little things. Everyone likes to feel appreciated, so don't neglect buying candy or flowers or other things for your spouse. A little affection could only help.

Here are some ideas to reignite that spark from a list titled "Making the Most of Your Marriage," published by Ohio State University:

➤ Start each day with a big hug.

➤ Send a card or love note to your spouse.

➤ Telephone to say "I love you" during the day.

➤ Give the gift of listening: Refrain from judging or giving advice.

➤ Complete daily chores together and let this time become special sharing time.

➤ Put on a slow song and dance before retiring for the evening.

➤ Give your spouse a list of 10 terrific memories.

➤ Share a brief stargazing experience.

➤ Assure your spouse often that you care, and show you care by how you act.

➤ Thank your partner for compliments and kind gestures, and you'll get more of them.

➤ Help without being asked.

➤ Always take each other's feelings into consideration.

➤ Make having fun together a priority.

➤ During tough times, recall why you initially fell in love and dwell on those things.

➤ List all the ways your partner enriches your life and share your list with your spouse.

Just the Two of Us

Imagine having someone who is interested in your thoughts, dreams, and ideas, and for whom you have the same interests! This is what relationships are about: two people coming together to try to understand each other and work through the hard times. Changing your relationship into a positive one can be a fun endeavor, and with time, can actually become easier.

The Least You Need to Know

➤ You and your partner must both be willing to change and put forth effort, to ensure that you understand each other.

➤ Classes can teach you how to improve the weak points in your marriage.

➤ If you take a course, and you don't perceive results immediately, don't give up.

➤ Often, it's the little things that mean the most.

➤ Never lose sight of why you got married in the first place.

Chapter 22

In-Laws and Outlaws

In This Chapter

➤ Your family relationships

➤ How to make family relationships better

➤ Seeing things through their eyes

➤ Doing it with a smile

Sometimes the hardest part of reinventing yourself is with family members. This chapter focuses on how to break free from old stereotypes and redefine yourself to your family.

Is That All There Is?

Often, people become stuck in redundant relationships with family members, in which parents, in-laws, aunts and uncles, nieces and nephews, and even spouses and children begin to play and replay worn-out roles. Parents, for example, regularly tend to play the same role in their child's life as they did when he or she was a kid. If you've ever stayed at your parents' home after years of living on your own, you may have found yourself falling back into familiar patterns:

➤ Perhaps you're trapped by old customs that need to be updated.

➤ Perhaps your parents criticize or nag you and you respond.

➤ Perhaps your communication pattern reverts back to when you lived there as a child, a teenager, high school student, or young adult.

Caution

The privileges some relatives take with their siblings' children is appalling at times. Despite the fact that we are adults, our relationships with aunts and uncles often are predicated on a 30-year-old dynamic—our relationships with them as children. Sometimes our relationships with our nephews and nieces are similarly mired.

Droll Old Roles

Even aunts and uncles sometimes maintain the influence that they had when you were a child. When I was growing up, one of my aunts thought she had a God-given right to pinch my cheek and tell me what a big boy I was becoming. Supposedly, this was a gesture of affection. However, it hurt and I did not enjoy being five inches away from her face. Come to think of it, she was my least favorite aunt!

I also had an uncle who felt that he needed to convey his strength and vigor to everyone via his handshake. When he shook my hand once, it felt like he had crushed my bones together. I tried to withdraw my hand from his grip, but could not.

Do your spouse's parents play the role of the enemy, treating you as an outsider? If this problem didn't persist, Hollywood movies and endless TV sitcoms would not profit from milking "mother-in-law" scenarios and jokes decade after decade.

Locked in Time and Feeling Insecure

The reasons that in-laws often treat their daughter's or son's spouse this way are many, and they often predate their arrival on the scene. You need to be a sleuth to find the reason(s) or you may not be able to reinvent the relationship. For example your in-laws may …

➤ Regard you as someone who has invaded their nuclear family, even if their son or daughter is a full-fledged adult in society, left their household more than a decade ago, and chose a partner wisely.

➤ Be insecure about their relationship with their son or daughter and feel you may represent some type of threat to that relationship.

➤ Never warm up to anybody, and you just happened to marry into their family.

➤ Have unrealistic expectations about the kind of partner their son or daughter would find in life, and try as you might, you'll never live up to those expectations.

➤ Have trouble conceding that you had a life before you met their son/daughter and, hence, regard you as something less than a fully functioning human being.

➤ Have always had trouble communicating with their son or daughter and now are extending that inability to include you.

➤ Subconsciously never have wanted their child to marry. After all, that's a signal that they're aging.

➤ Have liked someone else whom their child dated before you and wanted that person to be part of their family. Thus, anyone who comes after, in their minds, never will completely live up to their expectations.

➤ Be prejudiced about your background, education, religion, social status, ethnic origin, or some other personal characteristic.

➤ Have connected you with someone else who made them feel uncomfortable.

➤ Resent compromises their child has made to be in a marital relationship with you. For example, you may have ended up moving far from the in-laws' home, or you're in a profession that demands odd hours or prolonged travel. This contributes to problems that their child experiences.

➤ Feel they never see their child enough, and now they will see him or her even less with you in the picture.

➤ Feel their ability to communicate with their child was unique and special and that anyone else in the "channel" is a distracting or disruptive element.

➤ Have not had a happy marriage, and they project onto your marriage the same misery and misfortune. Thus, without knowing you or attempting to get to know you, they surmise that you will be the cause of much misery for their child.

➤ Vigorously disapprove of some aspect of your life—i.e., you smoke, drink, have a large dog, or drive a pickup truck, and they have let this single factor cloud their perception of you.

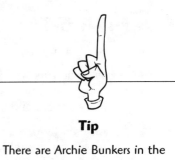

Tip

There are Archie Bunkers in the world, even though, miraculously, their children sometimes grow up to be nice people.

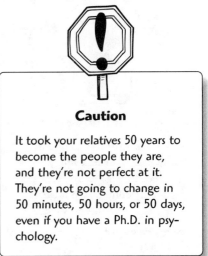

Caution

It took your relatives 50 years to become the people they are, and they're not perfect at it. They're not going to change in 50 minutes, 50 hours, or 50 days, even if you have a Ph.D. in psychology.

Realistically, you're not going to change your parents or in-laws. The easiest way to understand and, in turn, create better relationships with family members is to put yourself in their shoes.

R-E-S-P-E-C-T

To reinvent your relationship with your in-laws, you must first gain their respect.

One way to do this is to stop apologizing left and right for things over which you are not sorry, or over choices you've made about your time or level of participation. Be yourself with them and away from them. Do not compromise yourself.

Also, don't get involved in your spouse's battles with his or her parents. Their previous ideas of you should recede as they learn more about you, and their view of you will gradually be reinvented.

Let's Get Grounded

When we are *grounded*—that is, when we stay in control of our emotions, not allowing others to get to us—we have a greater potential for happy relationships. In their book *How to Keep People from Pushing Your Buttons,* Dr. Albert Ellis and Dr. Arthur Lang note the importance of realizing that other people don't control our emotions.

Word Power

To be **grounded** is to figuratively have your feet firmly planted, to engage in life or simply an encounter with a clear head, balance, and perspective.

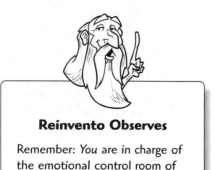

Reinvento Observes

Remember: *You* are in charge of the emotional control room of your life.

We're All Adults Here

It is important, especially with our parents and their siblings, to remind others, as well as ourselves, that we are adults. Speak to your parents adult-to-adult. Don't fall into any role that you might have played when you were 6, 11, or 19.

Be secure in your role as an adult, and your parents will have no choice but to respond to you as an adult. Avoid being manipulated by guilt as in the situation when you call your mother and she says, "Oh, hi. I was so surprised. You hardly ever call anymore!" Hint: Don't fall for it.

If she wanted you to call more often, then each time you called she would only need to say something like:

➤ It's wonderful to hear from you.

➤ I'm so happy when you call.

➤ The sound of your voice is comforting to me.

➤ How are you doing? I've been thinking about you!

If she never figures this out for herself, then maybe you need to coach her, but whatever you do, don't get defensive in the face of her *guilt-proving language*. All that will do is trigger another seemingly endless cycle of discussion that prevents both of you from communicating anew, in the here and now.

Got Guilt?

If you're face-to-face with your parents and they attempt to make you feel guilty, don't respond to it. Suppose one of your parents says, "Is it too much to ask you to blank blank blank?" If you say "Yes," you contribute to a climate of potential hostility and hurt feelings. If you say "No," you capitulate to his or her wishes and set yourself up for further manipulation and feelings of guilt. What would be a more appropriate response? How about, "What's the real issue behind all this?"

Don't allow your parents to offer prolonged criticism. Because they're your parents, they may feel entitled to criticize you, and some criticisms can be objective, valid, and even helpful. It's too easy to fly off the handle in the face of criticism from your parents, especially when you're an adult.

I've Got to Be Me

Present yourself as an adult to your aunts and uncles. They are the siblings of your parents, and, thus, are due the same measure of respect as any of your relatives and anyone older than you. Yet, they don't automatically earn rights and privileges over you because you happen to be their brother's or sister's child.

Caution

While gaining respect may be important, take heed. "When we worry too much about what others think of us or about getting respect, failing, or making fools of ourselves," says Dr. Ellis, "we forget we're really the ones in charge of ourselves."

Word Power

Guilt-proving language is full of terms and phrases that are used to induce feelings of guilt in another person.

Conversely, while your nephews and nieces are the children of your siblings, they don't have the right to run amuck when visiting your home, playing with your children, or otherwise occupying the same space as you. For example …

➤ If they play too loudly, ask them to play more quietly.

➤ If they make a mess, ask them to clean it up.

➤ If they leave something on, ask them to turn it off.

Caution

If you revert to childlike communication with your parents, chances are it will evoke responses from your parents similar to those of the past.

Given that your nephews and nieces are temporarily in your care, apply the same household rules that you apply with your children. Make the exception of respecting any norms or rituals that your brothers or sisters employ in raising their children of which you may not know or be informed. For example, their children may be allowed to have snacks close to dinner time, whereas your children are not. Treat them as fully functioning human beings who are simply smaller and younger than you.

But what if, however, your siblings never exercise any limitations with their kids? Does that mean you have to let them run wild in your home also? No! You still get to establish and set down your own ground rules for another's child.

Nearby Is No Easier

It seems equally as hard, at times, to maintain a healthy, growing relationship with our immediate family members. Perhaps sheer proximity is the culprit. It's easy to fall into the mindset that you know all about them—what their views are, how they'll respond, what sets them off, and how you are set off by them—because you see them so frequently. For example …

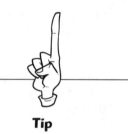

Tip

Don't reciprocate with anger or criticize in return. Instead, maintain a balanced and even tone. Your parents will get the message that you're not willing to engage in the same old unproductive behavior patterns anymore, and you may be on the road to a new relationship with them.

➤ You're having a discussion with your spouse about where you want to go on your next vacation. Your spouse says the mountains, and you say the shore. You present your case; your spouse presents his or her case. Neither side listens, and the conversation degenerates into a spat. In an era in which divorce rates are high and domestic quarrels make the evening news, it's safe to say that it's difficult for many spouses to interact effectively with one another.

➤ You tell your child to straighten up his room and he barely lifts a finger. You raise your voice, and he moves a little faster. You come back in a few minutes and he's dawdling again. You repeat what you want him to do. Now, however, you sound like your parents when they talked that way to you 28 years ago.

Standing in Their Moccasins

To reinvent your relationships within your family, let family members know that they're important to you. Listening to them is the best way to convey this.

Many of our family members have a history that we'll never know—the time they spend away from us. Author Thomas Moore suggests that instead of trying to diagnose or predict the behavior of our spouse, parents, or children, we should better spend our time appreciating them for who and what they are. That in itself undoubtedly would improve family relations.

A Smile as Your Umbrella

To achieve satisfaction within your family relationships, say things to make people feel good, but in addition to the words, let your body language express your glee. Widen your eyes. Perk up. Smile!

This is especially important when interacting with your spouse and children. Show interest in what they have to say, rather than being immersed in the affairs of the workday, and show it by your actions. After all, you're not talking to Alyson in marketing, Hal in logistics, or Jennifer in the Springfield division.

Language Kids Don't Want to Hear

When you speak to another person in your office or around town, do you use language similar to the following?

➤ "Because I know what's best for you ..."

➤ "Because I said so ..."

➤ "I don't want to say it again ..."

➤ "If I have to ask/tell you one more time ..."

➤ "Never mind what *I* do ..."

Reinvento Observes

In his book *Care of the Soul*, Thomas Moore says that human beings are "infinitely complicated and profound." He observes that our family relationships might either be good or not-so-good, but in either case, we could understand them better if we more often acknowledged just how complicated and profound other members of our family can be.

Caution

When making a request of a stern nature, your body language, posture, and demeanor don't always need to be stern. You can say some things with a smile or twinkle in your eye and be much more effective because the other party found your approach more palatable.

The answer to the question above is that you never use such language with other adults. Why? Because it simply doesn't work. You know they'd look at you, roll their eyes, and tell you to take a flying leap (and that's the most polite language they might use). Why would you believe such language would be effective with your children?

The Family That Plays Together, Stays Together

When you boil it all down, spending more time with your family members is the key to reinventing your relationship with them. The problem with too many families today is that they may be in the house physically, but not mentally or emotionally. Having everyone sit on couches and chairs and watch a TV show together can be somewhat uniting and comforting, but it's not the same as actively interacting with one another at the dinner table, playing a board game, or engaging in some athletic or outdoor activity.

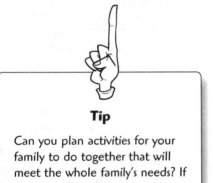

Tip

Can you plan activities for your family to do together that will meet the whole family's needs? If not, can you plan activities that will meet some of the family members' needs, and then rotate activities so that everybody's needs are met?

If there's one part of the day when you want to be sure to give your children your undivided attention, it should be dinner. Serve them and then sit with them—for the whole time. Talk to them, just like in the old days, as your parents did for you, or if that was not the case, as their parents did for them. Give them a strong, clear message that the rapid pace of the world does not diminish your family's ability to have an engaging dinner together.

I know one family that keeps a bulletin board by the dinner table, and each day, anyone can post a note that says what they want to talk about at dinner the next night. This gives everyone a day-long lead on what they might say about the topic. Long before the age of television, conversation with family, guests, and even strangers passing through town was the only way people received and shared news and information.

Reinvento Observes

Even if your kids don't seem wildly enthusiastic about what you're saying, the lessons of your life sink in with them and resonate on a high level.

Time for the Kids

When was the last time you saw your child play soccer or tumble in gymnastics? If it has been months, then maybe it's time to rearrange your schedule so that you can drop in on them. Perhaps you can get to work earlier, so that you can leave earlier or take time off. Perhaps you can rearrange your lunchtime.

Children have a built-in Geiger counter, and when their parents show up to see them at a sports activity, it's like striking gold. The same holds for piano recitals, school plays, and anything else in which they're involved. They want to perform, and they want you to be there to see it.

Letting Your Kids See You at Work

Have you talked to your kids about what you do on your job—what you *really* do on a day-to-day basis? The more your children know and understand what you do, the more they can support you in your quest for achieving balance. If you have older children, share with them stories about what you did as a child, your goals and aspirations then versus now. Talk to them about your training and education. Tell them what courses you took and what special experiences you've had.

If you can, take your children to work. Most will be fascinated by what you do, even if it's so much old hat to you. If there's anything you can delegate to them, let them help you for a few minutes. Here are some other things you can do:

➤ Take them to lunch in the company cafeteria.

➤ Walk them through the halls.

➤ Show them the conference room, the telecommunications center, the copier, and even the kitchenette.

➤ Give them a hands-on tour.

The next time they speak to you by phone while you're at work, they can picture where you are and what you might be doing.

Are there tangible aspects of your work? If you create products, or simply write reports, let your children see them. Then, talk to your children about what they saw and what they learned. You might ask them these questions:

➤ What impressed them the most?

➤ How did their visit stack up with what they had imagined?

➤ Do they have any new goals as a result of this visit?

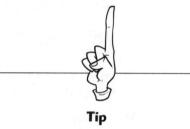

Tip

Kids feel very special when you introduce them to your co-workers and boss. It makes them realize how significant they are to you.

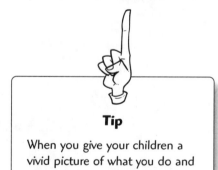

Tip

When you give your children a vivid picture of what you do and why you do it, you really can't lose. You get closer to your children and they get closer to you.

If you want to establish a better relationship with your kids, show them that you respect them. Most important, show them that you love them by spending time with them and reinforcing good behavior with attention and approval. After all, children are perfect mirrors of our own behavior.

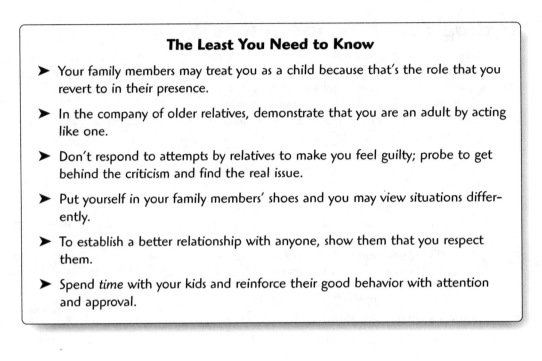

The Least You Need to Know

➤ Your family members may treat you as a child because that's the role that you revert to in their presence.

➤ In the company of older relatives, demonstrate that you are an adult by acting like one.

➤ Don't respond to attempts by relatives to make you feel guilty; probe to get behind the criticism and find the real issue.

➤ Put yourself in your family members' shoes and you may view situations differently.

➤ To establish a better relationship with anyone, show them that you respect them.

➤ Spend *time* with your kids and reinforce their good behavior with attention and approval.

Chapter 23

You Gotta Have Friends

In This Chapter

➤ The pace of life and maintaining friendships

➤ Friends help keep you healthy

➤ Putting friends among your top priorities

➤ Friendships are part of a full life

In the classic movie *It's a Wonderful Life,* Jimmy Stewart plays a young banker who finds out just how many friends he has when a crisis befalls him and his bank. It's a heart-warming story of life and friendship in a small town. Today, in a totally wired world, with all the people who come into and out of our busy lives, it's easy to lose sight of the importance of the relationships we have with friends and neighbors. Yet, the relationships that you can have with them are an integral part of your life. Reinventing your relationships with your friends is one of the wisest investments you can make.

Where Have All Our Friendships Gone?

With the pace of everyday life increasing rapidly, people are constantly faced with finding ways to make more time. Unfortunately, it's becoming more common for people to find this time by taking it away from their friendships, which seem less important than the more pressing commitments of work and family.

Many people feel it is unavoidable that the extra time they need should come from their friendships. After all, you can't take it from your family and you can't take it from work, right? Well, yes and no. Chances are that you're already working longer hours than you would have in the past, and chances are even greater that you're more connected to work than ever before—even at home, in the car, and in virtually every other facet of your life.

Weekends Used to Be the Solution

Even when the weekend rolls around, many people still have work to do and they must devote some time to family activities. Families who take trips to weekend homes are taking themselves even further out of the reach of their friends.

As author Robert D. Putnam points out in his book *Bowling Alone,* people are less likely to join groups than ever before and they feel little sense of community these days. Putnam warns that our stock of social capital—the very fabric of our connections with each other—has plummeted, impoverishing our lives and communities. He draws on evidence including nearly 500,000 interviews over the last quarter century to show that we ...

Caution

Work is not the only factor standing in the way of vibrant friendships. Our society also has a recent trend toward social disengagement—a mass movement away from social life in general.

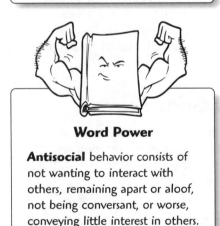

Word Power

Antisocial behavior consists of not wanting to interact with others, remaining apart or aloof, not being conversant, or worse, conveying little interest in others.

➤ Sign fewer petitions.

➤ Belong to fewer organizations that meet in person.

➤ Know our neighbors less.

➤ Meet with friends less frequently.

➤ Socialize with our families less often.

Countless other sociologists and researchers have devoted time to proving this theory, but even without the research the notion is easy to understand.

Think of the people you know. Among your group of acquaintances you likely notice that people are less interested in politics, they attend church-related functions less, and they have fewer casual gatherings and dinner parties than years ago. I've witnessed countless instances in which organized groups have been reduced to nothing more than a monthly mailing list or other formality that doesn't require physical participation.

Are We Losing Our Social Inclinations?

There are many suspected reasons for any *antisocial* trend looming. Surely, increasing time pressure at work is a factor. More compelling: The current generation of young to middle age adults grew up watching television and now is more committed to their viewing habits than to their community life.

How many people do you know, including yourself, who express having little time for social activities, but always have time for *Ally McBeal* or *Friends* each week? You could argue that watching a show is easier than relating to others—you merely sit there, in your space, in whatever attire you prefer. Many people plan their schedules around their favorite television shows, while becoming more withdrawn from their social lives.

Friends for Life?

Many of the reasons that friendships are so important are obvious. Recent evidence, however, suggests that maintaining close friendships may actually help you live longer! Studies have shown that people with close friends have a lower risk for health problems and recover faster when they do have problems. These health benefits increase with age and are thus especially noticeable in senior citizens.

If you lose touch too often with your friends early in your adult life, they might not be there when you need them most. At any age, when you make the mistake of putting your friendships on the back burner, you lose an important emotional support network.

Reinventing Your Friendships

What can you do to reinvent the once-vital relationships in your life? Moreover, how can one rediscover the friendships that have been put on hold?

Make Friends a Priority

Caution

Too many people today have actually substituted real friends with less demanding television friends. This phenomenon can be seen in virtually any workplace or gathering when you hear people talking about television show characters as if they actually know them.

Caution

Even if you presently have few problems and can't foresee any in the near future, the truth is, you never know when you will really need a friend. You might find out too late when a crisis looms or tragedy arises that you have isolated yourself from your friends to the point that no one is there when you need support.

Reinventing your friendships may necessitate adjusting your priorities. If you've lost touch with friends because of other time commitments, figure out a way to make time for your friends! Friendships require effort. It's erroneous to believe that if you neglect a friendship, that friend will be there to pick up where you left off when it's convenient for you. Few friendships can survive utter neglect for extended periods of time.

Word Power

Rekindle means to renew, reignite, or, in general, reinvest your time and energy.

Tip

It's okay to put friends among your top priorities, along with work and family, because that is right where they belong. You don't have to feel guilty about finding ways to make time for your friends.

Reinvento Observes

You have to eat lunch anyway, right? So why not include a friend and make the time more enjoyable with conversation and laughter? You might find yourself feeling less stressed when you head back to the office.

Chances are that when a friendship has been neglected, both parties are involved—especially with the busy schedules that are so common today. Someone has to take the first step toward making the friendship a priority. It may require juggling your schedule to accommodate your friend's schedule, and faith that they'll juggle their schedule for you the next time.

If you intend to *rekindle* your friendships, you can't feel guilty for taking time away from other things to invest in them.

Scheduled Shared Events

Ideally, you can adjust your schedule to create time to spend with just your friends. Unfortunately, however, many times this ideal scenario does not work out. So, you might have to be a little creative and incorporate time with your friends into your routine. Many married couples have a regularly scheduled "date night," so they can spend quality time together away from the business of home and work. It would be easy to include friends in these events once in a while.

If TV viewing admittedly is a big part of many evenings, why not adopt a show that you and a friend both enjoy, and watch it together each week? You don't have to give up your commitment to your favorite show, and you get to share it with a friend. You can enhance the evening by adding coffee or dessert after the show. That will allow time to discuss the episode and simply see where the conversation leads.

The Lunch Bunch

Lunch breaks from work might also be a good time to try to sneak in some time with your friends. While it may be hard to do this because of conflicting schedules and distance, there may be some times that it works out. If you and a friend can take a lunch break at the same time without too much effort, and your jobs are not too far from each other, you could plan to do it once a week or once every two weeks.

Baby, Workout

Another idea for getting friends more involved in your life's routine is working out together. If you already work out regularly, it would be easy to invite a friend to join you. And, if you don't already work out regularly and have been putting off getting into the habit, a friend might be just what you need to get motivated! Many people depend on their workout partner to keep them motivated, especially when they find themselves *not* feeling like working out.

Your workout can take many forms—an evening walk or time in the gym. Whatever the routine, it will enable you to spend time with a friend doing something you both enjoy.

Doubling Your Pleasure

When you think about it, you can integrate friend-ships into your busy schedule in countless ways:

➤ If you spend time reading, you and a friend could agree to read the same book and then discuss it at a mutually convenient time.

➤ You could invite a friend to your children's sports events.

➤ You could do your grocery shopping together.

➤ If you work for the same company, you could carpool.

Virtually anything is a possibility as long as you're spending time together.

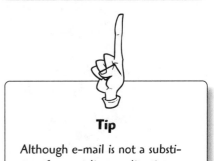

Tip

Many of the things that have to be done anyway can become more enjoyable if done with a friend—and, meanwhile, your friendship is no longer being put on hold.

Maintaining Touch

When all else fails and there are times that you just can't physically get together with your friends, avoid losing touch altogether for long periods of time.

If there is a stretch of time during which you can't get together with friends, drop them an e-mail to let them know they're still in your thoughts even when you're busy. Friendships thrive on little things, and a simple e-mail to say, "I'm thinking about you" can make a big difference.

Tip

Although e-mail is not a substitute for spending quality time with a friend, it *is* better than *nothing!*

Even better than e-mail is a phone call, even a short call or a message left on voice-mail. Speaking with a friend, to suggest meeting in the not-so-distant future, helps keep the friendship alive. It serves to show the friend that he or she is among your top priorities even when life is demanding.

Avoid Exploiting Your Friends

Short of betrayal, the worst thing you can do is to get in touch with a friend only when you need something, such as a shoulder to cry on. Sure, your friends are whom you go to when these things happen, but you have to devote some time and energy to the friendship outside of crises, too.

You probably know of friends who have treated you this way, and chances are that you didn't appreciate it. No one likes to feel that his or her friendship is only important when times are bad. If you effectively nourish your friendships, your friends will not mind being there for you in times of need—they'll probably be more willing to lend the shoulder.

Caution

Don't rely on e-mail and voice-mail to the extent that they become the *only* time you devote to a friend. However, they can be helpful when longer periods of time are hard to find.

Spicing Up Friendships

Even the best friendships are susceptible to rifts. Perhaps you know the person so well that he or she seems predictable, and even your activities and correspondence are becoming predictable and routine. Fortunately, you have many ways to spice up existing friendships. You can probably generate ideas more specific to yours if you spend some time on it, but the following are some ideas to get you started.

Joining Together

One idea for spicing up a friendship is joining a new group together. Undoubtedly, you and your closest friends share some interests, and more than likely a group or club somewhere promotes these interests. You might have to do some research to find the right group, class, or team.

Reinvento Observes

Becoming a part of a new group with your friend might lead you to see a different side of your friend, or even of yourself.

If it's within your interest area, perhaps you can find a group that meets to play games once a week, have a dinner party, offer poetry readings, do volunteer work, or undertake virtually anything that is new and different for you both.

Divide and Conquer

If you find yourself always spending time with your closest friends as couples—you with your spouse and your friend with his or her spouse—you might try planning times that you can spend together without the significant others.

Trying a New Setting

A relationship that seems routine and forced in a large group setting might flourish as a true friendship in a different, more intimate environment. A new environment might serve to put some life back into any friendship.

Go somewhere that neither of you has been before, or that only one of you has been to and can "show" to the other. Do something that you've never done together. Though you have many common interests, each of you has individual interests and can share them to liven up the friendship.

Although friendships can be held together by phone calls and e-mails, they also need some personal, face-to-face contact. A somewhat spontaneous weekend getaway might be just what your friendship needs.

Reinvento Observes

Perhaps you feel like you're in a rut because you're always doing the same things together in the same places. A friend might appear to be becoming too predictable when it's actually just a result of the predictable surroundings and encounters.

Empty Nesters Need Friends

Many people discover that after their children leave home, or after retirement, they have more time and energy to devote to their friendships. This is a common time for people to reunite with friends that they've seen sparingly, or to make new friends.

At this point in life, you will be more available to take vacations with friends, join groups with them, and have regular dinner parties without so many conflicting schedules.

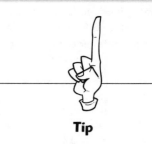

Tip

If your friendship is in a rut, or you only communicate over the phone and computer, you could come up with a vacation for just the two of you.

Resurrecting a Friendship

If you've lost touch with a friend because of a disagreement, but still feel that the relationship is worth saving, there's no better time to act than now. Someone has to make the first move toward repairing the friendship, even if it means swallowing your pride.

Sometimes a cooling-off period in itself is enough to solve the problem. If the issue was minor, you may find that when you call your friend you don't even have to discuss it! Whew! You're off the hook!

If the problem needs to be discussed, you have to respect your friend's opinion, even if it differs from yours. No one ever said that friends have to see eye-to-eye on everything. Indeed, it may be the differences in your personalities that make you complement each other so well.

Caution

A cooling-off period after an argument is perfectly natural, but if you let it go for too long the issue might fester or you might lose contact all together.

Tip

The only way for both parties to feel better is if you both get to say how the situation made you feel. Even if you don't agree with each other, at least you are each being heard.

In any case, you both have a side of the story. If you're a good listener, your friend will likely be a good listener in return.

Talk through the problem, discuss what the friendship means to both of you, and find some common ground to begin rebuilding. If the wounds are not too deep, the foundation will still be there.

When Reinventing Means Ending

Don't give up easily on a good friendship! They are not so easy to replace. However, there are times when ending a friendship is inevitable. If continued efforts to repair a friendship are futile and both parties are aware of the futility, perhaps it's better to recognize the end.

Often friendships end by simply dissipating over time, while others end suddenly after a fight or betrayal of trust. In any case, the most common reasons that friendships end are that one or both parties were harboring unexpressed expectations, there was a lack of communication, or one friend ceased paying attention to the other. Each of these root causes seems to arise when there are major changes in people's lives—for example, when one friend gets married and the other is still single.

Feelings of neglect and jealousy are common in such situations. Friendships are more likely to last when either the friends stay much the same as when they met, or when they change in similar directions. It's when friends change and grow in different or opposing directions that the friendship may get lost along the way.

A Friend Indeed

What would life be without friends? Friendships define you as a person as much as your role as a parent, a child, and an employee. There are countless poems, stories, songs, movies, and novels about these special relationships. When they flourish, they have the power to brighten everything in our lives. When they die, they have the power to torment us.

Reinvento Observes

The ending of friendships is a natural phenomenon, and very much a part of life. It's a painful process for both people, no matter what the reason. It's important to allow yourself to feel the pain, understand it, and learn from it. Your current and future friendships might benefit from your understanding of a lost friendship.

Yet, no one can tell you what friendships should mean to you and how you should begin, repair, and end them. The answer is different for everyone. What is true for all friendships is that they deserve your time and attention—your friends deserve to be a priority in your life and you deserve to be one in theirs.

The Least You Need to Know

➤ Too many people today have actually substituted real friends with less-demanding television friends.

➤ If you've lost touch with friends because of other commitments, figure out a way to make time to put into your friends. Friendships require effort.

➤ If you don't put time into your friendships, you might find yourself needing someone and nobody will be there.

➤ Becoming a part of a new group with your friend might lead you to see a different side of your friend, or even of yourself.

➤ Your friends deserve to be a priority in your life and you deserve to be one in theirs.

Part 6

Reinventing Other Aspects of Your Life

I couldn't conclude this book without addressing your relationship with money. After all, money is a part of your life, maybe too little a part, and it's likely to continue to play a role for the rest of your life. Reinventing the financial aspect of your life may be a pressing issue!

Part 6 also focuses on discovering or rediscovering hobbies—you know, the things you used to do before life got so hectic. I also discuss charity. Whether you give your money or your time, it can transform your life. Finally, I'll close with a chapter on becoming the person you always wanted to be—a goal that is within your grasp. There is no reason why you, with your strengths and weaknesses, skills and capabilities, and all the other things that go into the unique individual you are, can't move from point A to your desired point B.

Chapter 24

Reinventing Your Relationship with Money

In This Chapter

➤ Understanding your values

➤ Setting monetary goals

➤ Learning to manage financial risks

➤ Checking on your insurance

Money is one of the most powerful forces in our lives; for some of us, it is the main force. In our capitalistic society, money represents power, pleasure, security, and status. But money also brings fear, guilt, insecurity, greed, and selfishness. Perhaps you have been haunted by these feelings.

Earning as You Learn

Jerry Bennett, my certified financial planner (CFP), is an author and lecturer as well as a highly respected financial counselor. He is president of the Bennett Financial Advisors, based in Fairfax, Virginia (reachable at 1-800-663-0717 and on the Web at www.bennett-financial.com). This chapter reflects Jerry's insights and advice on reinventing your relationship with money.

"Money is a paradox," Jerry says. "It enslaves, yet it frees; it is intensely private, yet very public; it measures worth, yet is not a measure of real worth; it destroys, yet it creates. If your standard of rich and poor is based on your ability to buy all that you want, then you will always be poor; for there is always something too expensive."

Your Money Autobiography

A challenging and crucial step in understanding both your behavior and the powerful feelings that money may invoke in you is writing a money autobiography. Even if you find a money autobiography difficult to write, reflecting on money and your life's journey with it will yield insight and a deepened awareness.

Here's a list of questions to help you get started. There's no need to answer them all, but do address those questions that seem to "pop out" at you. Keep in mind that it's vital to focus on your feelings and relationship to money as well as on your factual background with it.

Reinvento Observes

Reinventing your relationship with money requires self-awareness and self-knowledge of how you feel and relate to money.

Tip

Examine your thoughts, feelings, and behaviors that relate to money. As you discern the ways people earn, inherit, invest, spend, give, or waste money, often without conscious choice or a deliberate stance, you will be enabled to direct your own life more fully.

➤ What is your happiest childhood memory in connection with money?

➤ What is your unhappiest memory?

➤ What attitude did your mother have toward money?

➤ What attitude did your father have toward money?

➤ What was your attitude toward money as a child?

➤ Did you feel poor? Or rich?

➤ Did you worry about money?

➤ What was your attitude toward money as a teenager?

➤ What role did money play in your life as a young adult?

➤ What role did money play in your life as a parent?

➤ At age 45? 50? 65?

➤ Did your attitude or feelings shift at these different stages of your life?

➤ How do you feel about your present financial status?

➤ Are you generous or sparing with your money?

➤ Do you feel guilty about the money you have?

➤ Do you feel covetous about the money of others?

➤ Do you take risks with your money?

➤ Do you worry about money?

➤ Does having or not having money affect your self-esteem?

➤ When you eat with friends and there is a group check, are you the one to pick it up?

➤ Do you make sure that you pay your share and that it includes the tip?

➤ If you lacked money, how would you feel about others helping you to pay rent or mortgage, or treating you when you went out and you were not in a position to reciprocate?

➤ How has your approach to money and its use been shaped by being a woman or by being a man?

➤ How have your thoughts about money and your giving behavior been shaped or hindered by your faith?

➤ In what ways is your relationship to money a training ground for your spiritual journey, or an expression of your deepest values?

Your answers may surprise you! Perhaps something that you did not realize until now has emerged.

Putting Your Money Autobiography to Work

Writing your autobiography about money will probably reveal some patterns. It may also show a lack of continuity between the story you create and the life you want to lead. Are you following rules you've inherited from your parents? Are they in line with your goals and lifestyle? Have you set unrealistic goals for yourself? Where did these goals come from?

Learning About Money

You have many ways to broaden and develop your knowledge about money. Here are a few:

➤ Take a class on investing, money management, or personal finance. Check with your local college or adult extension service. Watch the newspaper for seminars.

➤ Read at least three books a year about money.

➤ Every day resolve to learn one new thing about money. Within a year you will be one of the most knowledgeable people in your community on the subject.

➤ Join an investment club, or start one.

Understanding Your Money Values

Understanding your values is not the first thing you normally think of when it comes to money. However, money is not an end in itself. It's a tool to help you achieve a particular goal or goals. If the way you handle money conflicts with your personal values, you're going to be frustrated, unhappy, and definitely unfulfilled.

So, ask yourself this question: What's important to me about money? Keep in mind that values—independence, freedom, security, enjoying family—are intangible and don't carry a price tag. Once you've identified your values, it's far easier to set goals.

How to Set Money Goals (or Goals for Anything Else!)

Write your goals down. Make your goal specific and measurable. For example, suppose one of your values is providing financial security for your family, and a supporting goal you've chosen is to accumulate $10,000 by the end of the year. Your goal statement might read, "By the end of December 31, 200X, I will accumulate $10,000 in cash." Next, make up a log or chart to track your progress and measure how well you're doing.

Tip

Make your goal challenging but achievable.

Consider a few things here: you want to start by making sure your goals are within the realm of possibility. And then you want to take steps to make sure that you really achieve them. The first thing to do is to take some sort of action within 48 hours. For example, if your goal is to buy a home in San Diego, you could start by calling the Chamber of Commerce in San Diego and getting the name of some real estate brokers there. You've taken action.

Sharing and Daring

Also, your goals will be more achievable if you share them with someone you trust. It's human nature to want to keep goals to yourself. You may be afraid of people not taking you seriously or of putting pressure on yourself to reach the goal. But if you talk about your goals, they'll start to become more real and people around you may be able to help you achieve them.

Make sure your goals align with your values. That's obviously very important, and that is why we started with values. Identify your top five goals and write them down. So, think about the progress you've already made—you've looked at your values and a goal system to make your values real.

A Financial Check-Up from the Neck Up

What are you really worth? Be honest with yourself. Do you know your net worth? Do you know where your money is? These may sound like obvious questions, but many people don't have a clear picture of their finances.

Determining Your Net Worth

Your net worth is simply everything you own minus everything you owe. Here is a simple form to help you get organized.

What You Own: Current Value

Liquid Assets

Checking accounts	$_____
Saving accounts	$_____
Money market funds	$_____
Cash value of life insurance	$_____
Other	$_____
Total Liquid Assets	*$_____*

Investment Assets

Stocks	$_____
Bonds	$_____
Mutual Funds	$_____
Certificates of deposit	$_____
Retirement plans	$_____
IRAs	$_____
401(k)	$_____
Pension plans	$_____
Other	$_____
Total Investment Assets	*$_____*

Personal Assets

Residence	$_____
Vacation Property	$_____
Jewelry	$_____
Art/Antiques	$_____
Other	$_____
Total Personal Assets	*$_____*

Total Assets (Liquid + Investment + Personal) = $_____

---

continues

257

continued

What You Owe (Liabilities)

Credit Card	$_____
Banks	$_____
Car Loans	$_____
Personal installment loans	$_____
Education loans	$_____
Mortgages	$_____
Other	$_____
Total Liabilities	$_____
Total Assets – Total Liabilities = Your Net Worth	$_____

Determining Your Cash Flow

Cash flow is also an easy term to grasp. Cash flow means all the cash you receive minus all the cash you spend. The accompanying Cash Flow Planner will help you determine your cash flow.

Cash Inflows

Wages, salary, commissions	$_____
Dividends and interest	$_____
Annuities, Social Security, pensions	$_____
Rents	$_____
Other	$_____
Total Cash Inflows	*$_____*

Cash Outflows

Housing	$_____
Food	$_____
Clothing	$_____
Transportation	$_____
Utilities	$_____
Taxes	$_____
Insurance	$_____
Education	$_____
Child care	$_____

Entertainment	$_____
Vacations/travel	$_____
Gifts/donations	$_____
Other	$_____
Total Cash Outflows	$_____
Total Cash Inflows – Total Cash Outflows = Net Cash Flow	$_____

Subtract your estimated cash outflows from your estimated annual cash inflows. If the result is a plus, you'll likely finish the year with money left over. If the result is a minus, you're spending more than your income and are headed for trouble.

Working to Become Debt Free

Make a list of every debt you have. Be specific about the amount, when it will be paid for, the interest rate, who the lender is, and the monthly payment. Take the debt with the highest interest rate and determine how much extra you can pay to achieve the payoff date. Make a chart if it helps to track your progress toward being *debt free*.

Once you've paid off the first debt, add that monthly payment amount to your second debt payment, and apply the total of both to the second debt. Once the second debt is paid, take the total of the payment amounts from the first two debts and add them to the payment of the third debt. You'll soon be paying your debts off faster and faster.

Word Power

To be **debt free** is to have no lingering short-term financial obligations and only those long-term obligations that support long-term asset investments, such as a mortgage loan for a home.

To Become Rich, Pay Yourself First

While it's fun to spend money, and it's often necessary, a dollar spent today is gone forever! Paying yourself first means paying yourself when you have the most money—before Uncle Sam takes his tax bite. Do you know how much actually comes out of your paycheck? Typically, it's 28 percent for federal taxes, then 5 to 6 percent for state taxes, then 7.65 percent for Social Security.

Tip

The first debt is the hardest to pay off, but your resolve and hard work will see you through. While you are becoming debt free, get in the habit of paying cash for everything.

259

The only way to pay yourself first (before taxes) is to take advantage of tax-deductible investments. A certified financial professional can give you the best advice based on the specifics of your situation.

Building a Million by Age 65 at 10 Percent

Age	Daily Savings	Yearly Savings
20	$4	$1,440.00
30	$11	$3,960.00
40	$30	$10,800.00
50	$95	$34,200.00

If you don't think you can save money every day, try the "coffee and donut-a-day" savings plan. Simply determine how much you'd save if you skipped that cup of coffee, donut, diet coke, or candy bar. Keep a log for one week to see how much money you can save.

For example, if you cut out expenses of seven dollars per day, that totals $210 per month, a substantial sum. If you invested that $210 over a period of 20 years, before taxes, at 10 percent interest, it would result in a total of $159,467.00!

Tax Deferred Earnings Add Up Quickly

The importance of tax deferral cannot be over-emphasized. Here's an example of $1,000 invested at 10 percent interest, with column A showing the effect of combined federal and state income of tax at 33 percent. Column B shows *compounding* without taxes.

Importance of Tax Deferral

Column A	Year	Column B
$1,383.00	5	$1,610.00
$1,912.00	10	$2,593.00
$2,645.00	15	$4,177.00
$3,658.00	20	$6,727.00
$5,059.00	25	$10,834.00
$6,997.00	30	$17,449.00

Accumulating your wealth before taxes is the way to go.

Managing the Financial Risks in Your Life

You need to protect yourself and your family from financial risks. Protecting them will also give you peace of mind to actively pursue the goals in your life. To protect yourself you need to have a cash reserve for emergencies and unplanned contingencies, to have the proper legal documents in place, and to make sure that you are properly insured.

Have a cash reserve of 3 to 24 months' worth of expenses set aside for emergencies. Where you fall in that range depends on how long you think it would take you to get a new job if you lost yours.

Word Power

Compounding is the arithmetic increase in funds as time passes as a result of accumulating interest paid by the institutions with whom you have invested money.

If you think you could easily get a new job within three months, your reserve should be three months' worth of expenses. If it would take longer, your reserve should be bigger.

Caution

Where you keep your reserve should be a key focus when planning. Don't make the mistake of keeping your money in a low-interest checking account. If you don't know what your checking account is paying, call and find out. If you've got an account that's paying 0 to 1 percent, consider putting the money into a money market account, which works very much like a checking account and which is currently earning 4 to 5 percent.

Wills and Trusts

You need to have a will or living trust to protect your family in case of your death. A living trust is basically a legal document that accomplishes two things. It enables you to transfer ownership of any of your assets to a trust while you are still alive, and it designates who should be given those assets after you die. You definitely need to speak with a qualified financial counselor to set these up.

Reinvento Observes

The main advantage of a living trust over a will is that with a living trust your assets won't have to go through probate (a legal proceeding to determine how your assets should be allocated to your heirs), which can save your family thousands of dollars in attorneys fees and enable you to maintain your estate's privacy. Once an estate goes through probate, all details become a matter of public record.

Make sure your will or trust is up to date. If you haven't had it updated in the last five years, it's probably out of date. Also …

➤ Make sure beneficiaries are up to date and accurate, especially if you're in a second marriage.

➤ Make sure your family knows where your will or trust is located. This seems obvious, but many times it's in a safety deposit box or safe. If it's in a safety deposit box and your family doesn't know where the key is, it could take three months and a court order to get it out.

Caution

In most states, no adult, not even spouses, can make medical decisions for another person without the healthcare power of attorney. As a practical matter, your physician may listen to your next of kin, but why take the chance?

Healthcare Power of Attorney

The healthcare power of attorney—also known as the medical power of attorney, healthcare proxy, and durable healthcare power of attorney—is a special kind of power of attorney activated only in the event of your incapacity or incompetence. The power requires hospitals, nursing homes, doctors, and other healthcare providers to obey your designated agent's decisions as if they were yours.

The healthcare power of attorney must include the word "durable," as in "durable power of attorney." Note that powers terminate in the event you become incompetent unless they include the word "durable."

Durable Power of Attorney

Once a person becomes legally incompetent, the only way to arrange for the management of that person's property is to follow a court proceeding to have a conservator or guardian appointed. This is often a time-consuming and expensive procedure and may be very unpleasant for the heirs. A more effective and simpler alternative is to have the individual prepare a durable power of attorney.

A guardianship is likely to be more expensive than a durable power of attorney. And because a durable power of attorney contains the magic word "durable," it does not terminate if you become unable to communicate or are otherwise incapacitated. However, it does terminate on your death.

Living Will

The person named in your healthcare proxy becomes involved if you are unable, even temporarily, to make a healthcare decision. The person named in your living will becomes involved only if you are near death.

A living will is an advance directive that describes your end-of-life wishes concerning life-sustaining medical treatment and procedures in the event you become incompetent or unconscious. The living will enables you to describe the physical conditions that trigger the document's provisions, as well as the types of treatments and/or procedures to be avoided.

It is highly recommended that you seek legal counsel for drafting the above-mentioned legal documents.

Making Sure You Have Proper Insurance

If someone depends on you for income, then you probably need life insurance. Also, if you have a large estate, life insurance is an excellent way to pay estate taxes at your death. What else might you need?

Caution

Often when the court appoints a guardian, it is an attorney who has an idea about how you would want your life managed. The guardian may end up just paying bills, rather than making appropriate decisions that might incur liability. In addition, a court-appointed guardian requires compensation from your estate, adding another cost.

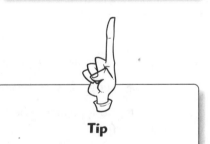

Tip

A living will becomes effective only as the final statement of intent when the person who executed it is unable to make or express his or her own decisions concerning medical care.

➤ **Disability insurance.** This insurance provides income in the event you are unable to work due to an accident or sickness. This coverage, while available individually, is often offered through employers on a group basis.

➤ **Health insurance.** You absolutely need to have it. You have choices between an HMO and a PPO, and the pros and cons vary among individual plans. Take the time to research it and spend a few extra dollars a month for a better policy, if you need to.

➤ **Long-term-care insurance.** This covers at-home nursing care or nursing home costs. The cost of long-term care can be $30,000 to $70,000 a year. If you're over 55, you should take a look at it.

Letting Your Dream Be Your Guide

"Everyone has dreams of doing certain things if only they had the money," says Jerry Bennett. "What are your dreams? It can be anything from retiring early to traveling to Hawaii. Stop for a few minutes and visualize your dreams, and then write them down."

"Once you've written them down, decide how much money it will take to make the dreams turn into a reality. Remember these are your dreams, so you can decide just how much you can save now. The great thing about saving for goals is that it makes saving exciting. It will motivate you."

Use Jerry's principles described in this chapter to reinvent your relationship with money. See if you aren't a happier and wealthier person!

The Least You Need to Know

➤ Learning more about money could be the key to making more of it.

➤ Set goals as to how much money you want to make, and try to achieve them.

➤ Do a financial check up, which includes determining your net worth and cash flow.

➤ Try to eliminate your debt. Pay off the loan with the highest interest rate first.

➤ Get qualified professional assistance in preparing wills and trusts.

➤ Make sure you have the right life, disability, health, and long-term-care insurance.

➤ Let your dreams be your guide.

Chapter 25

Discovering or Rediscovering Hobbies

In This Chapter

➤ Remembering the way things used to be

➤ Hobbies old and new

➤ Trial and error works

➤ Exploring the options

Remember those days as a kid when you had a hobby or two, like building model airplanes, playing with dolls, collecting stamps, drawing pictures, or building little gadgets out of scraps from the tool shed? Having a hobby is a bond common to nearly all children and is part of the world they create—a world where the rules are their own (and where words like "productivity" and "efficiency" do not exist!).

Kids at Heart

In a manner of speaking, we are all children, and we all have a desire to go out and simply play.

My nephew, Jimmy, started a coin collection last year—not anything particularly grand or extensive. It started when he found some old pennies lying around the house and asked if they might be worth anything. In 12 months, Jimmy has accumulated coins from all over the world. Probably none are worth more than their current face value, but it's amazing to see the smile that comes to his face when someone brings him a new coin for his collection.

Reinvento Observes

There is no reason that each of us cannot rediscover that child latent within our hearts, bringing him or her back to the surface to simply "play" again.

Reinvento Observes

Possibly the greatest lesson that we can learn from children is how to be children ourselves. It has always been customary that the young learn from the old, but why can't the old learn from the young?

Jimmy has devised his own cataloging system (which only he understands!). He's also researched the background and value of some of the coins on the Internet. More important, when Jimmy is "working" on his coin collection, he hasn't a care in the world. You could talk to him for 20 minutes and he wouldn't hear a word you said. He is in another sphere entirely, where he is the top coin collector and where no one can interfere with that.

Taking Your Cue

We can learn a lot from children, the ways that they occupy themselves, and the ways that they find such happiness in activities that to an observer don't seem like much.

In fact, why can't our children teach us? This is not to say that we must become children again in a literal way, forsaking our responsibilities and obligations. It simply means that we can benefit, both physically and mentally, from rediscovering those pastimes that we once held as children. We can even rediscover childhood pleasures and give them an adult twist.

The Play's the Thing

It can be amazing to observe how much people change when there is no pressure on them to perform, no pressure to be the best, and no expectations to fulfill. They invariably become happier, freer. So, what hobbies can you discover or *rediscover?*

Let Me Count the Ways

Doctors can alleviate stress with strong medication, but playing with the fervor that you did as a child can offer satisfaction and relief no drug could provide. Let's examine a number of benefits that hobbies offer.

A Diversion from Daily Routines

Do you get so caught up in the endless routine of work, commuting, and family that you seemingly have no opportunity for anything else? Having a hobby is a nice diversion to the stresses often associated with a daily routine.

The hobby can extend beyond diversion, however, offering you a chance to create a world entirely your own, at least for a few minutes at a time.

New Social Opportunities

Suppose you always wanted to learn to ride a motorcycle, and in doing so you join a local motor club. This type of interaction will be with people who share your passion and may be individuals with whom you thought you had nothing in common.

Maybe cultivating a new hobby will spark an old friendship, or give you and your friend something new to do outside of your daily interactions.

Reinvento Observes

Peter Berger, a renowned sociological theorist, argues that play is one way people escape, or "transcend," the mundane world and find some kind of order in the chaos that the world can present.

Health Benefits

Hobbies can potentially offer both physical and mental health benefits. If you've always wanted to learn the art of mountain biking, but never "found the time," by giving yourself the opportunity to learn, and by cultivating that skill, you'll be having fun and getting exercise at once! Isn't that what everyone seeks in an exercise program—exercise and fun at the same time?

Your newfound hobby may require great patience and concentration, as when learning to sail, but this is a *benign* mental exercise, and not the kind that gives you a headache at the end of the day.

Word Power

If something is **benign,** it is good for you, or at least not harmful.

Straight from His Holiness

In contemplating a new hobby or pastime, consider the teaching of His Holiness, the Dalai Lama, spiritual and political leader of Tibet. In his book *The Art of Happiness,* he says that with any decision you face in life, ask yourself one important question: "Will this bring me pleasure, or will this bring me happiness?" He advocates that you make decisions not based on what will bring you pleasure, but on what will bring you happiness (in which pleasure could be a component).

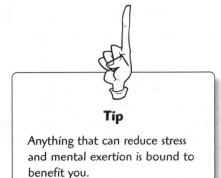

Tip

Anything that can reduce stress and mental exertion is bound to benefit you.

According to the Dalai Lama, things that bring you pleasure will eventually bring you displeasure because eventually they will end. Decisions based on what will bring you happiness will, if they truly make you happy, last indefinitely.

We may change jobs several times, have several cars, or live in several different houses, but eventually we lose all that "stuff." When lying on your deathbed will you be able to say, "I had pleasure" or "I am happy"?

Caution

Most of the time, we face decisions as to what will yield temporary pleasure—what clothes to buy, which car to own, what kind of house to live in, and so on. These eventually get old and fade away.

Reinvento Observes

As you reinvent yourself through a hobby, if only in a small way, engage in something that will bring you happiness, not just temporary pleasure. In the end, happiness is all you really have.

What Are My Hobby Options?

As with so many avenues of inquiry in the Internet Age, you have resources for learning about a hobby. If you're not Internet savvy, call a local hobby shop, or look in your local newspaper for announcements about club meetings or classes relating to your hobby.

Here's a brief summary of a handful of the hundreds of hobbies and pastimes that you may find to be *more* than worthwhile!

Learning to Play an Instrument

Can you teach an old dog new tricks? You may need a little more patience and a little more time than you did as a child, but anyone can learn to play an instrument. Learning to play doesn't require special knowledge. All of that comes in time.

Not all good musicians are child *prodigies*. You'd be surprised how many professional musicians didn't begin playing their instrument until they were far beyond childhood.

Once you learn how to play an instrument, you'll better appreciate the music you hear on the radio because you'll understand the effort required to produce it. Also, having learned to play, think of how great it will be to come home after a long day at work, sit on your couch, and pick up your guitar, or sit at your piano and get lost in the power of music. It is a power that can move your soul and make your heart leap for joy.

Sculpting

When Michelangelo finished his sculpture *David,* imagine the immense pride he must have felt for having made something so beautiful. While you don't have to be Michelangelo to be a good sculptor, creating something "out of nothing" can offer endless benefits. You become the designer and the creator. You unleash your artistic talents and passion in a way that you haven't been able to express before.

Word Power

A **prodigy** is genius, a wizard, a master at something.

You can learn to sculpt in two basic ways. You can teach yourself by picking up some basic equipment and experimenting. Eventually you'll find your own style.

Or, you can seek out local sculptors who might be willing to give lessons. Ask around, visit exhibits, make some calls and see what you can find! Great discoveries await!

Painting

A friend told me that she liked nothing better than to sit with a paintbrush in her hand, not to create grandeur, but simply to "doodle" on canvas. The finished product was always masterful, especially for just a "doodle." She had never taken formal lessons or read any books on how to paint. She simply painted!

Tip

Fortunately, there are many ways that you can learn to play an instrument, and many teachers who want to help you to feel the inspiration they do while playing. Visit your local music store and ask about area teachers. If no one offers lessons on how to play your instrument, look for instructional manuals or videos that might help you learn.

Painting was her chance to sit and do something enjoyable—free of television, the Internet, the noise of the world. She easily could have taken classes at the local arts center, or the community college, but she chose to teach herself. You can also do either.

Allow yourself the time to play around with your painting and you'll find yourself more relaxed and less stressed.

Photography

Nearly everyone likes to take and keep photographs, but often it seems that pictures don't do our memories justice. By learning how to take great shots, you can "immortalize" your memories.

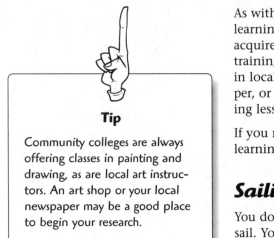

As with the other pastimes discussed in this chapter, learning how to take good photos is a skill anyone can acquire; you simply need enough practice or the right training. Finding a teacher will be the hard part. Look in local college catalogs, the Yellow Pages, the newspaper, or listings at the local arts center for people offering lessons in photography.

If you really want to take good pictures, the process of learning will be fun.

Sailing

You don't have to be a nautical genius to learn how to sail. You just have to have a passion for the open sea. The rest you can learn. Many people out there can help you, and you can use resources to make the dream a reality. At SailNet.com (www.sailnet.com), you can learn anything you ever wanted to know about sailing, as well as find ways to learn in your part of the country. In addition to SailNet, many sailing associations and clubs offer people the chance to learn how to sail, as well as a way to contact other enthusiasts with your same passion.

Another sailing Web site is www.ussailing.com.

Aviation

Wilbur and Orville Wright once had a dream to fly. After several failed attempts, they discovered a way to make their dream a reality, and the powered airplane was born. Today, aviators from all corners of the globe who love the open air are thankful for the opportunity to see the world from a different perspective.

You, too, can make this dream a reality. Learning to fly can be expensive. Visit a local municipal airport or research any local aviation clubs that might offer lessons. Also seek out *The Complete Idiot's Guide to Flying and Gliding,* which offers good tips on getting started. When you've mastered the art of flight, your view of the world and of life changes.

Motoring

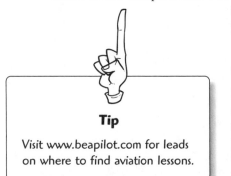

Driving is something that you may have to do everyday, and may often dread. Motoring—hitting the open road, and seeing where it takes you—is a different experience altogether. Whether your passion is antique cars, hot rods, or motorcycles, millions of miles of open road await you.

Once again, there are many organizations, clubs, and associations of people who share your passion, and finding them is easy. Start with these resources:

➤ **American Motorcyclist Association:** www.ama-cycle.org

➤ **10%er Brotherhood:** www.10percenterbrotherhood.com

➤ **Antique Automobile Club of America:** www.aaca.org

Sewing

What type of sewing do you want to learn? Quilting, cross-stitch, crochet, or clothing creation? Check at your local fabric store or quilting shop to see if they offer classes. If not, find a class via the Web (starting perhaps at www.sostre.com) or a book, to teach yourself.

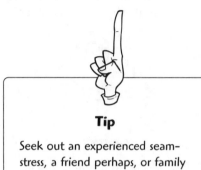

Tip

Seek out an experienced seamstress, a friend perhaps, or family member who can help. To help you get started, visit www.sewing.com.

Gardening

Beginning your own garden can be a terrific diversion from your daily routine! Gardening offers a chance to cultivate and nurture something, and a way to beautify and decorate your home in a relatively simple way.

Whether you decide to grow flowers around your house or plant an indoor herb garden, the hobby is a simple one, requiring only a few seeds, good soil, some good sunlight, a bit of water, a little time, and a lot of patience. The results can be quite fulfilling, and even delicious (garden vegetables always taste better than store-bought ones!).

Many Web sites and books offer advice on beginning your own garden, and the local plant shop will most likely have information on how to better care for the plants in your garden. Here are two Web resources:

➤ **Self Sufficient Gardening:** www.poplaracre.com

➤ **Indoor Herb Gardening:** www.herbgardening.com

Cooking

Cooking is an art form, although your creation doesn't last long (at least that's what every cook hopes for). Mastering the art requires balancing a delicate combination of ingredients and spices. Learning to cook is not so hard, despite the lamentations of novices.

If you would like to learn to cook or to cook better, there are thousands of books that can help you. Besides learning from books, a cooking class, or one-on-one with a

271

veteran cook, the best learning method is trial-and-error. Through this method you learn to cultivate your own styles and techniques. If you mess up, try again. When you succeed, enjoy it!

Carpentry and Renovation

Whether you're seeking to redecorate your house, build a new deck, or finish that project you started last year, you need a good plan and the time to accomplish your goal. There are many resources on how to begin and execute home projects, but if you have a good plan and know what you want to do, half the battle is already won. Here are a few sites worth visiting:

Caution

One of the worst feelings is that a project will never get done. Set your sites realistically on what you want to do, and the amount of time it will take to finish.

➤ **Hometime How-to-Projects:** www.hometime.com/projects/howto/

➤ **Aquarium Construction:** www.homearts.com/depts/pastime/

➤ **Tree House Construction:** www.guest. btinternet.com/~fulton/choosing.htm

Work slowly and patiently toward each goal. Eventually, the work will get done and you can appreciate your creation.

Hobbies and Renewal

Any way you cut it, hobbies offer wonderful opportunities for relaxation, fun, renewal, and reinvention. Why not rediscover one of your old hobbies or find a new one that is sustaining and rewarding?

The Least You Need to Know

➤ We are all kids at heart and often need to rediscover favorite pastimes.

➤ Hobbies can offer stress relief that is superior to any medication.

➤ With the advent of the Internet, finding supporting resources has never been easier.

➤ Seek long-term happiness over fleeting pleasures.

➤ The options for hobbies are endless, such as music, art, sailing, and carpentry. It's just a matter of finding what you enjoy.

Chapter 26

Reinventing Yourself Through Civic Participation

In This Chapter

➤ Following your path

➤ Serving others

➤ Donating money and other goods and services

➤ Local, regional, and national activism

A report by the National Commission on Civic Renewal found that, "Too many Americans are passive and disengaged ... In a time that cries out for civic action, we are in danger of becoming a nation of spectators." Too many feel powerless and they lament, "What can we do?" Too many look to others to resolve the country's social issues.

As the ever-increasing, high-paced culture of the American (and now globalizing) work force proceeds into the future, more people are seeking new paths toward fulfillment and happiness, as well as new ways to channel their energies.

Fulfillment Is a Do-It-Yourself Proposition

Some say that society has become too *pluralist* and chaotic to presume that government or institutions can effectively fill the gap for citizens between feeling fulfilled and feeling empty (if they ever could!). To find meaning and purpose in life, you have to find them by yourself and within yourself.

What do you seek? What do you think will make you happy? Most important, what will you do, as Captain Jean Luc Picard of *Star Trek* says, to "make it so"?

Something More, Something Better

Undoubtedly, you've had feelings intermittently, if not continually, that you need to be doing something more, something better, something for yourself, or maybe something for the rest of humanity.

Don't worry about what others may say, think, or do in response to the path you've chosen to follow, provided it is lawful and would not destroy society if everyone decided to follow it (a neat viewpoint my mother gave me!). It's your path, and, when all is said and done, you'll have the satisfaction of finding what you were seeking or perhaps the satisfaction of having given the attempt your best efforts.

Your path may come from serving others in your community, perhaps in a variety of capacities. If so, the remainder of this chapter will be of help to you.

Volunteering

Volunteering to help charitable organizations could hold vast potential for being a "win-win" situation for both you and those to whom you are giving your time.

According to the American Red Cross, on the Web at www.redcross.org, volunteering offers you the following benefits:

➤ Satisfaction and fulfillment in helping others

➤ The chance to travel to interesting places

➤ The opportunity to meet diverse groups of people

➤ The opportunity to socialize and network with fellow volunteers

➤ The chance to work according to your own schedule

➤ The opportunity to gain new training in unfamiliar fields

➤ The chance to gain new leadership opportunities

While these potentially positive benefits can all be valid incentives for volunteering, the most important benefit, and the one volunteers must not lose sight of, is the positive effect they will have on their communities, states, and country.

Adopting a Charitable Organization

Local, regional, and national charitable organizations are *always* looking for new help. For many organizations, volunteers are the lifeblood that keep them up and running.

Suppose you like animals and you volunteer to help out a few hours a week at the local chapter of the Society for the Prevention of Cruelty to Animals (SPCA). Although it may not seem like much to offer your time doing some clerical work, and perhaps no one even acknowledges your contribution, your efforts help keep that chapter running. Hence, they can continue to rescue and care for animals.

Caution

Without volunteers, most charitable and nonprofit organizations would crumble and disappear.

No One Loses

When you volunteer to help an organization, large or small, no one loses even if you have only a few hours a month to offer. Your time, energy, and experience usually are graciously accepted. Invariably, you feel good about yourself and the contribution that you're making. You also *demonstrate to yourself* that you are in control of your life—not every second is taken up by routine. You have the ability to carve out the space and time to help others. You'll gain a measure of happiness from doing so.

The charitable organization, as a result of your contribution, comes one step closer to reaching its goal, or perhaps merely keeps its doors open for another day. In any case, the result is highly positive.

Let Me Count the Opportunities

Regardless of where you live and what interests you, there are thousands of organizations to which you can offer your time and services. Whether it's volunteering at the animal shelter—feeding the animals or cleaning cages—or participating on a letter-writing campaign to stop the destruction of our national forests, you have only to identify your interests and then match them with the work done by a plethora of organizations.

Getting United with United Way

A good place to start locally is the United Way, listed in the white pages of your local phone book. United Way offices maintain rosters of all the social, civic, and charitable groups in the area and what each group is seeking in terms of volunteer help. In as little as 30 minutes, you can determine what might work best for you.

Each organization publishes its own literature, and virtually all have a Web site that spells out the organization's mission, objectives, and programs. If the objectives of a particular organization match your own, contact that organization and find out in what capacity they could use your help.

Paying a Visit

If you think that the work may be the right kind for you and your schedule, then take the next step and visit the organization and actually schedule an initial time to volunteer.

With so many worthy organizations and so many volunteer possibilities, we can only cover a smattering here, but such summaries may spur your thinking, lead you to further exploration, and ultimately be the catalyst for your connecting with the group that is right for you.

Reinvento Observes

Studies show that children paired with mentors are more confident in their school work and personal life, and that they get along better with their family, friends, and peers. How's that for making an impact?

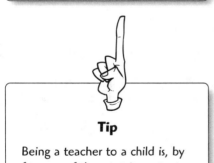

Tip

Being a teacher to a child is, by far, one of the most important jobs in the world. The great part in doing this is that you can have so much fun!

Being a Mentor

According to the Office of Research at the U.S. Department of Education, mentoring is defined as "a sustained relationship between a youth and an adult … Through a continued involvement, the adult offers support, guidance, and assistance as the younger person goes through a difficult period, faces new challenges, or works to correct earlier problems."

We've already discussed the role mentors can play in helping you along in your career (see Chapter 15, "All the Right Moves"). Another type of mentor, as discussed here, can play a crucial role in child development where parents are either unavailable or unable to be of much help. Practically speaking, adults are paired with children from the local community who need a role model, someone from whom he or she can learn, talk to, and consider a friend.

Mentoring programs have had a dramatic impact in decreasing the likelihood that a child will turn to illegal drugs or alcohol, skip school, and engage in violence as a means to resolve conflict. The adult who mentors is offered the opportunity to play a lead role in children's lives: teaching them, giving them support, and educating and guiding them through a sometimes cold and uncaring world.

Mentoring Options

There are many different ways to serve as a mentor to a child. With approval from his or her parent(s), you can simply befriend a local neighborhood child. You might take this child out to a ballgame, to the theater, or to a ballet. Perhaps you tutor the child, helping with schoolwork or simply listening to the child's view of the world.

You may want to get involved with a more structured program such as Big Brothers, Big Sisters, on the Web at www.bbbs.org. Started more than 90 years ago, this program offers children the chance to experience things that they may otherwise never get to do. Mentors are expected to meet with their "little brothers or sisters" a few times a month. When mentors meet with their brother or sister, the agenda is to be determined by the participants.

You might opt for the position of "Scout Leader" or "Troop Leader" in an organization such as the Boy Scouts (www.bsa.scouting.org) or Girl Scouts (www.gsusa.org). Being a mentor to children in such groups emphasizes learning in a different way, be it through a service project in the local community or hiking down a trail.

Reinvento Observes

No matter how you choose to be involved with a child, you have the potential to make a positive impact on the child's life, your life, and the whole community.

Local, Regional, and National Activism

Activists will tell you that working for change on any social issue is a wonderful way to invest your time and energy, and a great way to find new meaning and happiness in your life. Many different organizations fight for social, economic, and environmental change, but sometimes, as with other forms of civic and social participation, it can be difficult to find one for whom you want to work.

Besides selecting what group to work with, you have additional decisions regarding what kind of support you wish to offer, be it through letter-writing campaigns, petitioning, marching, participating in public forums, or even running for office.

Picking Your Fight

What you are actively fighting for will be determined by what you find most important to you. Getting involved is the easy part, because activists

Reinvento Observes

Taking up a social cause on top of your other responsibilities in life can prove difficult and strain you mentally, physically, and emotionally. However, such efforts can also prove to be some of the most rewarding and inspiring work that you will ever do.

are *always* looking for more support. In return, you'll find that activism can be inspiring and a great alternative to the stress and "hum-drum" of daily life. It can definitely be a major step toward reinvention. Here are some notable groups:

➤ **Greenpeace** (www.greenpeace.org), often regarded as a radically active environmental group, works to publicize environmental concerns such as global warming, food toxins, oil drilling, and whaling. Greenpeace is known for taking direct action against companies that harm the environment—for example, by forming "human chains" on logging roads and in front of oil barges and large fishing boats.

➤ **The Sierra Club** (www.sierraclub.org) and the National Wildlife Federation (www. nwf.org) are politically oriented environmental groups that organize petitioning and letter-writing campaigns. These groups offer many ways to get involved if you're on a limited schedule or simply not inclined to confrontative action.

➤ **The National Coalition Against Domestic Violence** (www.ncadv.org) is an organization that fights for better legislation against domestic abusers and stalkers.

➤ **The Survivors and Victims of Tobacco Empowerment Project** (SAVE) (www. tobaccosurvivors.org) is one of the first comprehensive, ongoing, programs in the nation to serve those affected by the number one preventable cause of death—tobacco.

International Volunteering

Do you want to see the world while donating your time and energy to the betterment of humanity? If so, many organizations offer short-term (one to three weeks), medium-term (one to six months), and long-term (six months to several years) volunteer opportunities. Such organizations range from the Sisters of Charity to the Peace Corps. Many benefits come from doing international volunteering and there are many ways to go about it.

Caution

Working internationally requires you to make more of a commitment to a particular organization and its goals. You may need to learn another language or another way of living. Consequently, this type of service is not meant for everyone.

Decisions, Decisions

Among the many factors to consider when deciding to volunteer internationally is where you want to go. This will help determine what type of organization you choose, the sort of work you'll do, and how much time and money you'll have to commit.

The philosophy and goals of an organization, obviously, as well as types of people with whom you will be working, will vary greatly depending on the organization's orientation.

Would you like to participate with a secular or religiously affiliated organization? Here is a resource list for both religious and secular organizations:

➤ **Catholic Network of Volunteer Service:** 212-529-1100, www.cnvs.org

➤ **Transitions Abroad:** 1-800-293-0373, www.transitionsabroad.com

➤ **Visions in Action:** 202-625-2353, www.visionsinaction.org

➤ **U.S. Peace Corps:** 1-800-424-8580, www.peacecorps.gov

Donating Money and Material Goods

If volunteering your time doesn't fit into your schedule, there are many other ways to give to and get involved with charitable organizations, and to find new meaning in your life through them. According to *Consumer Reports,* in 1999, "giving by individuals topped $130 billion, accounting for some 87 percent of all contributions nonprofit organizations received." Making informed and responsible donations of money and other goods to charitable organizations is an act of giving not to be discounted!

With so many organizations to which you can give money, it's important to plan your giving:

➤ To whom will you give?

➤ How much will you give?

➤ How often will you give?

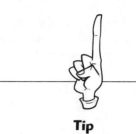

Tip

Some religious groups do not place any emphasis on evangelization. Some even discourage anything of that sort, focusing entirely on the needs of the people being served and not on their religious preferences.

Reinvento Observes

By planning your donation, it becomes a personal project to which you can responsibly devote some time and energy and, in that sense, it can offer a welcome diversion to the daily tribulations of life.

Donating your money, or even clothing or appliances, to charitable organizations will not only make you feel better about yourself and your investments, but is a practical way to help keep these good organizations in business.

Checking Your Budget

When giving money to organizations, decide how much of your budget you're willing to devote. Also, avoid spreading your donations too thin—decide on a small number of organizations to which you will make larger donations, rather than a large number of organizations to which you will make small donations. This makes life easier for you and offers a greater measure of assistance to the recipients.

Consolidating a significant portion of your giving among fewer groups also makes your gift more cost-effective for the recipient to administer, increasing its impact.

Y'all Come Back Now

After you make your donation, follow it—see how the organization progresses and try to determine if it is using your money effectively. Since most organizations must publish profuse data on their financial transactions, having them "show you the money" is not difficult.

If you've decided that a particular organization merits your continued donations, stay with it over the long-term, if you can.

Spotting the Winners

To help distinguish among organizations and potentially spot those who are not making good use of your money, get in touch with one or both of the following:

National Charities Information
19 Union Square West
New York, NY 10003

American Institute of Philanthropy
4905 DelRay Ave., Suite 300
Bethesda, MD 20814

Also visit the Nonprofit Locator on the Web at www.nonprofits.org.

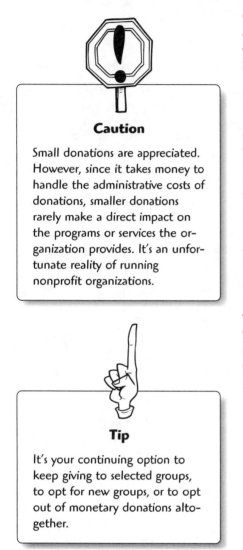

Caution

Small donations are appreciated. However, since it takes money to handle the administrative costs of donations, smaller donations rarely make a direct impact on the programs or services the organization provides. It's an unfortunate reality of running nonprofit organizations.

Tip

It's your continuing option to keep giving to selected groups, to opt for new groups, or to opt out of monetary donations altogether.

Socially Responsible Investing

Are you looking for a profitable investment and also one that meets certain moral criteria so that you can sleep better at night? Welcome to the world of *socially responsible investing*.

Socially responsible investing might not seem like a substantial way to "reinvent" yourself, but many people take great comfort in investing money both wisely and in tune with their moral convictions.

Looking Before You Leap

Socially responsible investing requires that you undertake in-depth research. Decide on your socially oriented priorities and how closely you want companies to conform to these standards. Such investigation will tell you how closely you may need to screen companies' practices.

Next, decide how much money you're willing to invest. As with any investment, you're assuming a certain amount of risk. Some of the companies that you regard as worthy investments may be smaller, newer companies and hence carry higher risk, but the investment may well be worth it in the end!

Here are some companies and Web sites that can help you identify socially responsible investments:

➤ **Calvert Group:** www.calvertgroup.com

➤ **Citizens Fund:** www.citizensfunds.com

➤ **Domini Social Investments:** www.domini.com

Word Power

Socially responsible investing is when you apply your beliefs and values to how you invest your money.

Tip

Many investment firms can help you with socially responsible investing and there are a number of mutual funds designed specifically to meet the needs of socially responsible investors.

Investing your money according to certain social and moral standards potentially benefits your finances and serves as a viable, if indirect, support system for your social interests and the community at large.

The paths to reinventing yourself discussed in this chapter are but suggestions, which may or may not be of help to you in discovering your own path. Listen to your heart and follow what it tells you. Ultimately, you know, better than anyone else, what is best for you.

The Least You Need to Know

➤ Giving to others makes you feel better about yourself, and aids in your personal reinvention.

➤ Volunteering, including mentoring, is rewarding for all participants.

➤ Donating money rather than time is another appropriate form of participation.

➤ Socially responsible investing is when you apply your beliefs and values to how you invest your money.

➤ Opportunities abound to act locally, regionally, nationally, or globally.

Chapter 27

The Person You've Always Wanted to Be

In this chapter, we'll explore some alternative insights on reinventing your life, such as drawing upon your emotional intelligence, having mission or vision, offering forgiveness, and accepting the immutable.

Another Kind of Intelligence

In his breakthrough book, *Emotional Intelligence,* Daniel Goleman, Ph.D., says that emotional intelligence reflects "the functioning of your emotional brain, the part that generates and regulates feeling and fear, mood and anger." Goleman regards emotional intelligence as being made up of five closely related factors:

➤ **Self-awareness.** Feelings have a major influence on all our decisions.

➤ **Mood management.** Depression, anxiety, and anger interfere with working memory, your brain's ability to integrate facts and ideas.

➤ **Motivation.** This is the ability to maintain hope and optimism.

➤ **Empathy.** Sensitivity to other people's feelings is key to understanding their needs and modifying your behavior.

➤ **Social skill.** This is the ability to deal with the emotions of others, to harmonize, and to persuade and lead.

As you become more aware of the range of feelings and sensations that you have, your ability to manage your attitude increases markedly. Goleman suggests ways of increasing your emotional intelligence to have more control in every aspect of your life:

Reinvento Observes

A woman got on an elevator and noticed she was standing next to actor Tom Hanks. "What's it like living at the absolute top of the heap?" she asked him. He replied that life is just one darn thing after another, no matter where you're living.

➤ Make a habit of self-awareness. More times throughout the day, check in on yourself and try to notice how you're feeling. Use these moments as mini assessments. As simple as it seems, many people don't do this even once a month. They simply feel what they feel, as if there were no option for having any other type of experience.

➤ Learn skills to calm anxious feelings. Having come this far in the book, you've gotten a boatload of these skills in your arsenal to get you started. If you're fearful or feeling blue, draw upon your skills to motivate yourself and lift your spirits.

➤ Fine-tune your empathy by discussing your spouse's or close friend's feelings. This makes practical sense—your life is made up of many people, and focusing your attention on someone other than yourself (as important as you are) can give you great perspective.

➤ Improve specific social skills. Goleman suggests heightening harmony in your domestic life by listening and speaking to others nondefensively. My book *The Complete Idiot's Guide to Assertiveness* (Alpha Books) offers considerable assistance in this area.

➤ Increase motivation by nurturing happiness: When your confidence dips, set a new goal immediately.

Mission: Possible: Focusing on Goals Can Keep You Chipper

Martin Edelston, publisher of *Bottom Line/Personal,* makes the observation that if you really want to be candid about your life, then three facets are worth dwelling upon:

➤ Where you happen to be

➤ Where you choose to be

➤ How you plan to get there

Caution

Failure to self-reflect and control one's emotional intelligence factors could be a hazard faced by young achievers. Researchers at the University of Cape Breton in Nova Scotia found that among 162 presidents and prime ministers, those who took office at an earlier age in life died an average of nine years earlier than those who took office at a later age. The same held true for Nobel Prize winners, Supreme Court Justices, and popes.

As we discussed in Chapter 3, "Assessing Where You Are," assessing where you choose to be, and determining how you plan to get there can help you to start working toward reinventing your life. Think about goal-driven, mission-oriented people you know. Sure, they hit stumbling blocks similar to the rest of us and their efforts are hindered at times. Instead of giving up, though, they switch gears and find another way to proceed, relentlessly pursuing their goals. More often than not, they feel a sense of pride in their accomplishments because they didn't allow circumstances to deter them from their chosen path.

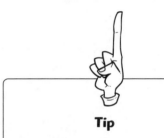

Tip

Sit down alone to create a vision for yourself, of yourself, in the next year, 5 years, and 10 years. You don't have to map out your life to the minute; simply chart an overall course for yourself. When you're feeling stressed, confounded, or disheartened, refer to your goals and get back on track.

... Grant Me the Serenity

No matter how hard you may wish or try, some situations are unavoidable and unchangeable. Instead of getting down about something that is out of your hands, change your attitude about that situation. For example, if your morning commute is characterized by bumper-to-bumper traffic and shaking fists, why not use that time for reflection rather than reaction?

Instead of getting frustrated about your slow pace, organize your thoughts before you reach the office. You can't make the traffic disappear, but you can turn an otherwise trying situation on its head and use it to your advantage.

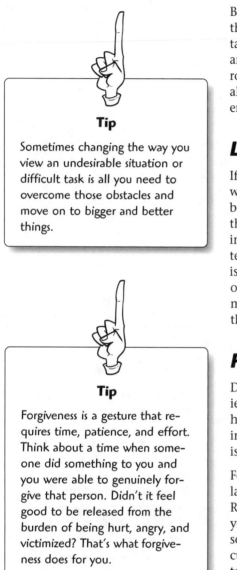

Tip

Sometimes changing the way you view an undesirable situation or difficult task is all you need to overcome those obstacles and move on to bigger and better things.

Tip

Forgiveness is a gesture that requires time, patience, and effort. Think about a time when someone did something to you and you were able to genuinely forgive that person. Didn't it feel good to be released from the burden of being hurt, angry, and victimized? That's what forgiveness does for you.

By making the conscious choice to think about something in positive terms, you better the odds of maintaining some semblance of control over the situation and letting go of the residual negative energy surrounding it. If you leave the negative behind, you're already reinventing your life by fostering positive energy and happiness.

Letting It Pass

If you're having a hard time finding the positive in what seems to be a completely bad situation, remember the saying, "This, too, shall pass." Not much in this world stays the same for long (think of how boring life would be if it did!). Giving up the futile attempt to control your surroundings at every moment is a profound way to reinvent your life. Admit that the outcome is not always in your hands, and in the meantime, keep looking out for the positive in everything!

Forgiving and Moving On

Don't forget about old-fashioned forgiveness. It's easier to "get back" at somebody than to actually forgive him or her; don't we all cheer when the transgressors in the movies get what they deserve? Yet, forgiveness is ultimately far more redeeming.

Forgiveness is a necessary element in the success of relationships (as discussed in Part 5, "Reinventing Your Relationships"). Think of forgiveness not as something you do to maintain relationships with others, but as something that benefits you and your life. As with focusing on the positive, forgiving someone enables you to release the negative tension you've harbored in your life.

Joan Borysenko, author of *Seventy Times Seven*, says, "Forgiveness is not condoning ignorant or harmful behavior." Nor is forgiveness "a sense of false humility that makes us better than somebody else."

Forgiving and Unlocking

If you have trouble forgiving others, you may find yourself locked up in other areas of your life. The inability to forgive is synonymous in many ways with animosity, resentment, and even hostility. Any unresolved anger you carry toward another person can be poisonous to your spirit.

Starting with Yourself

Self-forgiveness can be the most spiritually uplifting forgiveness of all. If you've ever heard someone say, "I just can't forgive myself for XYZ," you know that person is living in a self-imposed prison of guilt, shame, and personal condemnation. When you forgive yourself, you acknowledge the limitations of your human experience as well as contribute to your spiritual growth.

Forgiving "is an attitude that sets us free," says Borysenko, and enables us to "live in beauty and in balance, without judgment or expectation toward self or others." Instead of allowing something you or someone else did to you cause you tons of anguish, forgive yourself or that person, and let go of that unnecessary *emotional baggage*. You'll feel less burdened, and happier. As time passes, you may find that you have less and less to forgive of others, and perhaps more important, of yourself.

Wellness for the Self-Loved

Michelle Lusson, creator of the "Creative Wellness Program" in Vienna, Virginia, once offered an affirmation which, I believe, has a broad application to great masses of people in society:

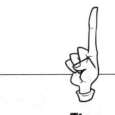

Tip

While it may be hard to embrace at first, forgiveness is actually the key to dissipating and vanquishing the poison. When you forgive, it must be unconditional, complete, and total. You don't have to forget, or condone, but rather, make it an act of moving on from a point at which you have been stuck.

Word Power

Emotional baggage is feelings and sensations left over from previous experience that surface in the present.

> "I acknowledge that in my past I have not lived the true meaning of self-love as an integrated expression of mind and body. Due to my lack of understanding I accept that I have made life difficult in emotionally securing myself.

> "I now pledge to transform myself so that my innate, loving qualities may shine forth from me, and bring balance to myself and support to others."

As you read these words, think how you, too, can fully embrace the notion of appropriate self-love. People who care for themselves in a nurturing and supportive way are less likely to have long-term, insidious bouts with unhappiness or dissatisfaction in their lives. To be sure, no one is immune to the ravages of life's ups and downs, but the negative effects of these experiences on those with self-love tend to be less harmful than those experienced by people unaware of the concept of self-love.

Every Day Is Precious No Matter How Long You Have

Have you ever encountered the suggestion to pretend you have only six months to live? Supposedly, such pretense would cause you to live your life on a higher plane. What's really important would emerge. Secondary goals would drop by the wayside. You'd spend more time with loved ones. You'd engage in activities that you truly enjoyed doing.

Maybe.

In reality, it's one thing to pretend and another to truly have only six months. If you pretended you had six months to live, when otherwise nothing led you to that conclusion, things might unfold quite differently. You might quit your job. You might sell your house and use that money to travel the world. These are activities that would get you in deep trouble if you actually had another 30 to 50 years to live after spending all your money, selling your house, and so on. The point here is that "pretending" might not be enough by itself to make you truly realize the important things in life.

Remember that "someday" comes sooner than you think. Someday, you *will* have only six months to live. If you treat each day as precious now, you're likely to live more fully all the way through your life.

Honoring Others While They're Still Around

One day—soon for you, I hope—you'll come to realize that your life is your own and that you have limitless possibilities for making it different and better. Freed from the clutches of energy-draining, unrelenting complacency, you'll see life in a different way. Often you realize that there are people in your life to honor.

That's Hollywood

Too many movies contain scenes depicting a surprise party thrown for someone who is, indeed, totally surprised. Yet the movie plots invariably fail to convey the true value of throwing a surprise party.

When someone is reaching a milestone birthday, graduating, retiring, or anything in between, throwing a party in honor of that person is something he or she is likely to remember *for the rest of his or her life*. The gesture takes on greater meaning, however, when it's done *for no special occasion*. In other words, you're honoring someone simply for his or her contribution to your life or the lives of others.

Making Your Plans Now

I seek to live without many regrets in this life, but one of mine is that I didn't honor my father in such a way. He died a little before age 61. He was scheduled to retire at 62, and I had planned to throw him a big retirement bash at that time. It never occurred to me that he wouldn't make it.

Honoring Thy Parents

I had two wonderful parents; I was lucky. I know that many people are not so fortunate. Perhaps one or both of your parents was missing during your formative years. Nevertheless, chances are that you have a surrogate parent, be it an uncle or an aunt, a step-parent, a grandparent, or perhaps even a coach or teacher who, in one way or another, fulfilled parental functions for you.

> **Tip**
>
> Perhaps you're more fortunate than me; perhaps you have the opportunity to honor a parent or someone else right now, while the going is good. If so, why not honor this person within the next month or two? If you wait, you may not get the chance.

Neither of my parents was highly religious in the strict sense, yet both achieved an admirable measure of spirituality before the end of their days. After my father passed away in 1977, my mother reinvented herself—she took on a much greater role in my life, and spirituality took on a greater role in hers.

At the time of my father's death, my mother was on the road, driving from her home in Connecticut to visit her sister in Florida. My brother, my sister, and I determined that when my father passed away, she had at least reached Washington, D.C. We called our aunt there and told her the harrowing news, instructing her, when our mother called her, to say only that father was "very ill and to return home immediately."

Later, we learned that my aunt had instead wisely chosen to tell the truth. When my mother made a routine call to her from Lorton, Virginia, my aunt said, "The children wanted me to tell you that he was gravely ill and you should go back to Connecticut immediately. But, the truth is that he is gone."

Time to Reflect

As my mother told us upon her return home, she needed that eight-hour drive to reflect on her and my father's 34 years together. With no warning, he was gone and at nearly 53, my mother was suddenly a widow. Fighting the tears while driving, she prepared herself for the forthcoming events and her life thereafter. Eight hours alone on the highway, on the way back to an empty home, must have seemed like an eternity.

The following year, another loss befell our family. Judy, my older sister, died suddenly. Yet, the tragedies and sorrows in my mother's life never dominated her. In many ways, she was lucky. She kept working almost right up to the end. Her memory remained sharp and she pursued new interests vigorously. She maintained a watchful, motherly eye on her children. As the end of her life approached, there was no question that she would face it with the same courage she had shown for years.

If Spring Comes Again

Even in the face of bad news, she was optimistic—she bought coats for the coming Spring, and she took out a long-term healthcare policy. When it became clear that her days were numbered, she faced the music like a soldier. The days dwindled, but she never let down her guard. She showed no fear. She put her discomfort aside and, as she had always done as a faithful mother and wife, showed interest in everyone else's lives.

My mother believed in living her life on earth while she had one. She didn't believe in the afterlife, but she didn't believe in the great void either. In closing, to re-honor my mother, I offer a Native American verse that was among her favorites. To this day, many years later, I still get choked up when I read it, but more than anything else it typifies my mother, Shirley Leader Davidson, and the sense of reinvention she took with her when she left this earth.

> Do not stand at my grave and weep.
> I am not there. I do not sleep.
> I am a thousand winds that blow.
> I am the diamond glint of snow.
> I am the sunlight on ripened grain.
> I am the gentle autumn rain.
> When you awake in the morning hush,
> I am the swift, uplifting rush,
> of quiet birds in circling flight.
> I am the soft starlight at night.
> Do not stand at my grave and weep.
> I am not there. I do not sleep.

The Least You Need to Know

➤ Cultivate the behaviors of the emotionally intelligent.

➤ Gain serenity by letting go of the past, and through forgiveness of others as well as of yourself.

➤ Seek to live every day with some sense of serenity.

➤ Honor others while you can.

➤ Constantly reinvent yourself as you age.

Glossary

antisocial behavior   Not wanting to interact with others, remaining apart or aloof, or conveying little interest in others. In extreme forms, it can involve doing harm to others.

aromatherapy   Use of essential oils and herbs to treat specific health and stress-related conditions.

axiom   A truism of life, a premise that people accept as valid.

balance   To bring into proportion or harmony; to be in equilibrium.

benign   Something that is good or favorable for you, or at least not harmful.

book clubs   Groups of individuals who meet to discuss a book that all have recently read.

career curriculum   That combination of on-the-job training and mentoring, shadowing, and 4-V programs that will enable you to progress in the direction you desire.

cherubic   Angel-like.

chiropractic   A method of treating disease through the manipulation of body joints, especially of the spine.

classic novels   Books that remain popular generation after generation.

compounding   The arithmetic increase in funds as time passes as a result of accumulating interest paid by the institutions with which you have invested money.

compromise   A settlement in which both sides make concessions, or a solution that is midway between two alternatives.

Continuing Education Units (CEUs)   A point system whereby professionals in an industry receive accumulating credits for courses and training that they have taken, of which may enable them to achieve or maintain certification or some other professional credential.

cranial   Related to the head and, more specifically, to one's skull.

debt-free   To have no lingering short-term financial obligations and only those long-term obligations that support long-term asset investments such as a mortgage loan for a home.

diaphragm   A dome-shaped muscle in your abdomen that helps regulate breathing.

diuresis   An excessive excretion of bodily fluids.

elucidate   To clearly explain something.

emotional baggage   Feelings and sensations left over from previous experiences that surface in the present.

empathy   The ability to relate to another person's situation, outlook, or disposition in a way that conveys some sense of caring and understanding.

entrepreneur   One who organizes a business undertaking, assuming a risk to earn a profit.

etymology   Charting the origin of something.

fascia   The strong, flexible, soft tissue that runs extensively throughout the body and helps the body to maintain its structural integration.

fasting   Abstaining from all or certain foods.

goal statement   An objective or desired result that is written down, measurable, and has a specific time frame.

grounded   To figuratively have your feet firmly planted, to engage in life or simply an encounter, with a clear head, balance, and perspective.

"halo effect"   When you benefit with those with whom you associate as a result of something you have already done, or some other factor otherwise unrelated to the merits of the current situation.

homeostasis   The state of balance and harmonious function characterizing all healthy, living organisms.

learning niche   One's preferred way of ingesting new information.

lifecycle   The typical course of events in a person's life.

lone rangers   Individuals who work on their own with little need and perhaps little desire to be involved in group efforts and team-related functions.

meditation   Quieting the conscious mind and enabling it to roam freely without intentional direction.

meditative   A contemplative state; immersed in deep reflection.

memoir   Basically a life story or some part of it.

mentor   A wise advisor, teacher, or coach.

networking   Developing personal contacts for exchange of information to further one's career.

neurotransmitters   Biochemical substances that transmit or inhibit nerve impulses within the brain.

obesity   Being 30 percent or more over the norm for one's height and body type.

olfactory epithelium   The area above the nasal cavity containing countless receptor cells that help you interpret aromas.

organic foods   Food grown without the use of harmful pesticides.

paradox   A situation where two seemingly independent items or events exist at the same time or in the same place.

perfectionism   The practice of attempting to make things perfect; often a disguise for not proceeding or for being discontent.

pilgrimage   A journey usually prompted by one's religious beliefs or convictions. People often travel to Holy Lands or the lands of their ancestors to better understand their origins and religious traditions.

pluralistic society   A society that offers citizens many ethnic, racial, religious, and social ideas from which to choose.

portable dictation equipment   The hand-held pocket tape recorders widely available in retail outlets that allow one to record anywhere from 30 minutes to two hours of dictated material for future transcription.

priority   That which is most important to you.

prodigy   Someone who is a genius, a wizard, or a master at something.

proverbial   Alleged or fictional, as opposed to real and tangible.

reinvention   Noteworthy movement from point A in your life to point B.

rekindle   In the context of a relationship, it means to renew, reunite, or reinvest your time and energy.

revving   Humming along or operating at optimum capability.

role model   A person who as a result of their position, expertise, actions, and/or personality serves as an example to other people as to how to conduct one's self.

sanctity   Refers to the holiness, virtue, or worthiness of something.

self-actualization   The quest for happiness and fulfillment.

self-transcendence   Independent of gratification of the self; an awareness of one's interdependence with the rest of the world.

socially responsible investing When one considers one's beliefs and values and applies them to how one invests money.

status quo The existing state of affairs, or how conditions are traditionally expected to be.

visualization The practice of forming a mental image to foster a sense of calm and a more ready focus on tasks.

yoga Yoga means "union," referring to the union of the mind and the body.

More
About
This
Stuff

Bibliography

Further Reading

Ackerman, Diane. *A Natural History of the Senses*. New York: Random House, 1990.

Angevine, Erma. *Instructions for Beginners in Genealogy*. Arlington, VA: National Genealogical Society, 1999.

Anthony, Robert. *50 Ideas That Can Change Your Life: An Indispensable Guide to Happiness and Prosperity*. New York: Berkeley, 1987.

Ayan, Jordan. *Aha! 10 Ways to Free Your Creative Spirit and Find Your Great Ideas*. New York: Crown, 1997.

Bennett, Jarrett. *Making the Money Last*. Dubuque, IA: Kendall-Hunt, 2000.

Bennis, Warren, Ph.D. *On Becoming a Leader*. Reading, MA: Addison-Wesley Pub. Co., 1989.

Birren, Faber. *Color & Human Response*. New York: Van Nostrand Reinhold, 1978.

Blakeslee, Thomas R. *Beyond the Conscious Mind*. New York: Plenum Press, 1996.

Caliandro, Arthur, and Barry Lenson. *Simple Steps: 10 Things You Can Do to Create an Exceptional Life*. New York: McGraw-Hill, 1999.

Cameron, Julia. *The Artist's Way*. Los Angeles: Tarcher, 1992.

Campbell, Joseph. *Power of Myth*. New York: Doubleday, 1988.

Chandler, Steve. *Reinventing Yourself: How to Become the Person You've Always Wanted to Be.* Franklin Lakes, NJ: Careerpress, 1998.

Condrill, Jo. *A Millennium Primer: Take Charge of Your Life.* Washington, DC: Goalminds, 1999.

Csikszentmihalyi, Mihaly. *Flow: The Psychology of Optimal Experience.* New York: Harper, 1990.

Dalai Lama. *The Art of Happiness.* New York: Riverhead Books, 1998.

Davidson, Jeff. *Breathing Space: Living & Working at a Comfortable Pace in a Sped-Up Society.* New York: Mastermedia, 2000.

———. *The Complete Idiot's Guide to Managing Stress.* Indianapolis: Alpha Books, 1999.

———. *The Complete Idiot's Guide to Managing Your Time.* Indianapolis: Alpha Books, 1999.

———. *The Complete Idiot's Guide to Reaching Your Goals.* Indianapolis: Alpha Books, 1998.

———. *Joy of Simple Living.* Emmaus, PA: Rodale Books, 1999.

Dlugozima, Hope, James Scott and David Sharp. *Six Months Off.* New York: Holt, 1996.

Dyer, Wayne, Dr. *You'll See It When You Believe It.* New York: Avon, 1996.

Easterbrook, Gregg. *A Moment on the Earth.* New York: Viking, 1996.

Eastman, Janet. *Simple Indulgence: Easy, Everyday Things to Do for Me.* Kansas City: Andrews McMeel, 1999.

Elkins, D. N. *Beyond Religion: A Personal Program for Building a Spiritual Life Outside the Walls of Traditional Religion.* New York: Quest Books, 1998.

Ellis, Albert, Dr., and Dr. Arthur Lang. *How to Keep People from Pushing our Buttons.* Secaucus, NJ: Birch Lane Press, 1995.

Freeman, Dave, and Neil Teplica. *100 Things to Do Before You Die: Travel Events You Just Can't Miss.* Dallas: Taylor Publishing, 1999.

Friedan, Betty. *The Fountain of Age.* New York: Simon & Schuster, 1993.

Fritz, Robert. *The Path of Least Resistance*. New York: Fawcett Columbine, 1989.

Gallagher, Winifred. *Just the Way You Are*. New York: Random House, 1996.

———. *The Power of Place*. New York: HarperPerennial, 1993.

———. *Working on God*. New York: Random House: 1999.

Goleman, Daniel. *Emotional Intelligence*. New York: Bantam Books, 1994.

Greene, Bob, and D. G. Fulford. *To Our Children's Children: Preserving Family Histories for Generations to Come*. New York: Doubleday, 1993.

Haley, Alex. *Roots*. New York: Doubleday, 1976.

Hay, Louise. *101 Power Thoughts*. Carlsbad, CA: Hayhouse, 1995.

Helmstetter, Shad, Dr. *What You Say When You Talk to Yourself*. New York: Pocket Books, 1990.

Jolley, Willie. *A Setback Is a Setup for a Comeback*. New York: St. Martin's, 1999.

Keyes, Ken Jr. *Your Road Map to Lifelong Happiness*. Coos Bay, OR: Love Line Books, 1995.

Kostner, Jaclyn, Dr. *Virtual Leadership*. New York: Warner, 1996.

Lawlor, Elizabeth. *Discover Nature Close to Home: Things to Know and Things to Do*. New York: Stackpole Books, 1993.

Massey, Anne. *Interior Designing of the 20th Century*. London: Thames & Hudson, 1990.

McCormack, Mark H. *Staying Street Smart in the Internet Age*. New York: Viking, 2000.

McKibben, Bill. *Hundred Dollar Holiday*. New York: Simon & Schuster, 1998.

———. *The End of Nature*. New York: Anchor Books, 1999.

McRae, Hamish. *The World in 20/20: Power, Culture and Prosperity*. Boston: Harvard Business School Press, 1994.

Monahan, Michael. *The Coming American Renaissance*. New York: Simon & Schuster,1996.

Patterson, James, and Peter Kim. *The Day America Told the Truth*. Englewood Cliffs, NJ: Prentice Hall Press, 1990.

Pelton, Warren, Ph.D. *Tough Choices*. Burr Ridge, IL: BusinessOne Irwin, 1992

Penwell, Dan. *101 Things to Do in the Year 2000*. Tulsa, OK: Honor Books, 1999.

Pinker, Steven. *How the Mind Works*. New York: Norton, 1997.

Powell, Colin, Gen. *My American Journey*. New York: Random House, 1995.

Putnam, Robert D. *Bowling Alone: The Collapse and Revival of American Community*. New York: Simon & Schuster, 2000.

Robin, Vicki, and Joe Dominguez. *Your Money or Your Life*. New York: Penguin, 1999.

Rubin, Lillian. *Just Friends*. New York: HarperPerennial, 1990.

Sachs, Judith. *Nature's Prozac*. Paramus, NJ: Prentice Hall Press, 1998.

Samaras, Thomas. *The Truth About Your Height*. San Diego: Reventropy Associates, 1994.

Scharma, Robin. *The Monk Who Sold His Ferrari*. New York: HarperCollins, 1997.

Schor, Juliet. *The Overspent American*. New York: HarperPerennial, 1999.

Sharma, Arvind, ed. *Our Religions*. New York: HarperCollins, 1993.

Siegel, Bernie, Dr. *Love, Medicine and Miracles*. New York: Warner, 1988.

Taylor, Maureen. *Through the Eyes of Your Ancestors: A Step-by-Step Guide to Uncovering Your Family History*. Boston: Houghton Mifflin Company, 1999.

Templeton, John. *Discovering the Laws of Life*. Radnor, PA: Templeton Foundation Press, 1995.

———. *Golden Nuggets*. Radnor, PA: Templeton Foundation Press, 1997.

———. *Is Progress Speeding Up?* Radnor, PA: Templeton Foundation Press, 1997.

Tye, Joe. *Personal Best*. New York: Wiley, 1997.

Vroon, Piet. *Smell: The Secret Seducer*. New York: Farrar, Straus and Giroux, 1994.

Wallace, Amy, and Robert Wallacinsky. *Book of Lists*. New York: Morrow, 1977.

Watson, Donna. *101 Simple Ways to Be Good to Yourself: How To Discover Peace and Joy in Your Life*. Austin: Bard Press, 1992.

Weider, Marsha. *Making Your Dreams Come True*. New York: Random House, 2000.

Weil, Andrew, Dr. *Spontaneous Healing*. New York: Knopf, 1996.

Williamson, Marianne. *A Return to Love*. New York: HarperCollins, 1992.

Wydra, Nancilee. *Feng Shui: The Book of Cures*. Chicago: Contemporary Books, 1996.

———. *Feng Shui in the Garden*. Chicago: Contemporary Books, 1997.

U.S. Department of Labor. *The Occupational Outlook Handbook*. Washington, DC: Government Printing Office, 2001.

———. *Statistical Abstract of the United States*. Washington, DC: Government Printing Office, 2001.

Young, Jeffrey, Ph.D., and Janet Klosko, Ph.D. *Reinventing Your Life*. New York: Dutton, 1993.

Zukav, Gary. *The Dancing Wu Li Masters*. New York: Morrow, 1979.

Index

M

magazines, gaining publication, editorial guidelines, 181-182

magnesium, 129

maintaining
  contact, rekindling friendships, 245
  momentum, actions to avoid procrastination, 56

making love longer, revitalizing your relationship, 227

management, financial risks, wills and trusts, 261-262

manipulation of the body, bodywork systems, 149
  Alexander Technique, 152-153
  Chiropractics, 151-152
  Feldenkrais Method, 150-151
  Rolfing, 149-150
  Shiatsu, 153-154
  Trager Approach, 150

manuscripts, reprinting for mailing, trying to get published, 182

Market Your Career and Yourself, 200

marketability, career, staying current on your marketability, 163

marriages
  all-time shortest marriages of celebrities, 223
  records (genealogical research), 95
  types, 222

martial arts, physical activity, 139
  T'ai Chi, 139
  yoga, 139-140

Maslow, Abraham, self-actualization, 7

massage versus aromatherapy, 62

mate changes, as impetus for change, 21
  after mate change, 22
  avoiding desperation, 22
  before mate change, 21-22

MBAs, necessity in leadership role, 195-196

McClelland, Dr. David (hierarchy of human needs), 7

McCourt, Frank, 88

McGuire, Mark, 75

medals of honor, General Colin Powell, 13

meditation, resting mind and body, 68

meditative state, 75

memoirs, writing, exercising the mind, 88

memory trigger, aromatherapy, 61

mental
  exercises (as incentive tools to begin reinvention), 9
  obstacles, sabbaticals, 210

mentoring, 276-277

MentorU University Web site, 203

Meyers-Briggs personality indicator test, 34

milestones, career, as impetus for change, 20-21

military records (genealogical research), 95

Milken, Michael, 133-134

mind (reinvention of), 71-101
  exercising, 83
    book clubs, 86
    building your vocabulary, 89
    classic novels, 83-85

  discussion groups, 98-99
    journaling, 86-88
    learning a foreign language, 100-101
    reading schedules, 85
    structured education, 90
    writing a memoir, 88
  genealogical research, 93-94
    computerized databases, 96
    outside resources, 95
    talking to family members, 94
  internal focus, 72
    breathing, 75-76
    creating a sanctimonious space, 73
    deeper sense of self, 73
    dreams, 78-80
    flotation therapy, 78
    spas, 77
    time for nonaccomplishment, 72-73
    trances, 73-74
  resting, 68
    aromatherapy, 59-62
    footbaths, 63
    hot baths, 63-64
    meditation, 68
    music, 65-66
    relaxation tapes, 67
    soaking, 64
    soothing sounds of nature, 66
    whirlpool baths, 63
  societal pressures, 71
  study of religion, 96
    beginning with your faith, 96-97
    expanding areas of study, 97-98
    narrowing your focus, 97

procrastination, 50
avoiding the impetus of
staying put, 48
changing now, 50
habitual behaviors, 49
motivation, 49
Newton's laws, 48
letting go of perfection-
ism, 51
self-imposed limits, 51
taking action, 50-51
delegating tasks, 54
easy wins, 53-54
eliminating distrac-
tions, 55
five minute option,
52-53
getting rest, 52
identifying lingering
issues, 53
jump-starts, 53
maintaining momen-
tum, 56
recruiting friends, 54
reframing the task, 54
rewarding accomplish-
ments, 55
prodigies, 269
professional magazines,
gaining publishing, editorial guidelines, 181-182
public speaking, 197-200
articulation, 198-199
becoming memorable,
204-205
combining logic with
emotion, 205-206
online training programs,
203-204
plain speaking, 198-199
practicing, 201
preparation, 200-201
reducing anxiety, 201-203
tools, 199-201
vocabulary, 198
publications, 177
benefits, 178-180
finding publication information, 179-180

generating article topics,
183-184
extracting material
from previous works,
184-185
in-house publishing, 179
learning more about
the company, 180
options for entry,
180-181
landing a publisher, 178
portable dictation equip-
ment, 178
professional magazines,
editorial guidelines,
181-182
pyramiding process, 182
reprinting manuscripts
for mailing, 182

Q

qualities of leaders, 193
connects with winners,
193
generates cross linkages
with other fields, 194
handles small decisions
quickly, 194
innovative, 193
offers no compromise on
quality, 193
quest for balance, maintaining objectivity, 40

R

Rahe, Richard, 15
RDAs (recommended daily
allowances), vitamins, 128-
129
reading
book clubs, exercising the
mind, 86
classic novels, *83*
Modern Library's list,
84-85

people, leadership, 189
promoting awareness and
objectivity, collecting
inspiring articles, 41
schedules, exercising the
mind, 85
real estate records (genealogical research), 95
reallocating time, finding
balance, 109
home environment, 110
thirty minutes a day, 109
work environment, 110
reasons people want to
change, 6
hierarchy of needs, 7
self-actualization, 7
Rebirthing (Breathwork therapy), 76
recommendations, obtain-
ing prior to cosmetic surgery, 148
recommended daily
allowances. *See* RDAs
recording
dreams, 79
thoughts, self-assessment
of where you want to
be, 35
rediscovering hobbies
aviation, 270
becoming child-like
again, 265-266
benefits, 266
diversion from routine,
266
improved health, 267
social opportunities,
267
carpentry and renova-
tion, 272
cooking, 271
engaging in an activity
that brings happiness,
267
gardening, 271
learning to play an
instrument, 268

317

319